THE CREATIVE GARDENER'S COOKBOOK

Director of Publishing Patricia A. Pingry
Cookbook Editor Teri Mitchell
Manuscript Editor Gail Kummings
Copy Editor Susan DuBois
Art Director Jennifer Rundberg
Staff Artist David Lenz

ISBN 0-8249-3057-6
Copyright © MCMLXXXV by Ideals Publishing Corporation
Previously published as *Das grosse Garten-und Kochbuch*
by Ceres-Verlag, Rudolf-August Oetker KG Bielefeld, West Germany
All rights reserved.
Printed and bound in West Germany.

Published by Ideals Publishing Corporation
P.O. Box 141000
Nashville, Tennessee 37214-1000

THE
CREATIVE GARDENER'S
COOKBOOK

ideals

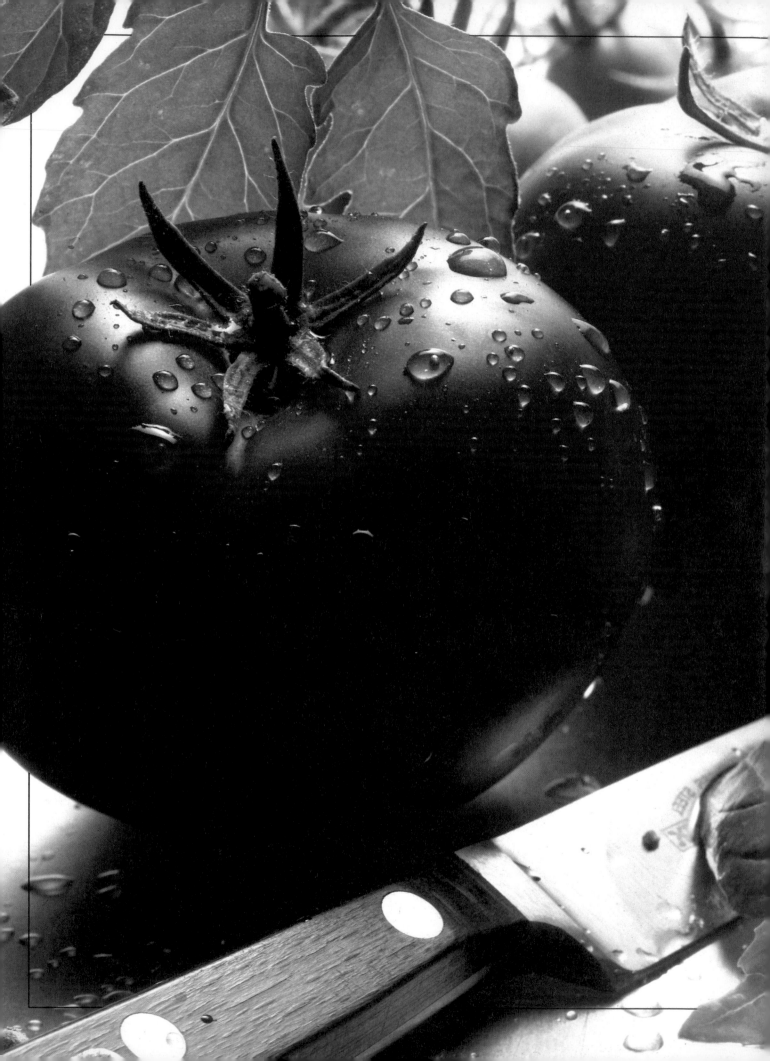

Preface

All of us envy the person with a thriving garden. The secret of such a garden is working in partnership with nature, and one way to learn how to do this is to consult the latest in gardening know-how. *The Creative Gardener's Cookbook* presents clear and richly illustrated instructions to guide you to a successful garden.

Once you have harvested your fruits and vegetables, you will want to prepare them in ways that will preserve their freshness and nutrition. The final section of this book presents over 350 recipes and suggestions for delicious meals designed to make the most of the results of your garden. Particular care has been taken to recommend the best cooking methods, temperatures, and techniques in order to protect and preserve the freshness and nutrition of the fruits and vegetables. We hope that this book will enable you to combine the enjoyment of working in your garden with the delight of dining on its harvest.

1. A Little Space Goes a Long Way

Suggestions for vegetable garden designs. Beds for small yards. Balcony gardening. Pages 1-7.

2. The Soil and its Significance

Basic soil composition. Improving your soil. Compost, cover crops, mulch. Working the ground; preparing seed beds. Useful garden tools. Pages 8-27.

3. Planning Your Garden

Seedbeds; mixed cultivation; hill beds; deep cultivation beds. Crop rotation for healthy soil and plants. Pages 28-35.

5. Sowing, Cultivating, Planting

Sowing outside. Raising seedlings for transplanting; hardening off. Cold frames; nursery beds. Pages 42-49.

4. Seeds, Seedlings and Seasons

Seeds; seedlings; sets. Catalogues. Pages 36-41.

6. Feeding Your Garden

Organic and mineral fertilizers. Plant nutrients: types and requirements. Deficiency symptoms. Fertilizing and the quality of your harvest. Pages 50-57.

7. Caring for Your Soil

Watering; weeding; loosening the soil. Appropriate tools for soil cultivation. Pages 58-61.

9. Harvesting, Storing and Preserving

Harvesting. Nutrition and the vitamin content of vegetables. Storage; salting; drying; freezing. Pages 68-73.

8. Caring for the Plants In Your Garden

Integrated plant protection: growth, intercropping, natural control. Chemical protection: insecticides, herbicides, fungicides. Rules for pesticide use. Pages 62-67.

10. The Garden in Winter

Time to reflect, relax, and plan for the next year. Pages 74-76.

Planting Advisor

2. Fruit-bearing Vegetables, Fennel and Rhubarb

Cucumbers, pumpkins, peppers, eggplants, sweet corn, fennel and rhubarb. Pages 86-93.

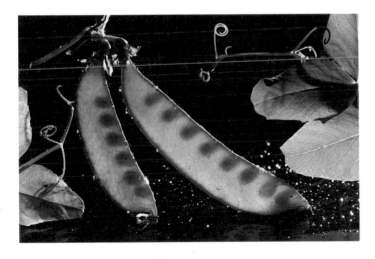

1. Legumes

Peas: Garden peas, sugar pod peas
Beans: Haricot Vert green beans, pole beans, scarlet runner beans, broad beans
Pages 78-85.

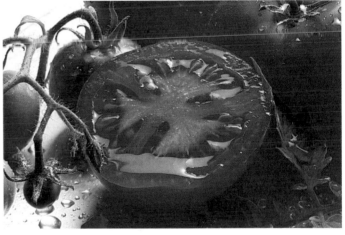

3. Tomatoes

Salad tomatoes. Beefsteak tomatoes. Italian tomatoes. Cherry tomatoes. Pages 94-99.

4. Potatoes

Selecting seed potatoes. Early and middle varieties. Digging the crop. Pages 100-103.

6. Varieties of Leeks

Spring onions, pearl onions, yellow onions, red onions. Shallots. Garlic. Leeks. Pages 112-117.

5. Brassicas

Cauliflower and broccoli. Kohlrabi. Savoys. Red and white cabbage. Brussels sprouts. Kale. Chinese cabbage. Pages 104-111.

7. Lettuces and Greens

Head lettuce, butterhead lettuce, leaf lettuce. Cos (Romaine) lettuce. Endive. Lamb's lettuce. Sugar loaf, radicchio, Belgian endive. Cress. Sorrel. Spinach. New England spinach. Pages 118-127.

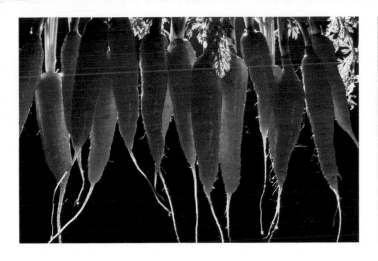

8. Young Root Vegetables

Turnips. Carrots, baby carrots, and parsnips. Radishes, red and white. Beets. Celery and celeriac. Salsify. Pages 128-135.

10. Berries

Strawberries. Raspberries. Blackberries. Red currants and gooseberries. Pages 148-153.

Gardening Encyclopedia

Pages 154-162.

Introduction and Cooking Guide

Preparation suggestions and herbal hints. Canning pickles and fruit products; jelly-making. Pages 163-166.

9. Garden-Fresh Herbs

Basil. Savory. Borage. Dill. Tarragon. Chervil. Lavender. Lovage. Marjoram. Parsley. Mint. Burnet. Rosemary. Sage. Chives. Thyme. Wormwood. Lemon mint. Pages 136-147.

Gardener's Cookbook

1. Legumes

Tender and delicate as butter. Plump and crisp in Parmesan dressing, with shrimp or ham. In soups, soufflés, or salads. As delicious fillings, and on toast. Tender and thin with mushrooms or bacon, as side dishes, stews, or salads, and salted, as in Grandmother's time. Pages 168-187.

2. Fruit-Bearing Vegetables, Fennel and Rhubarb

Wealth, variety, the staples of your garden...In old combinations and new. Cold in salads, cold and hot in soups, hot in soufflés. Delicate in stuffings, or tangy in vinegar dressings. Pages 188-207.

3. Tomatoes

Slices of summer sun...Classic dishes, and new combinations. As side dishes and main courses. Alone, or with other vegetables. With fish, meat, and cheese, on pasta and pizzas. As color in soups, sauces, or salads—and preserved as green pickles. Pages 208-223.

5. Brassicas

Multi-colored strength and vitality...Excellent with almond butter, cheese toppings, steamed, or stuffed. Nourishing and flavorful in stews and as a side dish. Fresh in salads, and steamed in soups. Pages 238-257.

4. Potatoes

Bounty from beneath the soil...Golden yellow in dumplings and soups. Golden brown in soufflés and potato pancakes. In old and new salads. Pages 224-237.

6. Leek Varieties

Long and delicious...Sharp and mild dressings, tangy combinations, and sweet-sour pickles. A refined addition to meats, a tasty main ingredient in soups and vegetables. Baked in savory yeast rings or pastries. Pages 258-273.

7. Lettuce and Leaf Vegetables

Sometimes raw, sometimes cooked...Cold as salads—sometimes sweet with fruit or nuts, sometimes savory with bacon, vegetables, or mushrooms. Hot as soups or accompaniments. Sometimes traditional, sometimes brand-new. Pages 274-297.

9. Herbs

Full of flavoring power...Added to salads, vegetables, eggs, meat, and fish. To sweeten and flavor soup, jellies, and punches. Pages 318-341.

8. Root Vegetables

To sink your teeth into...Plump and stuffed, as side dishes or main courses. Small and delicate in salads or sauces. Tasty in stews, surprising in cakes, healthy as juices. Crispy deep-fried and sautéed. Pages 298-317.

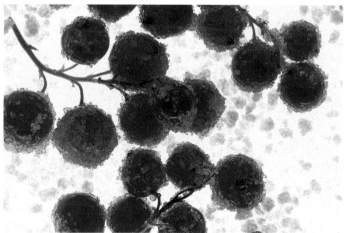

10. Berries

Fruits—a way to pamper yourself...Sweet as jams, ices, and custards. Tangy as sauces for game and poultry. In beverages, with and without alcohol. Pages 342-363.

Gardening Guide

The "Gardening Guide" gives clear and richly illustrated instructions to guide you to a thriving garden.

A Little Space Goes a Long Way

It's amazing how little space you need in order to harvest a wide variety of vegetables. In fact, even if your yard isn't large enough for a traditional garden, you can grow many herbs and vegetables in a flower bed or on a balcony or patio.

What's more, growing fruit and vegetables isn't just a paying proposition—it's also a lot of fun. Granted, gardening does take a little effort, but the work is repaid in full by the pleasure you feel when your crop flourishes a hundredfold at harvest time. Just watching your plants grow will whet your appetite for the coming feasts: tender green lettuce next to glowing red tomatoes, crisp green cucumbers next to colorful sweet peppers, and feathery parsley next to a multitude of other aromatic herbs.

A thriving garden doesn't just please your eyes. It also pampers your palate with crisp, fresh vegetables, bursting with vitamins and simply unsurpassed in flavor. Try it once for yourself. You'll hardly believe how easily it's all achieved.

To experience all this, you need only lay out a bed, sow seeds or set in small plants, add fertilizer and water. The rest is done by nature. Try not to be too ambitious with your first efforts. If your first plot is about 100 square feet, it will require little enough maintenance that the experience will remain a pleasure. A bed this size will require on the average no more than about 2 hours per week for its cultivation. In return you will be delighted with a multitude of freshly gathered, healthy garden produce the whole year through.

Once you have had the enjoyment and success of your first garden, you can decide on the size of the next one. Your expanding plans may well surprise you.

Laying Out the Garden

On pages 4-5 you'll find some suggestions for laying out your first garden plot. These should help you begin your own plans and give you some ideas about how to make the most use of a garden the whole year round. Of course, no plant mentioned here is a "must." Once you've read through the "Planting Advisor," you'll want to work out your own choices, especially if you have limited space.

No matter how much space you have, you'll enjoy your gardening experience the most if you make special efforts to combine the necessary with the beautiful. The design of many old vegetable and herb gardens illustrates that this idea isn't new. Years ago a kitchen garden was so artfully laid out that you could hardly tell the difference between it and a flower garden. It wasn't uncommon, for instance, to use herbs either in beds of their own or as partitions between one section of the garden and another. Only a few such gardens exist today, but numerous illustrations

and engravings show just how important such partitioning was.

A vivid example of the typical mixture of kitchen and flower gardens can still be seen on a large scale today in the formal Renaissance Gardens at the Chateau Villandry in France. Each bed, not only those for flowers but also the tracts containing vegetables and herbs, is bordered with hedges. Viewed from above, the intertwined, severe geometric shapes and the overall design of the so-called flower beds is obvious.

Of course, most of us have to settle for less display in today's limited space. But that doesn't mean that a garden must be square or rectangular, or that everything has to be planted in the same place. For example, circular beds of various sizes (about 50 inches) often work well in a modern yard. Border these beds with low bushy shrubs or summer flowers—or plant a border of parsley, just for decoration. Its loveliness will surprise you.

By the way...

There's a lot to think about when you plan a vegetable garden: Which kinds of vegetables do you want to grow? What should the bed look like? Do you want to plant a mixed garden? Where's the best place for an early bed? If you draw everything out long before you intend to plant, it's easier to make changes than if you wait until you're standing between half-planted rows. In the next chapter you'll find practical advice to help you plan.

Sample Garden Bed Size of garden: 15 x 22 feet

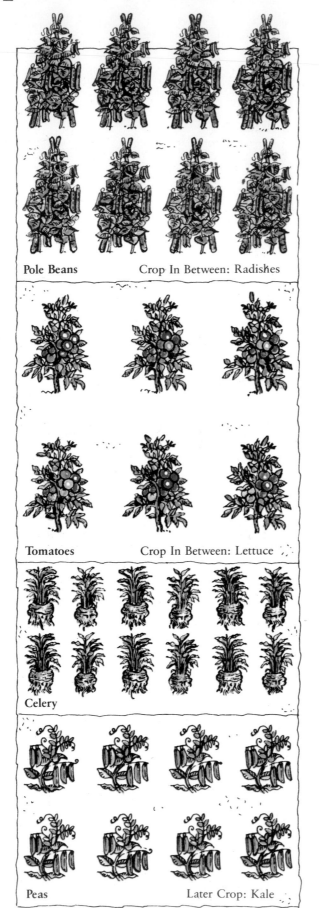

Pole Beans | Crop In Between: Radishes

Tomatoes | Crop In Between: Lettuce

Celery

Peas | Later Crop: Kale

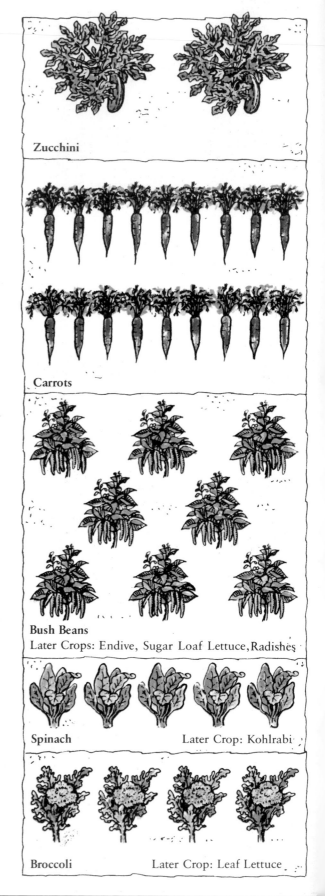

Zucchini

Carrots

Bush Beans
Later Crops: Endive, Sugar Loaf Lettuce, Radishes

Spinach | Later Crop: Kohlrabi

Broccoli | Later Crop: Leaf Lettuce

Individual areas: 15 x 5 feet Width of paths: 8 inches

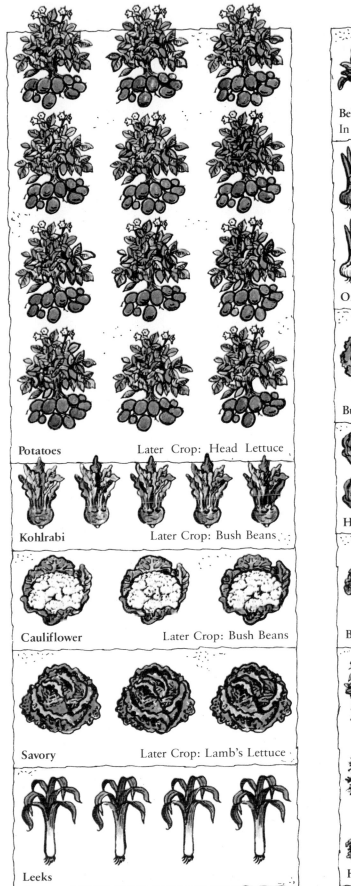

Potatoes   Later Crop: Head Lettuce

Kohlrabi   Later Crop: Bush Beans

Cauliflower   Later Crop: Bush Beans

Savory   Later Crop: Lamb's Lettuce

Leeks

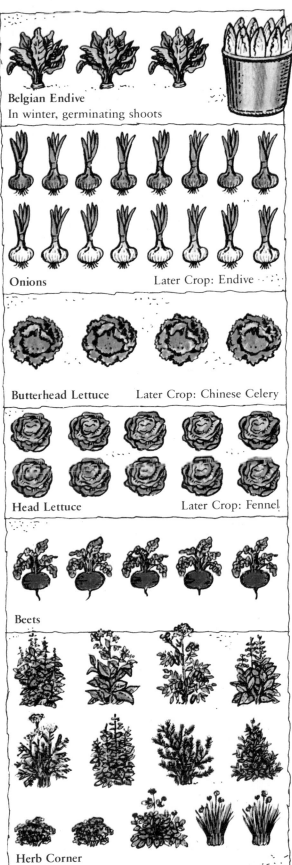

Belgian Endive
In winter, germinating shoots

Onions   Later Crop: Endive

Butterhead Lettuce   Later Crop: Chinese Celery

Head Lettuce   Later Crop: Fennel

Beets

Herb Corner

Don't be discouraged if you can't manage a large bed. Small gardens are almost as efficient as a conventional one, and cabbage heads look like blowsy flowers in them. An apartment dweller usually can find a place for growing herbs on a window sill or the smallest balcony. And thanks to the efforts of horticulturists, the balcony gardener doesn't even have to do without fresh fruits and vegetables. A decorative floor tub can hold flowers, or you can grow shrub tomatoes, carrots or even everbearing strawberries, which will bear three or more times a season. There is even a variety of miniature fruit trees. You won't have a gigantic harvest, it's true, but even the blossoming of the small tree and the growth of its fruit is an experience worth having.

The ornamental Renaissance Garden at the French Chauteau Villandry, where vegetable beds are hard to distinguish from nearby beds of flowers.

Plant a seed. Perhaps you'll lay the foundation for a hobby that isn't just fun, but also, in the truest sense of the word, bears "fruit."

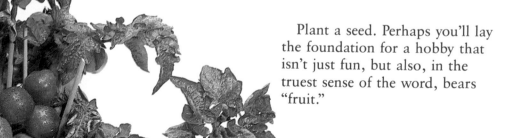

Shrub tomatoes in plant pots can grow well on balconies and patios.

Tomatoes or other vegetables grown in large plant pots can be tasteful, attractive additions to your landscaping.

A round herb bed in the lawn is, at one and the same time, a lovely and useful alternative to the usual round flower bed.

The Soil and Its Significance

The success of every gardening effort depends upon fertile soil. Even though at first glance a handful of soil may seem insignificant, it is still a highly complicated structure. Originating millions of years ago, and working in conjunction with water, soil made our great variety of plant and animal life possible.

Soil Basics

Soil is still being formed today, in the same way it has always been. Wind, water, heat and cold constantly erode the original rock. This raw mineral creates conditions favorable to certain kinds of plant growth. When these plants die, their decay gradually enriches the rocky substance with organic materials. Living organisms in the soil combine the organic material with the weathered stone to form fertile soil. Basically then, all soil consists of the hard original **mineral** (i.e. rock), the **subsoil**, which already contains eroded rock, and the fertile **top soil**, which contains all the elements necessary for abundant plant growth.

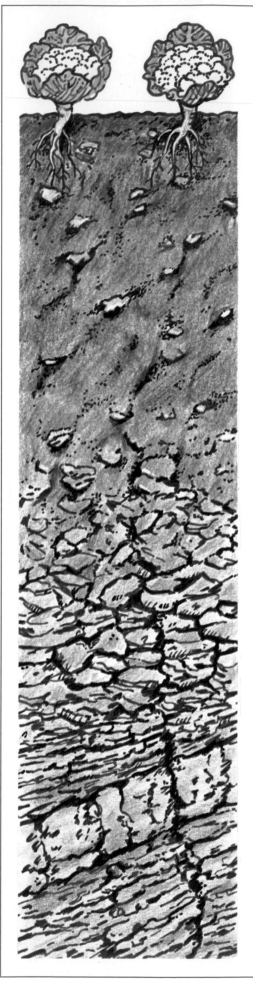

By the way...

You can actually see the type of soil you have in your garden. Put a handful of soil into a glass, fill the glass with water and stir vigorously. Then watch how the soil settles to the bottom. Sandy soil sinks swiftly, and the water remains predominantly clear. Heavy clay and loam soil settle slowly, so the water remains cloudy. You can recognize a soil containing a large amount of humus by the thin film of particles that float on the surface of the water.

Sand

Loam

Clay

Soil Types

It's especially important for a gardener to know the composition of the top soil of his or her garden. There are three basic types of soil:

1. Lighter soil = sand
2. Medium heavy soil = loam
3. Heavy soil = clay

Most soil contains a mixture of these types, such as sandy loam or clay loam.

The individual particles of the three soil types differ in size—sand particles are the largest, and clay particles are the smallest. Keeping these distinctions in mind, use a simple finger test to make a rough determination of your garden's soil composition.

Take a handful of damp soil from your garden and roll it between your palms. As you do, note the following distinctions:

Clay is "dirty"—it coats your skin. It molds easily into balls, and its surface is smooth, and slightly shiny.

Loam is less "dirty" than clay. Its texture is slightly floury or crumbly. It's less moldable than clay, and its surface is rougher.

Sand isn't dirty. It has a granular texture, and it isn't moldable.

The various proportions of each type determine the subdivision to which your soil belongs.

Improving Your Garden Soil

Together with climatic conditions, a multitude of interrelated factors determine a soil's fertility, and gardeners need to consider all of them in order to decide if their land is ideal for garden use or whether it should be improved. The most important characteristics are soil structure, porosity, friability, humus level, pH value, nutrient content and the presence of soil organisms.

Soil Structure and Porosity

There are two basic soil structures, **single-grain structure** and **crumb structure**. They are determined, for the most part, by the type of soil being discussed.

Single-grain structures are found mainly in clay and sand soils. The soil particles in these two types lie very loosely, but very closely, together. However, in terms of total volume, there's a crucial distinction between the structure of a clay soil and a sand soil. In a clay soil, the air spaces between the soil particles make up as little as 25%. In a sand soil, air spaces can take up as much as 60% of the total volume.

Crumb structures are found in loams and sandy loams. Here the soil particles are cemented together into very small irregularly-shaped crumbs. Because of the

Strong root systems can develop in well-prepared garden soil.

A loose surface denotes a well-prepared crumb structure.

irregular shapes, the spaces between the crumbs are different sizes. As a result, the particle-air spaces ratio is in better balance in loam soils.

The percentage of air space in a soil directly affects its ability to hold and release water. This characteristic is called **porosity.** Pure sand is easy to work because of its loose texture. However, it holds little water and dries out quickly. Pure clay soil, on the other hand, holds a lot of water, which makes it cold and heavy. It has brought many gardeners to despair.

Loams and sandy loams have advantages over both of the other soil types. The structure is looser than clay, so it's easier to work, but holds water better than a sand soil, so the proportions of air content and water are usually more favorable for cultivation.

A crumb structure also best meets the needs of cultivated plants; it supplies sufficient quantities of air and water.

It has enough body to provide roots with a firm hold but not so much body that roots can't penetrate it.

These conditions are found in sandy loam soils. Be happy then, if your garden soil consists of medium heavy loam.

Friability

Ideal soil is known as **friable** and is said to have **good tilth.** This state is achieved by encouraging your soil's crumb structure through clumping the soil particles together. It's also necessary to supply a sufficient amount of humus and lime, in order to ensure the correct soil make-up.

Correct soil cultivation promotes good tilth. Turning under

Loam soil containing a high proportion of clay is almost impossible to cultivate after an extended period of drought.

The ordinary brown soil common to most areas is well-suited for gardening.

a garden's topsoil in the autumn contributes to **frost mellowness** (see "The Soil and Its Significance," p. 21). **Shade mellowness,** achieved by growing what is called a "green manure crop," keeps the soil's surface moist and protects the crumbs from the impact of raindrops. Microorganisms in the soil also play an important role, because they "cement" the soil crumbs together.

Humus: A Garden's Necessity

A garden cannot thrive without humus. This comes in two important types: **nutrient humus** and **permanent humus**, which is commonly referred to as top soil.

Nutrient humus is all the fresh organic material that's supplied to the soil, such as compost, dung, peat, mulch, or the remains of plants. Whether these materials are dug into the soil or placed on top of it, nutrient humus serves as food for the soil creatures, it decays, and it finally becomes permanent humus.

Unlike nutrient humus, permanent humus has no recognizable structure, but it is very advantageous to the soil. It promotes *friability* because it loosens and slightly improves heavy soils, thereby enabling even soaking and aeration of the soil. The decay process transforms the nutrients in organic matter into a form that's soluble in water, so that plants can absorb them. Finally, because of its balanced composition, permanent humus helps maintain the biological equilibrium of the soil.

Permanent humus is formed in part through the activities of microorganisms that live in the soil. Their ideal environment is a well-aerated soil with a weakly acidic to a lightly alkaline pH value and an abundant supply of nutrients in the form of organic substances. The microorganisms also need soil that's not too wet or too dry. It's in your garden's best interest to supply these conditions.

Because of its importance to plant life, a healthy 8 to 12-inch thick covering of permanent humus is the best basis for successful gardening. As a result, every gardener should always work at maintaining a constant level of soil humus. This means that you have to replenish the supply constantly.

Compost—The Way to Supply Humus

In order to grow, plants remove nutrients from the soil. When the plants die, the normal decay process returns those nutrients to the soil. This is nature's natural cycle. However, the situation in a garden is a little different. There plants are harvested, so they can't participate in the natural cycle. The gardener's task, then, is to replace those nutrients and organic materials removed from the soil by the garden's crops. The best method for replenishing the humus content of the soil is **composting**. Composting artificially continues nature's natural cycle, compensating for human interference, and speeding up the process of organic decay, at the same time.

Practical Composting Tips

A well-maintained compost heap bears no resemblance to the commonly-held image of an untidy pile of rubbish in a far corner of the garden. Some people might consider one of its ingredients to be "rubbish," but the aim of composting is to turn that rubbish into valuable earth, and to do so in less time than would take place under normal circumstances. To accomplish this, you need a plan.

1. The Site. Several factors should dictate the location of a compost heap. Look for a clean, half-shaded spot that is, if possible, sheltered from the wind and easily accessible, both from the house and the garden. Set the heap directly on the soil so that the soil organisms there can enter the materials quickly.

2. The Size. The decay process in a compost heap causes it to generate heat. That heat in turn decays the heap's organic content more quickly than it would occur in nature. To ensure adequate heating the heap must have a base of at least 3 square feet, and a height of about 30 inches. The base can be larger than that, but don't let it get too large, or you won't be able to turn the heap during the year.

3. Appearance. Although many people simply build their compost heap out in the open, there are ready-made compost bins designed especially to hold the growing accumulation of organic materials. Commercially produced bins are available at garden centers and hardware stores, or, if you are handy, you can build one according to the designs provided by many gardening publications. And a composting bin can be valuable. From a strictly aesthetic point of view, it keeps the garden area looking tidy. What's more, most are designed to increase air circulation through the heap, and this hastens the decay process. One warning: whether you buy or build, don't have one that holds too much organic material, or you won't be able to handle the weight when it comes time to turn the contents. A single bin can handle the needs of a household of two or three people. Adjust your plans accordingly.

4. Construction. The organic matter in a compost heap comes from plant materials, such as dead leaves, grass cuttings, and garden and kitchen waste. To speed the process along, cut up or shred all large pieces before adding them in.

Build up a layer about 8 inches thick. Cover this with an equal layer of garden soil enriched with mineral fertilizer. To increase the rate of decay, sprinkle an application of lime between the layers. Repeat the layering until your heap is as high as you want. Then water the heap well and cover it with some air-permeable material, such as dried turf or peat. This top layer will protect the heap from becoming too moist, which encourages putrefaction, or too dry, which encourages mold.

Your compost will be ready for use in about a year. (A rule of thumb: if you can recognize the contents of the mixture, the compost isn't finished yet.) At least once during that time, you should turn the heap. This reinitiates the decay cycle, and keeps the composting cycle moving. (See also the chapter "The Garden In Winter," p. 76.)

Compost Heap Ingredients—Desirables and Undesirables

All easily decayable organic waste from the kitchen and garden can go into the compost heap, including corn stalks, bean vines and any other plant that has completed its growing cycle. The heat generated by the decay process will kill many seeds, so weeds can go in the heap also.

There are exceptions, however. Meat wastes, such as fat and bones, don't belong in a compost heap—they cause odor problems as they decay and they attract animals. Do *not* place cabbage root stalks in a compost heap. There is danger that they may carry the extremely resistant cabbage hernia virus, which causes club root disease (see "Brassica Plants," p. 111). If any plant has had any sort of disease or insect infestation, it also has *no* place in the compost heap. The heat level will destroy some diseases and insect eggs, but others are unaffected and can later reinfect other plants. And it goes without saying that there is no place in your compost heap for non-organic rubbish, such as glass, tin, wire, rubber or plastics.

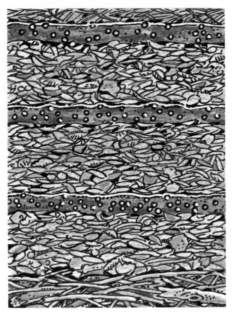

Layer a compost heap in this way.

(see diagram)

By the way...

You can also compost leaves. Layer them in the same way as other organic waste matter (see diagram). However, don't include the leaves from fruit trees in a compost heap—there is too great a danger that they might carry diseases.

Compost bins provide neat and convenient storage containers and are well-suited for a garden.

Cover Crops: Green Fertilizers

Green fertilizing with legumes is an ideal way to improve the soil. The bacteria that live in their roots have the ability to take nitrogen from the air and make it available to plants.

The value of letting a field lie fallow for all or part of a year has been known for a very long time. During this period, the land is allowed to rest, no plants are grown or harvested, and whatever seeds that are already in the ground can flourish. At the end of the fallow period, the surface is turned under, plants and all, in order to enrich the soil with humus from the plant materials.

Letting a field lie unused does cause problems, however. Exposed ground is always subject to erosion, and no gardener wants to see valuable top soil blown or washed away. Weeds proliferate on an open field, and when you plow under their seeds they'll come back to haunt you for years. To gain the advantages of a fallow field and still control these problems, plant what is called a *cover crop* as a mid-season or late crop. This is called a **green fertilizer** or a **green manure** crop.

Garden centers and seed companies sell specially designed

Turn green manure under the soil by autumn at the latest. By spring the plants will have decayed, enriching the soil with nutrients.

green manure seed mixtures. Legumes are especially valuable in green manure mixtures, because nitrogen-fixing bacteria live in their root nodules. These bacteria convert nitrogen in the air into a form that can be absorbed by plants, and when the plants are plowed under they add this valuable nutrient to the soil (see "Nitrogen," p. 54). In addition, legumes build up a large plant and root mass in a relatively short time, which yields an abundant supply of organic substances.

Green manure plants have deep root systems, and these open new layers of subsoil to release their nutrients to later crops. The leaves shade the soil's surface, thus keeping it moist and protected (shade mellowness). And, by reducing the amount of light that hits the soil's surface, green manure crops reduce weed growth.

Broadcast the seed sometime between April and mid-August (see "Broadcasting," p. 44). After about six to ten weeks, or whenever you need the ground again, simply cut off the plant growth. Use the cuttings as a layer of mulch on the other beds (see ("Mulching," p. 18), or add them to the compost heap. Or, dig the plants directly into the soil. The plants, together with their roots, will decay and become food for your new crop.

Read the label carefully before you select your green fertilizer to be sure that these mixtures are free of cruciferous plants, such as mustard. All kinds of cabbages also are members of this family, and their use in green manures increases the danger of cabbage hernias (see "Brassica Plants," p. 111). Look for green manure mixtures containing small-seeded legumes and annual grasses such

as various types of clover, lupins and annual willow grasses. They are easy to sow and are easy to work into the soil.

Here grass cuttings form a layer of mulch.

By the way...

Grass cuttings, which are always available, make an excellent mulch. Black plastic film is valuable as a mulch for many plants, especially ones like strawberries and cucumbers. It functions just like a "natural" mulch, and it also keeps the fruit from rotting.

Mulching

Mulching, another natural way to fertilize the soil, lies between composting and green manuring. A mulch is a layer of organic material that protects the soil from too much sun and wind, which can cause fluctuations in evaporation and temperature, and from the silting effect of rain, which otherwise causes an accumulation of sludge around the plants.

To mulch, spread an easily decayable organic material such as grass cuttings or foliage around the plants and between the rows. Some gardeners layer spoiled hay, salt hay, or even evergreen branches between the rows. People who live on the coast can use seaweed. The depth of a mulch can vary, from 1 to 2 inches to as high as 6 to 10 inches.

During the growing season you'll have to replenish the mulch layer, because nature's decay cycle will break down the organic materials and draw them into the soil. So mulch not only protects the soil and lessens your work load, it also replenishes its humus.

Peat

Peat is made from a loose organic substance (predominately sphagnum moss) that's cut out of bogs and marshlands. It can loosen a clay soil and add more body to a sandy soil, but it isn't

Peat cannot be manufactured in a factory. It is, as it has always been, dug out of bogs or marshy areas, and the supply has become limited.

a magic fertilizing agent in a garden. Because of peat's watery origin, it's extraordinarily poor in nutrients, and the continual leaching that occurs in marshy areas makes the material acidic. As a result, too heavy an application of peat makes an acid, or sour soil, thereby restricting the development of soil life. Always apply it with caution.

One thing to keep in mind: peat cannot be manufactured, but must be dug out of already scarce marshland areas. That makes it relatively expensive, especially given its lack of nutrient content. There are other methods, longer lasting and less expensive, that can also improve your soil.

Lime

When soil is too acidic, microorganisms cannot develop properly, and the quality of the soil is reduced. Lime plays a predominant role in soil improvement, since it neutralizes surplus acidity, expedites transplanting processes, and makes available materials that are otherwise difficult for the plant to absorb. Compared to other fertilizers, it's also relatively inexpensive.

For all of these reasons, gardeners often apply too much lime, and too much does *not* improve a garden's soil. In fact, since both the animal and plant worlds generally favor a neutral pH range, an alkaline soil is just as unfavorable as an acid soil.

So, lime your soil only when it needs it. Should a soil test show that your garden is on the acid side, you need to rectify the situation. Even in this case, you can do without an annual liming. It's usually enough to apply about 6 ounces per square yard every three years. Then the best time for liming is October or November.

Should liming be necessary, please note: it's relatively easy to add lime to an acid soil, but if you add too much and the soil becomes alkali, you'll have a difficult time trying to get your garden back to a harmonized, neutral pH range.

The Seasonal Round: Working The Soil

Working the soil carefully is the basis for successful gardening. Not only does it help to create friable soil that's easy to work, it also creates the conditions necessary for the germination and growth of your valuable seeds. All your gardening work will be considerably easier if you work on your soil at the right time and with the right tools.

	Feb	Mar	Apr	May	June	July	Aug	Sep	Oct	Nov
1st Step	Harrowing									
2nd Step		Crumbling								
3rd Step			Sowing/Planting							
4th Step			Aerating (see Care of the Soil)							
5th Step			Weeding							
6th Step									Turning Under	

The only way to achieve optimal growth conditions in your garden is to work the soil regularly. The table above shows you the basis of successful gardening in six steps.

Individual Work Steps

Turning the Soil Under

So that plants can take up sufficient water and nutrients during the course of their development, their roots must be able to penetrate the soil deeply and easily. When you turn the soil under, you break it up into clumps that are easier for roots to penetrate.

Autumn is the best time to turn the soil under thoroughly. Nature then continues the work through the winter. Water penetrates the clefts dug into the earth, then freezes with the first frost. As it freezes, it expands,

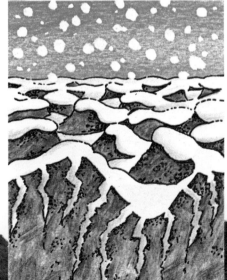

breaking up the large clumps of earth and creating new cracks. Sunlight rewarms the soil and melts the ice, the water penetrates the newly created cracks, and the cycle begins again. In this way, the clumps become smaller and smaller. Soil in this condition has the quality of **frost mellowness**.

By the way...

Don't break up the soil you turn under in the autumn. The clumps supply the frost with a larger area of attack, and the rain and melted ice and snow can penetrate the earth more easily.

Harrowing

In winter, soil soaks up water like a sponge. This water continually forces its way upwards through small channels called *capillaries*, similar to the way that oil rises in a lantern wick. In the spring, when the soil warms up, the water evaporates, the surface becomes encrusted, and the capillaries are solidly open.

At this time there's a danger that the sun and the wind will dry out the bed if it remains unworked. When the surface of your garden's soil becomes lighter in color, it means that the bed is drying out, and it's time to harrow the surface of the soil thoroughly. Breaking up the surface crust retains valuable winter moisture, and microorganisms can fully develop in order to release new nutrients for new growth. Harrowing also allows better aeration and more thorough warming.

The cultivator is a valuable tool for harrowing crusted soil or for loosening and aerating the soil.

Hair-thin veins, called capillaries, pass through all of the soil. The physical laws of nature cause water to rise in them continually.

The capillaries in the surface soil must be broken up, so that water cannot evaporate out through them before the plants have an opportunity to use it.

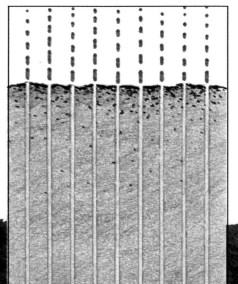

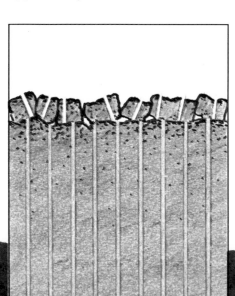

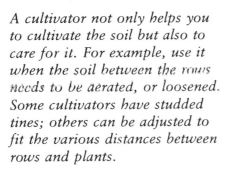

A cultivator not only helps you to cultivate the soil but also to care for it. For example, use it when the soil between the rows needs to be aerated, or loosened. Some cultivators have studded tines; others can be adjusted to fit the various distances between rows and plants.

Tilling

After harrowing, the earth is tilled to a fairly fine consistency. The loose layer of crumbs acts like a lid and keeps the valuable winter moisture in the root area. But use restraint—if the soil is too fine, it will create silt and you'll lose the crumb structure you need.

Tilling is the best soil preparation for planting. Only an evenly tilled soil offers the optimal hold to seed roots, a condition necessary for strong root formation and good growth.

Suitable Garden Tools

Just as every craftsman needs good tools, so a gardener needs good garden implements.

Well-made, dependable garden tools can lighten your work considerably and, as a result, save time. Badly chosen tools will soon have you complaining of backaches or blistered hands. Before you buy, examine them carefully.

Good garden tools should be made from *tempered, high quality steel* that holds its shape even under extreme stress. *Galvanized* garden tools are more costly, but they rust less easily and are worth the extra expense.

The shaft of the tool should be made of *hardwood* and should fit comfortably in your hand. Examine the joint between the tool head and the shaft. This shouldn't break, split or work loose, even under great expenditures of energy. A *steel core* connecting the tool to the shaft guarantees long-lasting stability, tensile strength and rotary resistance.

Improvements are made in garden tools all the time, so you may be surprised at some of the implements available. Many manufacturers advertise in gardening magazines and will send you a catalog of their supplies upon request. You also should investigate local garden centers and hardware stores.

For instance, consider the implement set that features a lock-on handle and several gardening heads. The heads attach quickly and easily to the shaft by means of a locking system that's roughly similar to the mechanism of a car safety belt. Just select a head and click it into position on the shaft, where it's held firmly. To release the head, press a button in the locking mechanism. A set requires little storage space and eliminates trips back and forth between the house and the garden.

Working on a garden can be a tiring proposition. Two things can help.(1) Take care to have the correct handle length. Your work will be considerably easier if you can stand upright instead of being forced to dig with a bent back. (2) Your work will be much easier if you use tools that

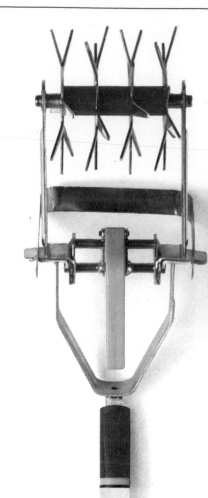

The lock-on system of some garden tools makes them versatile enough to cope with all light gardening tasks. The head on this universal milling-cutter can be exchanged with various other appliances (cultivator, Dutch hoe, hoe, curved weeder or grubber).

The "beating" method of working: bent posture makes gardening exhausting work.

The "gripping" method of working: an upright posture makes for non-tiring work.

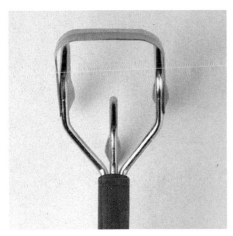

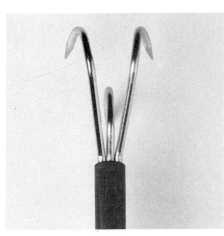

require a pulling motion rather than a pushing motion.

Your standard equipment should include the correct **spade**. It's suitable for all types of garden digging and for all types of soil.

Many experienced gardeners also like to work with a **garden fork**, since it has some advantages over a spade. Because the tines penetrate the soil more easily than the blade of a spade, you can work more quickly in heavy soil and disperse the clumps of earth more efficiently.

A **cultivator** is valuable when you are harrowing large clumps or breaking up encrusted earth. It can also be used for loosening and aerating the soil.

Tilling the surface soil is quicker and easier with a **universal milling cutter** than with a rake. With its help, you can even break up heavy soils to an adequate depth and texture. During the growth period, you can also achieve a fine loose tilth. The work doesn't take long, and you'll certainly be rewarded with a rich harvest.

A well-equipped tool shed is the pride of every backyard gardener. To begin with, of course, you'll manage with fewer implements.

Planning Your Garden

The way you lay out your garden depends on its size, its location and the natural features of your land's surface. However, your garden's appearance can be as individual as your personality. The most successful gardens are well-planned. Take enough time to set out beds and measure out paths. When everything's well thought out you save yourself work and the entire project will be much more enjoyable.

Bed Cultivation

The traditional way to lay out a garden is to establish several beds, one for each type of plant. Paths then run between the beds. If you plan to work your garden by hand, the ideal width for a path is about 10 to 12 inches.

However, if you intend to use a garden tiller, make sure the paths are wide enough to accommodate the blades.

In this design, the ideal width for a vegetable bed is about 4 feet—you'll be able to reach comfortably halfway across the bed from either side. The length is determined only by need or the overall size of your plot.

To grow vegetables in mixed cultivation, alternate the type of plants from row to row—or have several kinds of plants in the same row.

Mixed Cultivation

Traditional bed cultivation is a man-made invention. Mixed cultivation, on the other hand, is based upon the example of nature. If you look at a field or lot that's growing wild, you won't see fixed paths or set beds, but a mixture of plants, a community that ensures a healthy biological balance. Mixed cultivation follows this pattern—different types of plants are grown together in a bed for the mutual benefit of both. Mixed beds are likely to be more resistant to diseases and pests, so this technique is becoming very popular in private gardens.

The success of mixed cultivation depends on good planning. Certain crops, for instance, do well planted with some plants, but not others. You need to know whether plants are *compatible* or *incompatible* (see "Compatible and Incompatible Crops," p. 31). In addition, you need to keep several basic rules in mind.

1. Plan the distances between plants so that when they are fully grown they will lightly touch, or overlap. This will protect the soil.

2. Tall "thin" plants fit well beside short "fat" ones; deep-rooted plants between will grow well when paired with shallow-rooted ones.

3. Plants divide up into low, medium and heavy feeders, according to their nutrient requirements (see the table "Plant Varieties According to Nutrient Needs," p. 35). You can combine medium feeders with heavy or low feeders, but never put heavy with light feeders, because their demands are too different.

4. Stagger the harvest times of the various types and species so that the soil is never wholly uncovered and your harvesting chores don't pile on top of each other.

Compatible and Incompatible Crops								
Vegetable	Compatible	Incompatible		Compatible	Incompatible		Compatible	Incompatible
Brassicas	Beets	Chives	Garden	Beets	Celery	Radishes	Brassicas	Cucumbers
	Bush Beans	Garlic	Lettuce	Belgian Endive	Parsley		Bush Beans	
	Celery	Onion		Brassicas			Carrots	
	Cucumbers	Potatoes		Bush Beans			Lettuce	
	Endive	Rhubarb		Carrots			Peas	
	Lettuce			Comfrey			Spinach	
	Peas			Cucumbers			Tomatoes	
	Spinach			Fennel		Pole Beans	Brassicas	Beets
	Tomato (not red cabbage)			Kohlrabi			Celery	Fennel
Bush Beans	Beets	Chives		Leeks			Cucumbers	Garlic
	Brassicas	Fennel		Onions			Endive	Leeks
	Celery	Garlic		Peas			Lettuce	Onions
	Cucumbers	Leeks		Radishes			Radishes	Peas
	Kohlrabi	Onions		Tomatoes			Spinach	
	Lettuce	Peas	Leeks	Brassicas	Beets		Zucchini	
	Potatoes			Carrots	Peas	Tomatoes	Brassicas	Beets
	Radishes			Celery	Pole Beans		(except	Cucumbers
	Savoy			Comfrey			Red Cabbage)	Fennel
	Spinach			Endive			Bush Beans	Peas
	Tomatoes			Lettuce			Carrots	Potatoes
	Leeks			Tomatoes			Celery	Red Cabbage
	Lettuce		Onions	Beets	Beans		Leeks	
	Onions			Carrots	Brassicas		Lettuce	
	Peas			Cucumbers	Peas		Onions	
	Radishes			Lettuce	Potatoes		Radishes	
	Spinach			Parsnips			Spinach	
	Tomatoes			Tomatoes		Zucchini	Onions	
Celery	Brassicas	Corn		Zucchini			Pole Beans	
	Bush Beans	Lettuce	Parsley	Cucumbers	Lettuce			
	Cucumbers	Potatoes		Radishes				
	Leeks			Onions				
	Peas			Tomatoes				
	Runner Beans		Peas	Brassicas	Beans			
	Tomatoes			Carrot	Garlic			
Cucumbers	Beans	Potatoes		Celery	Onions			
	Beets	Tomatoes		Corn	Tomatoes			
	Brassicas			Cucumbers				
	Celery			Fennel				
	Fennel			Kohlrabi				
	Garlic			Lettuce				
	Lettuce			Radishes				
	Onions			Potatoes				
	Peas			Zucchini				
Fennel	Cucumbers	Beans	Potatoes	Broad Beans	Beets			
	Endive	Tomatoes		Bush Beans	Celery			
	Lamb's Lettuce			Kohlrabi	Cucumbers			
	Lettuce			Spinach	Onions			
					Tomatoes			

Mixed Cultivation Garden

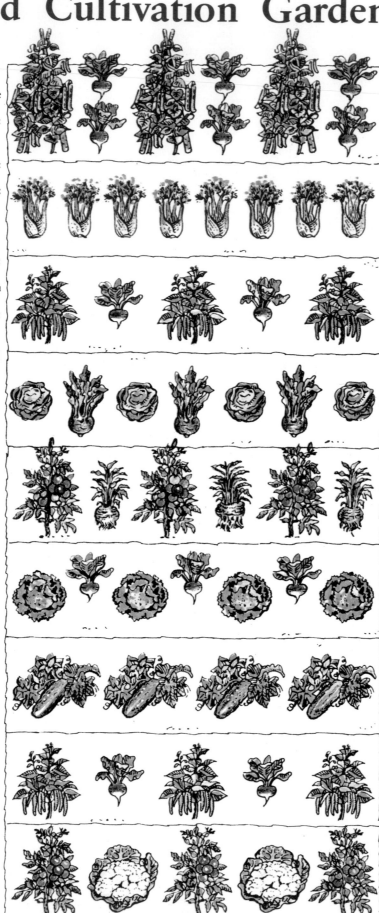

First Crop:
Radishes
Main Crop: Pole Beans
In Between Crop: Lettuce

First Crop:
Spinach
Main Crop: Fennel or Cauliflower

First Crop:
Radishes
Main Crop: Bush Beans
Next Crop: Chinese Cabbage

Main Crop: Head Lettuce and Kohlrabi
Next Crop: Radishes

Main Crop: Tomatoes and Celery

First Crop:
Butterhead Lettuce and Radishes
Main Crop: Bush Beans

Main Crop: Cucumbers

First Crop:
Radishes
Main Crop: Bush Beans
Next Crop: Head Lettuce

First Crop:
Lettuce
Main Crop: Tomatoes and Cauliflower

Main Crop: Tomatoes
In Between Crop: Spring Onions, then Basil

Main Crop: Carrots and Onions
Next Crop: Lamb's Lettuce

Main Crop: Beets
Next Crop: Lamb's Lettuce

Main Crop: Broccoli
Next Crop: Head Lettuce

Main Crop: Broad Beans
Next Crop: Sugar Loaf

Main Crop: White Cabbage
Next Crop: Butterhead Lettuce

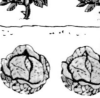

Main Crop: Zucchini
Next Crop: Radishes

Main Crop: Cauliflower and Celery

Main Crop: Peas
Next Crop: Fennel

Size of garden: 15 x 22 feet

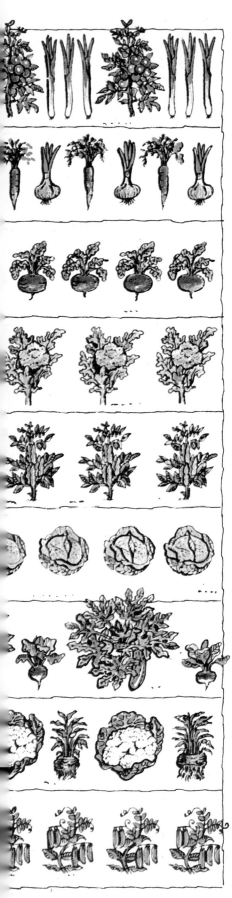

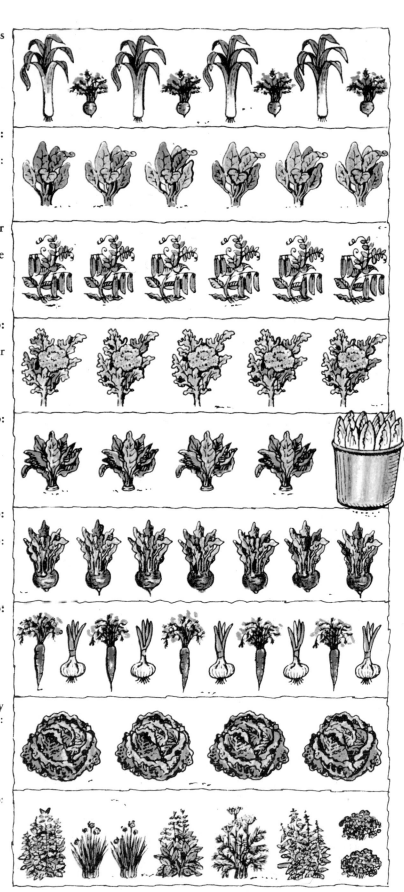

Main Crop: Leeks and Carrots

Main Crop: Spinach Next Crop: Brussels Sprouts

Main Crop: Sugar Peas Next Crop: Kale

Main Crop: Broccoli Next Crop: Sugar Loaf

Main Crop: Belgium Endive

Main Crop: Kohlrabi Next Crop: Butterhead Lettuce

Main Crop: Carrots and Onions

Main Crop: Savoy Next Crop: Endive

Main Crop: Herbs

Mound Beds

If you want to make the maximum use of your garden land—and are willing to invest a fair amount of work on it—you'll find mound bed construction an interesting and fruitful project.

The basic idea is simple: combine a plant bed and a compost heap in a single unit. You gain some space, since the mound-shaped surface enlarges the area of the bed. You also have longer growing and harvesting periods because the decay that takes place in a mound bed warms the soil. As a result, you can sow earlier in the spring and harvest longer in the autumn.

A mound bed is constructed in much the same way as a compost heap, although the two aren't interchangeable. The best time to do the work is in the autumn, when you have an abundance of organic materials to incorporate into the mound. First, dig a shallow ditch. Place in it, one after the other, twigs, leaves, woody waste from shrubs, and other autumnal garden and kitchen waste. Finally, cover the materials entirely with compost soil.

The bed will undergo substantial settling during the winter. By spring it will have settled enough that it shouldn't sink any further and will be ready to use. Decomposition will continue, however,

and the supply of nitrogen and other nutrients in the soil will be particularly high. As a result, don't plant leafy vegetables, such as lettuce or spinach, in a mound bed during its first year. There will be too much nitrogen fixing in these vegetables.

The organic materials in the bed will continue to decompose, just as in a compost heap, so you should offset any settling. The best way is to add well-rotted manure to the soil about every second year. After about four to six years, the mound bed will be completely level.

There is one precaution: If you have mice in your garden, don't construct a mound bed. It provides them with an almost ideal shelter.

Deep Cultivation Beds

Another way to achieve a substantial yield from a small space is to construct a deep cultivation bed. The plants in this kind of bed can penetrate deeply and don't need to branch out sideways. Plants in a deep cultivation bed can grow quite close together, and they still will be larger and stronger than in a normal bed.

Constructing a deep cultivation bed isn't difficult, but it does take some effort. The best width is 5 feet. Its length is up to you. First, cover the whole bed with dung or compost. Then dig a trench spade-deep along the width, and throw the earth into a wheelbarrow. Loosen the base of the ditch with a garden fork.

Now, dig a second trench next to the first, only instead of placing the initial layer into your wheelbarrow, throw the soil from the second trench into the first. Loosen the base layer again, and follow the same procedure. When you have loosened the base of the last trench, empty your wheelbarrow load into it, and the bed is complete.

The following spring, loosen the soil again with a garden fork.

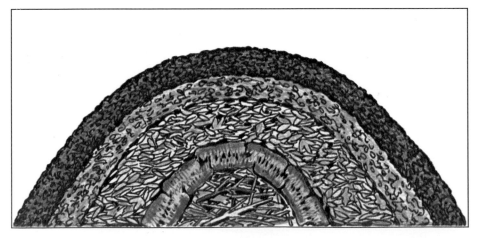

An example of mound bed construction: Begin with a layer of twigs that's about 20 inches high and 20 inches wide. Over this place about 6 inches of loose lumps of sod and turf. Then comes a 12-inch layer of leaves and about 6 inches of slightly decomposed compost. Lay about 6 inches of good humus soil over the top.

Alternating Crops to Keep the Soil and the Plants Healthy

Whenever you grow something on a patch of ground, you interfere with the soil's natural biological balance. If you plant the same plant variety in the same spot year after year, your garden will suffer from *soil fatigue*.

Soil fatigue is caused by a one-sided removal of nutrients. When the soil becomes imbalanced, it encourages pests and diseases, and plant roots have difficulty eliminating wastes. Plants are visibly smaller and the crops are reduced.

The best measure against soil fatigue is **crop rotation**, i.e., a regular changeover of plant varieties in the same bed. One way to rotate crops successfully is to divide the bed into four quarters. The first quarter can hold predominantly light feeders, the second medium feeders, the third heavy feeders, and the last a green fertilizer with legumes. By following heavy feeders with a green fertilizer, you will regenerate the soil before using it again. The accompanying diagram may give you some suggestions for your own garden.

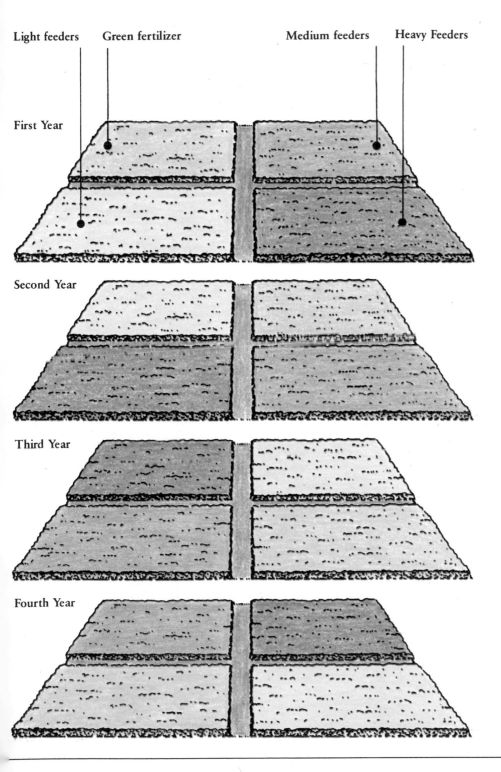

Light feeders Green fertilizer Medium feeders Heavy Feeders

First Year

Second Year

Third Year

Fourth Year

Plant Varieties According to Nutrient Needs

Heavy Feeders	Medium Feeders	Light Feeders
Beans, Broad	Beans	Cress
Cabbage	Beets	Herbs
Cauliflower	Belgian Endive	Lamb's
Celery	Broccoli	Lettuce
Comfrey	Carrots	Radishes
Corn	Cucumbers	
Eggplant	Endive	
Kale	Fennel	
Parsnips	Kohlrabi	
Potatoes	Leeks	
Pumpkin	Lettuce	
Rhubarb	Onions	
Savoy	Peas	
Squash	Potatoes, Early	
Tomatoes	Radicchio	
Zucchini	Spinach	
	Sweet Peppers	
	Swiss Chard	
	Turnips	

Seeds, Seedlings and Seasons

Winter is the time to plan your garden and to decide what to plant. Then you have the time to look over the hundreds of varieties listed in seed catalogs before you make your selections.

What to Plant, Where to Look

Seed and nursery catalogs are fascinating; they make their readers aware of a variety of plants that most people have never heard about. It's good to keep in mind that many fruit and vegetable varieties have become mainstays in our diets not necessarily because they are better tasting, but simply because they travel well or keep in storage for a long time. Varieties without these characteristics are less well known, but they sometimes offer more in both flavor and nutrition.

Seed Catalogs

Seed catalogs are easy to find. During the winter months, all the national gardening magazines will list one company after another, from all over the country. Most of the catalogs are free; a

In general, seeds should only consist of complete kerns, without impurities from the soil or bits or other plants.

few require that you enclose postage stamps to equal the cost of the mailing. Some do require a nominal payment (ordinarily around a dollar or so) and usually refund it with your first order. Most of the companies are more than willing to answer any questions about their products, so they supply customer service numbers, some of which are toll-free, and have representatives that can be very helpful.

It's worth your while to examine several catalogs. Some unusual vegetables are only offered by one company and they never reach the public market. For instance, there is a purple cauliflower that is winter hardy and is revered for its flavor by those who know it. Unlike many white varieties, it doesn't require that you tie the leaves in place over the forming head to preserve its whiteness, so it's less trouble to grow, although it does require a

bit more room. When cooked, it turns a pale greenish white, much like its cousins. This plant is only one example of the varieties that may tempt you to experiment.

Maturity Dates

Maturity dates are estimates of how long a certain variety must grow before it's ready to harvest. Those dates are important if you decide to make succession plantings. For instance, if you want to grow a fall broccoli crop, you need to know their maturity dates. In "The Planting Advisor" in this book, you will learn that broccoli needs to go through at least one frost to have the best taste, so you want to harvest in November. Then you figure backwards to determine when you must sow the seeds.

For instance, if your first frost is due in late October, you must plant in early July. During the spring and early summer you can grow a short or medium season crop, such as lettuce, perhaps peas, or even early scallions. By July, they will have finished their growing, and you can replant the space with your second crop, broccoli. With careful planning and an eye for maturity dates, you can often use the same space to grow two or even three different crops during the growing season.

Some vegetable varieties have been developed to meet special needs. For instance, there are cucumbers for salads and cucumbers for pickling. Lettuce usually does best in cooler weather, but there are certain varieties specifically designed to withstand the heat of summer. There are peas that can only be harvested when they have filled their pods—and

some that are harvested when the peas are very immature and are eaten pods and all. Some of the most recent varieties can be eaten at any stage of their development—as edible pods when the peas are immature, later in a manner similar to green beans, and finally at maturity, when the pods are shucked, just as with traditional varieties. Local garden centers can't offer the wide variety of a seed catalog.

If you have the space in your garden and don't want to plant more than once, take advantage of vegetables bred for staggered maturity dates. There are early, medium and late tomatoes, for instance. By choosing your varieties carefully, you'll be able to plant in the spring, and harvest all through the season. This is especially important with crops such as corn, which bear only once.

Investigating the Specialists

Not all seed companies are large. Many are small, often concentrating on one specialty. Some aim their products specifically at a given state or region. Others specialize in certain types of vegetables, such as unusual herbs or lettuces. There are companies that import seeds from Europe. Be sure that the company will include any necessary special instructions with their seed orders. You'll find that small companies offer an interesting variety unavailable elsewhere.

Nursery Catalogs

Not all seed companies include nursery stock for berries, and

Seeds purchased from reputable companies will germinate reliably and form true-to-type plants and crops.

those that do often have a relatively limited selection. Should you decide to plant a certain type of berry, you'll probably have to browse through nursery catalogs. These too are listed in gardening magazines. There may or may not be a charge for the catalog, and again, many of these are refunded with your first order.

Nursery catalogs offer the same advantage as seed catalogs. They present you with a variety that you can't find anywhere else. Some small companies specialize in varieties of apples or strawberries especially suited to a given climate or region. Both large and small companies are glad to help you in any way that they can, either by phone or by mail.

Garden Centers And Local Nurseries

Garden centers and local nurseries may not have access to the wide variety that national companies do, but they can still be a very good source of seeds, seedlings, and nursery stock. They are also close at hand, and this can be important when you are concerned about the wear and tear that long-distance shipping could cause to young seedlings. If you purchase seedlings from a local concern, you don't have to worry about hardening off a tender plant that's unaccustomed to your particular climate. Nursery stock that is locally produced, especially for a crop like strawberries, will have the special advantage of being resistant to locally prevalent diseases, and this is sometimes a valuable asset that no national company can provide.

Hybrids—Breeding for Quality

One thing that seed and nursery catalogs offer is access to the newest developments in plant breeding. Plant breeding is a very specialized profession devoted to improving vegetables in any of a number of ways. For example, a breeder will pair a plant variety that is valued for its fruit's flavor with another variety of the same plant valued for its disease resistance or cold hardiness. The goal is to develop a new strain that will exhibit both of those characteristics.

Most breeding programs concentrate on certain qualities, among which are:

1. Appearance

2. Flavor and aroma
3. Disease resistance
4. Fruit of similar size
5. Uniform, predictable yield
6. Increased vitamin and mineral content
7. Extended harvesting period
8. Uniform plant growth, height and size
9. Extended shelf life (period of storage)

These characteristics stem from the genetic heritage of the variety and determine the worth of a strain.

Developing new strains is costly and requires much patience and time. A successful product is patented, just like any other new invention, to protect the rights of the developer. The system works, for new strains are offered every year. The way to find out about them is to search for them in seed catalogs.

The Seasonal Round—or, Will It Grow Here?

Because of their inherited tendencies, certain vegetables are more suited to some climates than others. Rhubarb prefers cold weather and needs the dormant period that comes with the freezing temperatures of northern winters. Sweet potatoes and peanuts, on the other hand, need a long growing season, and seem to prefer to be planted in the same place that they will grow. The more you learn about vegetables, the more you realize that they have very specific needs.

Different vegetables also require their own individual weather conditions. Lettuce and peas germinate well when the weather is cool, whereas corn won't thrive until the soil is well warmed. Some crops can survive the worst of winters with little or no protection, and will grow in the spring, as soon as the sun reaches the right angle. Still others will die at the first touch of frost in the air. Some plants, like catnip, are so persistent and spread so rapidly, no matter what the conditions, that some gardeners resort to burning to get rid of it. As a result, both climate and weather conditions must influence your planning.

Father: resistant to disease

Mother: firm flesh

You must pay attention to the special requirements of each vegetable. If you ignore the weather requirements of your garden crops, the only result will be failure. To have a thriving garden, every gardener must know about seasons and growing zones.

Offspring: resistant to disease; firm flesh

Examples of Hybrid Cultivation

Varieties that are the result of F_1 hybrid breeding exhibit the positive charactersitics from two parents in one offspring. In order to breed true, all hybrid seed must be fertilized carefully, often by hand methods. To be sure that you'll grow what you intends, only use hybrid seeds from a reputable seed company. Those you grow at home often inadvertently cross-pollinate with other varieties and the qualities you desire will be lost.

Sowing, Cultivating, Planting

To garden is to experience the germination of seeds, the development of the first leaves, to observe the formation of the blossoms and the ripening of the fruits of your labor.

Sowing in the Open

Before sowing your seeds, you need to prepare the soil properly. It should be loose and finely tilled to ensure good seed emergence (see "The Seasonal Round," p. 41).

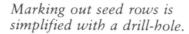

Marking out seed rows is simplified with a drill-hole.

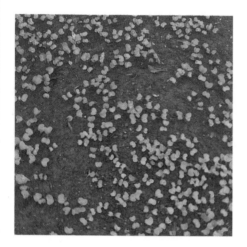

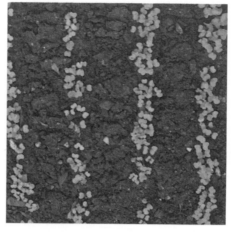

Broadcasting

There are two techniques for sowing seeds: broadcasting or sowing in rows. To broadcast, simply toss the seeds in all directions and let them, more or less, fend for themselves. Under certain circumstances, as, for instance, when you sow a lawn or plant a cover crop, this technique is quite effective.

When the seeds germinate, you'll find some places where there are no plants at all, and others where the plants are clumped far too closely together.

The plants that do come up will inhibit each other's development, and their care and cultivation will be unnecessarily difficult.

Sowing in Rows

Even though it seems to require more work, you should sow your garden seeds in rows. This method will give each seed enough living space, and will lighten your work load later on.

The soil should be relatively dry before you sow. That will make it fairly easy to handle, so you will have more control over the depth and evenness of the layer of soil you place over the seeds.

To begin, draw regularly spaced furrows in the soil. A string stretched between two sticks, one at each end of the row, is an easy way to keep your row from wandering as you draw your line. Spread the seeds evenly along the furrow.

After sowing the seeds, cover them lightly and tamp the soil gently but firmly. Then water the soil well. Do this carefully so you don't silt in the furrow.

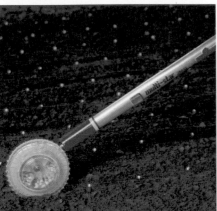

A seed dispenser is designed to sow seeds of varying sizes with the correct spacing.

To sow rows quickly and surely, first mark the furrows with a drill hole, then sow the seeds with a seed dispenser. Finally firm the soil lightly over the seed rows.

Appropriate Tools

The simplest way to draw seed furrows is to use a drill hoe. This useful tool can mark either narrow or widely spaced furrows, and it simplifies the task of making them even.

To sow seeds evenly and quickly, try using a seed dispenser. The opening adjusts to any seed size, from coarse to fine, and you can check its contents anytime through its transparent face.

Seed-Starter

If you live in an area with a short growing season, or you want to shorten the time between planting and harvest, cultivate seeds in a seed-starter. With a seed-starter you can begin growing your important vegetables and flower plants long before they could survive out in your garden. Then, when the weather is right, plant the seedlings out in the open. A seed-starter can make you absolutely independent of the weather.

Garden centers carry every-thing you need to start seeds, such as starting beds, or *flats*, peat pots, crushed rock for drainage and starting soil (this mixture is designed to meet all the needs of germinating seeds). Purchase the items separately or buy an entire seed-starting kit. To plant, cover the bottom of the flat with crushed rock and cover this with the soil. To settle the soil, water the flat, then plant your seeds thinly in rows about 2 inches apart. Cover the seeds with a thin layer of soil. Water the flat thoroughly, and cover it with a sheet of plastic wrap to hold in the moisture until the seeds germinate.

Place the flat in a warm, light, airy place. Once the plants break through the soil, remove the plastic and keep the seedlings well watered. You may have to thin out some of the plants to give the remaining ones enough room to grow and develop. Retain the plants with the healthiest development.

When the seedlings are strong enough (usually when they have at least one set of true leaves), transplant them into your garden or a cold frame.

Some seed-starter kits come complete with safe, powerful 16-volt heaters. This system creates a mini hot-house in which both temperature and humidity are regulated. You can then decide for yourself, independent of the weather and outside temperature, when to grow young plants.

Cultivating plants in a seed starter is a nice exercise for children. They can experience for themselves how a young plant grows from a seed. It may be the first step to an interesting, diversified, leisure-time activity for your entire family.

Growing Seedlings to Transplant

You can raise young plants in a seed starter, a cold frame or in an open-air cultivation bed. All of these methods can make your gardening independent of weather and season to some extent.

Sowing in a seed starter, or flat.

Planting in a flat.

Replanting in a cold frame.

When you transplant seedlings, you move them from the dense growth of a flat into small pots or into a cold frame. This encourages strong development and the growth of a healthy root ball.

Hardening Off

Even if all signs of frost are gone, conditions inside a house and in a garden are hardly similar. The shock of being transplanted straight from house to garden bed can kill susceptible seedlings. The process of acclimating them to the outdoors before placing them in a permanent bed is called **hardening off.**

One way to harden off seedlings is to place them outside in the shade for one or two afternoons so that they gradually become accustomed to direct sunlight, wind, and temperature changes. Then plant the seedlings in their permanent bed, preferably late in the afternoon, so they won't have to tolerate direct sunlight right after being moved.

Plastic film cloches, sometimes called *hotcaps*, can help seedlings make the transition. Plant them in their permanent bed and place wire hoops around them. Cover the hoops with plastic film and fasten it with clothespins or something similar. Garden centers carry ready-made cloches.

Transplanting into the Garden

Seedlings are usually transplanted into the garden in the spring, once the danger of nighttime frosts is past. However, some plants, such as many brassicas, some lettuces and peas, aren't frost-sensitive and can be planted earlier (see pp. 76-153).

Again, check the information on your plant packets for crops that are frost-hardy.

If the seedling's roots are in a peat ball, moisten the root ball, then place the seedling in its hole. Press the earth firmly around it with your hands. If the

seedling is in a peat pot, water it well, split the sides of the pot, and set the seedling, pot and all, into the earth, with the lip of the pot just below the surface.

If the seedling has no ball of earth protecting its roots, spread the roots gently and set the plants carefully into a hole that you have made with a dibble or a trowel. Then firm the earth gently around them.

Once the seedlings are in place, water the young plants carefully to assure quick rooting. Some gardeners cover the new plants with plastic cloches for protection the first few days, until the seedlings have taken hold. To advance the harvest date, cover the bed with plastic film after transplanting.

Using a Cold Frame

Another way to harden off seedlings is to transplant them into a cold frame, an enclosed outdoor bed that's designed to

Ready-made plastic film cloches come in many different designs. When buying, take care that the film is stable and that it is easy to raise or drape for ventilation.

be, in principle, a "miniature greenhouse." Because the glass that covers a cold frame causes more efficient utilization of solar energy, the temperature inside the frame is higher than it is outside. The glass over the frame can be lifted to allow air circulation during the day and lowered during the cold evenings. Every day leave the glass open longer and longer. After a week or so, you can safely move your seedlings to their final, permanent bed.

A cold frame can also lengthen your growing season. By using it as a large, outdoor seed-starter, you can plant earlier in the spring and harvest longer in the autumn. Since the frame automatically hardens off seedlings, it increases successful transplanting.

A cold frame is easy to construct. The simplest requires only a glass window laid over a wooden box, with some provi-

sion for ventilating the frame so that strong sunlight won't overheat the interior. The most sophisticated design is only a variation of this basic format.

If you have neither the time nor the inclination to create your own, there are commercial models available. Some come with unbreakable double panes that have a considerably better insulating ability than ordinary glass panes (up to 35%). Some models have thermostatically controlled ventilators; others come with heating coils that are buried in the soil to ensure even heating. Any of these models enable you to start your seedlings long before the final frost.

Whether you build or buy, it pays to acquire a cold frame. It's more expensive than a plastic cloche, but it lasts considerably longer.

Open-air Nursery Bed

Some gardeners prefer to start seeds directly in a nursery bed in the garden, and they continue to raise seedlings there throughout the growing season. That way they always have young plants on hand. As a bed is harvested, they replant the area immediately.

The size of an open-air nursery bed depends on the number of plants you wish to start off at one time. If you do decide to have a nursery bed, it's a good idea to begin every year by enriching the soil with a little compost and digging in peat to loosen it up. Early in the growing season you can use a row-length portable "greenhouse" covered with plastic film to protect the growing seedlings.

A nursery bed requires little special care. Always keep the soil well loosened and evenly watered. Since you'll transplant the young plants to their final location when they are strong enough, you can plant them more densely in an open-air nursery bed than in a normal bed.

The elements in mineral
fertilizers are all natural in
origin. Nitrogen comes
predominantly from the air.
Phosphate and potash salts come
from natural deposits.

Feeding Your Garden

Nutrients are substances necessary for maintaining the life of an organism.

Plant nutrients are all the irreplaceable elements required for healthy plant growth.

The Significance of Nutrients

Plants are unique because they have the ability to manufacture their own food. Through the process of *photosynthesis*, plants use solar energy to form organic substances such as starch and sugar from the elements they take from the soil and the air. The starches and sugars are then

used to build up their roots, leaves, stems, flowers and fruits. A sound fertilizing program is based upon the fact that plants cannot manufacture the nutrients needed to create those starches and sugars. For photosynthesis to take place, those nutrients must already be present in the air and the soil.

The basic framework of all organic substances is based upon carbon, hydrogen and oxygen. Plants breathe in both oxygen and carbon, in the form of carbon dioxide, from the air. They take both hydrogen and oxygen from water.

Plants take the rest of the nutrients they need for growth and development from the soil, in the form of mineral salts. Their presence depends upon the activities of microorganisms in the soil. As a rule, the soil's natural store of nutrients can't support healthy plant growth over a period of years, so you must replenish the mineral supply regularly. Not only does fertilization ensure the presence of nutrients, it also improves the soil's structure.

Soil minerals are crucial to plant nutrition. That means that if you fertilize your garden, you can ensure a healthy crop because your plants are receiving the nutrients they need in the correct amounts and balanced proportions. Either a mineral or an organic fertilizer will do the job, since plants absorb their nutrients through a process that is biologically determined. Plants utilize mineral fertilizers in exactly the same way as those occuring naturally in the soil.

Organic Fertilizers

Fertilizers are called "organic" because they supply organic materials to the soil. We have already discussed the value of natural organic fertilizers such as compost and green manures in the chapter "Improving Your Garden's Soil" (see pp. 12-20).

Compost and other organic fertilizers also contain plant nutrients, but in relatively small quantities. Their minerals are present mainly in forms that are insoluble in water, so soil microorganisms must break them down before plants can absorb them. The advantage of organic fertilizers is that they minimize the danger of *leaching*, a process by which minerals are literally washed out of the soil.

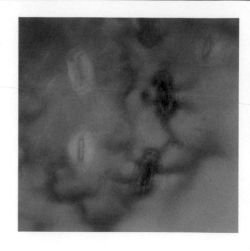

Every leaf has "stomata." Too small to be seen with the naked eye, these openings are found, almost without exception, on the underside of the leaves. Stomata regulate gas exchange and water balance.

Commercially produced organic fertilizers work in the same way as home-grown compost or green manure plants. They contain nitrogen and phosphates in difficult-to-release combinations that are only set free through microbe activity.

Legumes grown as green fertilizer are turned under in the autumn. By spring, the decomposition of plants will have released the nitrogen in their root nodules and enriched the soil.

Mineral Fertilizers

Mineral fertilizers supply plant nutrients in inorganic form, at a much greater strength than commercially produced organic fertilizers.

Extensive testing has shown that mineral fertilizers have a beneficial effect on your garden and improve the quality of your yield—as long as they are used with common sense. If you pay attention to how much you are applying, these products maintain fertile soil and encourage good plant health.

Like human beings, plants get sick when they don't get the nutrients that they need. Mineral fertilizers specifically designed for vegetables supply your garden with a biologically sound, controlled source of nutrients throughout the growing season. These fertilizers contain nitrogen, phosphate and potash, as well as all the important trace elements that plants need, and the minerals

Plants that cannot obtain sufficient nutrients remain small and stunted. Correct fertilizing guarantees optimal growth.

are present in the correct amounts and proportions.

Mineral fertilizers also supply nitrogen in a form that plants can absorb. It is true that air is a source of nitrogen; however, these reserves are only available to plants through the action of nitrogen-fixing node bacteria. Legumes, such as beans, peas and clovers, have these bacteria at their disposal. Other plants can only absorb nitrogen that is present in suitable chemical combinations in the soil. The most important of these are mineral ammonium nitrites and nitrates. These two forms are found in

A spreading shovel is ideal for evenly distributing mineral fertilizers.

humus and in universal vegetable fertilizers.

When you add mineral nutrients, correct timing and exact dose are important. *More* is not better than *enough* when you are fertilizing a garden. If you add too much fertilizer, the plant cells acquire too many nutrient salts. The increased concentration inside the cells makes the plant become "thirsty," and it tries to compensate by increasing its absorption of water. The cell tissues then become diluted.

Plant Nutrients: Types, Requirements

There are two types of plant nutrients: (1) *main nutrients* are those elements needed in large quantities; (2) *trace elements* are those required in only minute amounts.

The main plant nutrients are nitrogen, phosphate, and potassium. In addition, even though

magnesium and calcium are needed in such small amounts that they should be called trace minerals, they are also considered to be main nutrients because of their importance for healthy plant growth and development.

Trace elements are boron, copper, manganese, zinc, molybdenum, and iron.

Nitrogen

Nitrogen is a basic element in chlorophyll, a basic building block in all plant proteins and the vehicle for photosynthesis. It is indispensable in the life of every plant and is one of the most important nutrients of all.

Nitrogen deficiency can shorten a plant's entire growth cycle. The plant grows poorly because it can't carry out photosynthesis efficiently. There are fewer fruits and seeds, and those that do form are small. Leaves remain a light green because they lack chlorophyll and they turn yellow before they should because of their meager amount of protein material.

However, *excess nitrogen* is also a problem. Too much nitrogen delays blossoming and rudimentary fruit formation. The leaves are dark green and abnormally large, due to their high chlorophyll content. Protein production is greatly accelerated. In order to accommodate this, the plant consumes carbohydrates at such a rate that it no longer has enough stocks at its disposal to build up its supporting tissues. As a

Regular applications of fertilizer have a positive effect on plants' growth and yield.

result, the plant's rigidity and hardiness suffer.

Nitrogen excess also makes the plant take in too much water, which increases its sensitivity to temperature fluctuations. That, in turn, makes it more susceptible to diseases and parasites. The increased formation of specific

organic bonds, such as asparagine and glutamine, often impairs flavor.

Phosphorus

Simply seen, phosphorus is an essential part of specific proteins (nucleic acids) in every plant and is involved with the production of new plant cells. Most importantly, phosphorus encourages the formation of the blossoms and fruit.

Ensuring that plants have an adequate supply of phosphorus is one of the most difficult tasks in plant nutrition because of the complicated way that phosphorus is broken down. Although phosphorus is found in abundant combinations in the soil, it can join with other substances in combinations that are difficult to

break in acidic or alkaline soils. If this does happen, the phosphorus is said to be *fixed*, and plants no longer have access to it.

As a result, to make phosphorus readily available to plants in a soluble form, you must take whatever measures are necessary to bring the soil into a neutral to weakly acidic pH range and to keep it there (see the chapter "Improving Your Garden's Soil, pp. 12-20).

Potassium

Potassium is not one of the building blocks in plant proteins or green leaves. Nevertheless, it plays an important role in plant metabolism, because it regulates the plant's water balance. Good water balance makes the plant more resistant to rain-free periods, temperature swings, and frost.

In addition, potassium plays a role in the production of starch and sugar, and thereby encourages the formation of roots and tubers.

When a plant suffers from *potassium deficiency*, it turns brown and withers. In the worst cases, the plant will literally dry up and die.

Our vegetables need relatively high amounts of potassium, so

you need to replace the mineral continually. Mineral fertilizers designed for vegetable gardens supply potassium in sufficient quantities to protect your plants.

Magnesium

Magnesium is the central building block of chlorophyll and is therefore extremely important in plant metabolism.

Potassium and magnesium

Calcium is a support element in the plant's "skeleton".

work in conjunction, and replenish each other through their own activities. An excess of one element can lead to a deficiency in the other.

Calcium

Strictly speaking, because a plant needs so little, calcium is actually a trace element. However, because of its importance in the life of all plants, it is regarded as a main nutrient. Its

Without magnesium, plants cannot make chlorophyll, and without chlorophyll no plant can survive.

The Most Important Deficiency Symptoms

Element	Where It Appears	Symptoms	Cause
Nitrogen	Older Leaves	Leaves become red, violet, yellow or pale yellow. Discoloration begins in the center. Plants are small; poor fruit formation or none at all.	Wetness, cold, badly aerated soil with little humus.
Phosphorus	Older Leaves	Reddish violet leaf and vein coloration. Loss of leaves. Grey to dark green. Thin, spindly plant growth, poor fruit formation. Rigidity (stiffness).	Fixing of phosphorus in alkaline soils. Reduced ability to absorb water.
Potassium	Older Leaves	Leaf coloration (edges and points) from yellow to dark brown, especially in lettuce. Poor growth; limp, floppy leaves.	Dryness in heavy clay soils.
Calcium	Whole Plant	Meager growth (small leaves, few roots). Young leaves become yellow-green and deformed. Potatoes are extremely small; tomato flowers die.	Acid soil (pH value under 5)
Magnesium	Older Leaves	Green leaf veins with light green areas between them. Leaves later become brown, beginning at the points. Corn gets whitish-yellow stripes on older leaves. Premature loss of leaves is common with beans.	Acid, soaked and sandy soil, or a surplus of potassium.
Manganese	Young Leaves	Green leaf veins with yellow-green areas between them. Small brown flecks in leaf centers.	Alkaline soils or prolonged damp periods.
Iron	Young Leaves	Similar to manganese, but more pronounced. Red coloring, especially common with strawberries and raspberries.	Alkaline soils.
Boron	Young Plant Parts	Badly developed leaf and flower buds; small, deformed leaves. Beets show corky places on the roots; cauliflower develops high, dark brown stalks.	Light sandy soils. Dryness increases boron deficiency.
Zinc	Whole Plant	Small, yellow-flecked leaves. Young shoots die.	Alkaline or very acid soils.
Molybdenum	Whole Plant	Insufficient growth. Leaf edges become yellow or brown on tomatoes, cucumbers and beans; in cauliflower the leaf edges become wavy or the leaves are long and thin.	Acid soils.

primary function is to join with lime in order to adjust the soil's acid-base relationship (its pH value).

Trace elements

Trace elements are as necessary as main nutrients for healthy plant development and for the growth and ripening of fruit. Trace elements also influence the harvested crops' mineral content, which is so important in human nutrition.

If a trace element deficiency is severe enough, a plant can die, so you must watch over your garden carefully. The best strategy is to provide your plants with all the nutrients they need, so that deficiencies can't occur in the first place.

A plant's growth pattern or appearance will signal when it's suffering from one deficiency or another. The accompanying table indicates symptoms to look for, and provides a key to the problems they indicate.

Fertilizing and the Quality of Your Harvest

The phrase *quality fruit and vegetables* can mean a number of different things, depending on who's using it. A seed company may value varieties that produce large fruits or a heavy yield, or are resistant to specific diseases, and so spend much time and

money developing varieties with those characteristics.

When you, as a gardener and consumer, judge the quality of your home-grown fruits and vegetables, your decision will probably be based on their flavor and nutrition.

The Law of Minimums

Although most gardeners don't start a garden with the idea of harvesting the largest crop they can, a rich harvest is certainly more welcome than a sparse one.

Therefore, a quick mention to the *law of minimums*. It states that the least available nutrient determines the size of your yield.

If, for instance, the soil contains a sufficient amount of nitrogen and phosphorus but too little potassium, the plant will take only enough nitrogen and phosphorus to balance with the amount of potassium at its disposal. Having limited its intake of all three nutrients, its growth is stunted and its yield is small. Increasing the supply of potassium increases the plant's intake

of the other two elements as well, thus increasing the yield.

Soil Analysis: Learning About Your Garden's Nutrients

Once gardeners realize that fertilizers can influence their harvest's quality, they often want to determine the best fertilizing program for their land. A soil analysis can give you that information quickly.

If you decide you need a soil analysis, there are two ways to go about it. Do-it-yourself kits are available in many garden centers and are sold through many gardening magazines.

You can also arrange for a soil analysis through the office of your local county agriculture agent. You will be instructed to take a soil sample from various places in the garden. The sample is then mixed together and about 2 1/2 pounds is sent off to be tested. For a relatively low fee, you will receive an exact soil analysis, along with fertilization recommendations.

Caring for Your Soil

Your garden will require care during the entire growing season. This chapter should help you become a good partner to nature.

the extra job of aerating the encrusted soil that comes from watering too heavily.

Sprinkling is best done with a simple garden hose fitted with a perforated nozzle, sometimes

called a *rose*. This system helps you water hard-to-reach places, and there's no danger of washing away rich earth or shallow seeds.

If your garden is large, use a lawn sprinkler, so you can water large areas automatically.

The best time to water is in the morning, or even better, early evening. During the day, and especially under the glare of the midday sun, the water evaporates before the plants can benefit.

Watering

Water is essential for healthy plant growth. It releases the nutrients in the soil so that plants can absorb them. It controls the production of sugar, starch and cellulose, and aids the leaves' breathing process. Plants that are given sufficient water are strong and well-formed. As soon as there isn't enough water, they wither.

Before you water your garden, you must prepare the soil. Only a loose soil can hoard water for a long time and retain it in the layers of soil near the roots. If the soil is encrusted, water simply runs off.

Apply the water in a fine sprinkle to keep the soil from silting up. Then you won't have

Weeding

Weeding certainly isn't the most pleasant task in the garden but it is the most indispensable.

Nature has so endowed garden weeds that they can grow absolutely anywhere, even in the cracks of a sidewalk. Vegetables and herbs aren't that resilient, so they have practically no chance against weeds. Since weeds are easier to pull from a clear soil than one that's completely overgrown, you must remove them whenever they appear. And you

Oscillating weeder

must weed any ground before you can resow it. An old saying goes: "One year seed, seven years plague." In other words, if you allow weeds to grow for one year, you can look forward to seven years of weeding before you banish their offspring from your garden.

Loosening the Soil

It's especially important, from the time you sow until you harvest, that the soil's surface doesn't become encrusted. It must continually be broken up, since loose soil is a prerequisite for the water retention and mellowness, and so air and warmth can reach the roots.

By continuing to till the soil, you establish weed control and promote growth in your garden. Loose, airy, and warm soil fosters the microorganisms that promote mellowness and release plant nutrients.

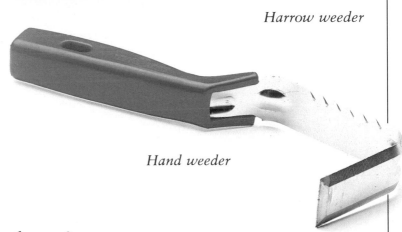

Harrow weeder

Hand weeder

Water evaporates from soil that hasn't been loosened before it is used. Level loosened soil retains water for the plant roots.

Tool Selection

Hoeing is the most efficient way to fight weeds—and certainly the one requiring the most effort.

There are new garden tools that can make this unpopular work considerably easier. In spite of this, even skillful gardeners make extra work for themselves by continuing to use obsolete implements. When they work, they "strike" the soil, a method that consumes a great deal of time—and above all, energy. Garden tools that rely on a "pulling" motion require less effort and are quicker.

A curved hoe, for example, is a tool with a double function: the hoe chops off the weed, and at the same time, three tines loosen the soil so that new weeds won't develop quickly.

An oscillating weeder is another help. As you swing it lightly back and forth, it cuts off all the weeds and loosens the soil at the same time.

The hand hoe is the correct tool for working in rock gardens and borders. It can be used with the hand grip as well as with the shaft.

A cultivator can help you prepare the soil and take care of it. For example, always use one when the paths between rows and the spaces between plants need to be aerated or loosened. Some cultivators have pronged tines, and adjustable cultivators adapt to the most varied distances between rows.

A grubber is a useful tool for stony or wet soils. With just a light pull, its rounded tines dig deeply into the soil. It's indispensable when you want to loosen and aerate carefully around roots.

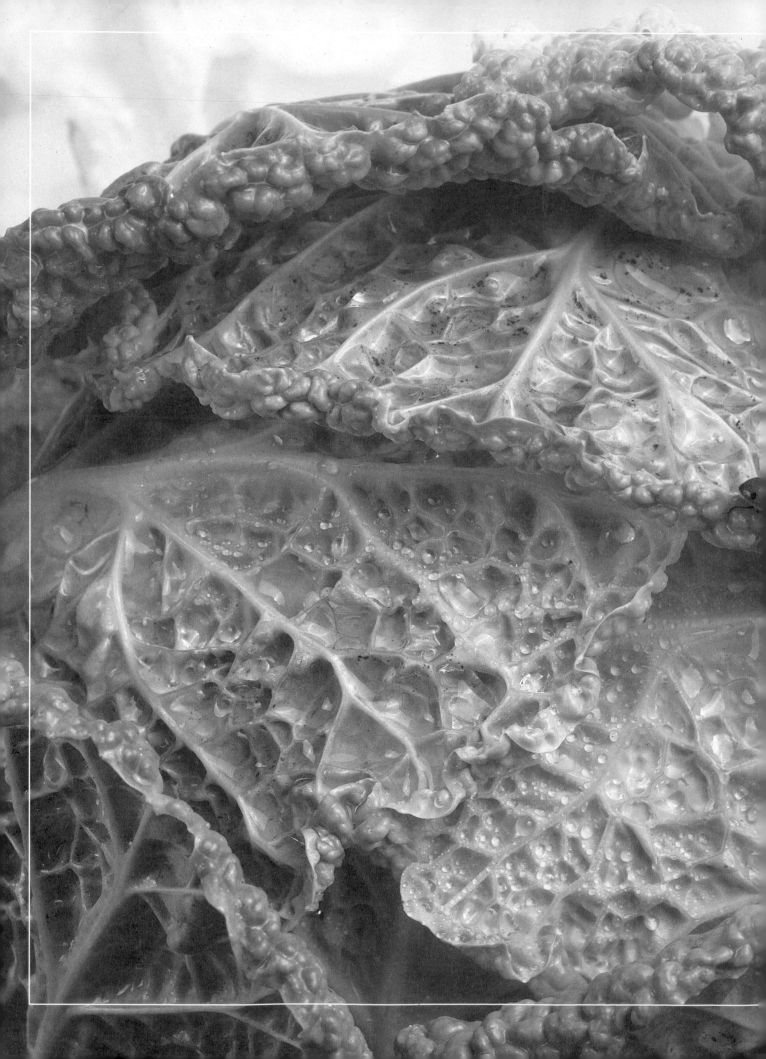

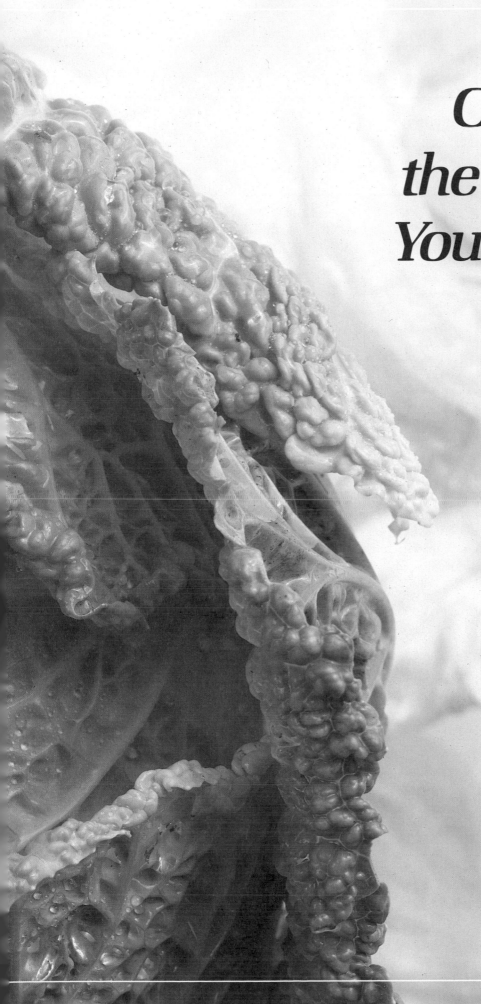

Caring for the Plants in Your Garden

To manage your garden, you must care for your plants, and this means protecting them from various pests and diseases. You can do this in two ways—with integrated plant protection and with chemical pesticides—and both have their advantages and disadvantages. However, in a small garden you rarely need to resort to powerful chemicals to deal with problems. There are some measures you can take, even when you are planning the garden's layout, that will help you prevent attacks from pests and diseases.

Integrated Plant Protection

There is no other place that's as easy to practice integrated plant protection as a vegetable garden. Integrated plant protection is a way of fighting pests and diseases without resorting to chemical measures. Instead, you use mixed cultivation, companion planting and the encouragement of helpful insects, ones that feed on predators that vandalize your plants. The following are counted among integrated plant protection measures.

Unimpeded Growth

Weak plants are much more susceptible to attack by insects and diseases than healthy ones. So, the more you do to encourage *unimpeded growth*—shallow loosening of the soil, mulching, regular watering, weed control, and careful fertilizing—the more protection your crops will have.

Planting Strategies

Special *planting strategies*, such as crop rotation and mixed cultivation, also protect your vegetables, since soil fatigue results in weak plants susceptible to attack. It is also important to maintain adequate distances between plants and to prune trees and shrubs so that their leaves dry quickly after a rainfall. If any plants do become sick or affected by any problem, remove them from the garden at once—but do not throw them onto the compost heap, throw them in the garbage.

Companion Planting for Pest Control

Plant	Effective Against	Remarks
Amaranth	Nematodes (thread worm)	Plant that attracts slugs
Garlic	Many pests	Grow between plants
Basil	Flies Mosquitoes Gnats	
Horseradish	Colorado Beetle	
Mint	Flea-beetle White Cabbage Butterfly	
Sage	Carrot Flies	
Nasturtium	White Cabbage Butterfly	Attracts black plant lice

Companion Planting

A great deal of research is being conducted on the practice of *companion planting*. This technique involves planting certain

crops together because one keeps away pests that feed on the other. (For some examples of these, see the accompanying table). Extended companion planting also includes growing windbreaks and special varieties that attract helpful insects and birds who prey on pests.

Natural Pest Control

Natural pest control relies on non-chemical ways to rid your garden of pests. One technique is hand picking. You examine your plants regularly for larger pests, such as slugs, caterpillars, and beetles, and remove them by hand. Or you can create an environment that the pest finds unpleasant, but doesn't affect your vegetables. For instance, because of their soft bodies, slugs avoid rough, stony ground. Some gardeners have found that a mulch of poultry-grade oyster shells is an effective deterrent to a pest that they'd really rather not handle.

Planting Resistant Strains

Seed companies spend much time, energy, and money developing plant varieties that are resistant to fungus attacks, and you should take advantage of their work. No one should plant a tomato variety that is not resistant to verticulum wilt, for instance. Strawberries are particularly vulnerable to a whole series of diseases, and these vary throughout the country, so it's better to buy plants from a local nursery rather than from a company in another region. Plants from your area will more likely be resistant to the area's particular problems.

Encourage Helpful Insects

It's an unfortunate fact that people in this country have a general phobia about insects and assume that any they see are harmful. If fact, most insects are actually beneficial, and you will harm your garden if you automatically assume every many-legged thing you see is after your vegetables. Many are not, such as ladybirds (or ladybugs), lacewings, and praying mantises. Instead, they feed on other insects, and are the enemies of sucking pests, such as plant lice, mites, and shield bugs. Ichneumen and bristle (larva) flies lay their eggs in caterpillars, which cause them to die.

Chemical Plant Protection

Even resistant strains have natural limits. There are, for example, no varieties of lettuce that are resistant to plant lice, and if there were, they probably

wouldn't be all that tasty. The time may come when you throw up your hands in despair and decide that you have to do something about the caterpillars that are feasting on your cabbages. But if you do decide to use any kind of spray, always go by the motto: "as little as possible, and only as much as is necessary."

Herbicides

Herbicides are poisons designed to combat weeds. Some are selective, i.e., they eradicate only weeds and spare cultivated plants. Leaf herbicides work on the already mature plant, and soil herbicides destroy weeds while they are still in the germinating stage. Total herbicides kill all vegetation.

Insecticides

Insecticides are substances that combat detrimental insects. They have several modes of attack. Some kill on contact, some work through the respiratory system, and others have to be digested to be effective. The so-called systematic insecticides are beneficial. They are absorbed by the plants and are carried to the roots or the surface of the leaves by the plant's transport system (i.e. in the plant tissues). This kind of poison kills sucking and chewing pests but doesn't damage the plant itself. Systemic poisons also don't harm useful insects that usually only use the leaves as hunting grounds as they stalk their insect prey.

Whenever possible, purchase insecticides that destroy only one distinct type of pest—this will protect useful insects. And do not spray into open blossoms, or you may kill those insects you need for pollination.

Fungicides

Fungi does not reproduce in the same way as other plants.

They produce no flowers, and after fertilization, they give off what are called spores. Fungicides combat fungal diseases by inhibiting spore growth. More and more, organic fungicides are displacing the chemical sulphur and copper preparations. Organic fungicides are just as effective, but are less dangerous to people and animals.

Basic Rules for Pesticide Use

1. The most important rule of all is this: **Follow the manufacturer's instructions exactly for applying any chemical, and under no circumstances exceed the concentrations specified on the label.** Never go according to the motto "a lot helps a lot."

2. While it is true that most cabbages are fair game for the caterpillars of white cabbage moths, never spray *just* because you suspect you have a problem or because you are afraid one may develop. This applies to the use of any pesticide.

3. Search out preparations that do not harm bees. These insects are essential for blossom fertilization, and without them some of your vegetables will never develop.

4. Read labels carefully, and try to find pesticides that are poison-free and have a short "life." A chemical's life is the amount of time that it takes for its effective substances to break down. Only after that period can you be sure that there are no more damaging residues present in the plant's tissues.

5. Be sure that there is an adequate *waiting time* between the time you spray and the time you harvest. Any systemic poison cannot be removed by simply washing the vegetable after harvesting it. Be sure there is enough time for the chemical to have broken down before you eat your vegetables.

To Avoid Overkill

Any plant protection measure that you use in your garden should be directed only against animal pests such as plant lice, caterpillars or slugs. If you purchase resistant plant varieties, you may never have to deal with fungus infections. Keep this in mind, since almost all active substances in fungicides have a relatively long life, their residues may wind up in your harvested crop.

You should also avoid using herbicides in a garden. Limit their use to weed control in your lawn.

Harvesting, Storing and Preserving

The reward for the work in your garden is your harvest, but even harvesting has to be learned. The main mistake of many beginning gardeners is that they harvest too early or too late. Then there is the question of what to do with what you've grown. This chapter provides special harvesting tips for the home gardener.

Harvest

The main rule for harvesting is to bring in your fruits and vegetables before they are over-ripe. Corn, for instance should be taken while you can still break the surface of the kernels with a fingernail. When your crops are fully ripe, a large proportion of their carbohydrates have already been changed from sugar to starch, and that usually detracts from their aroma and flavor.

Nutrition and Your Health

If you preserve your harvest carefully, you will retain the nutritional strengths of fresh produce and benefit your basic good health. In order to understand why this is so, you need some information about basic nutrition.

Although we are becoming more nutrition-conscious all the time, our diets are still too one-sided. We consume too many "empty" carbohydrates, such as refined sugar or white flour. Our calorie intake sometimes climbs dangerously high because we eat too many fatty foods. On the other hand, our diets do not fulfill our vitamin, mineral and roughage requirements.

All of these nutritional problems can be eased if you include freshly harvested vegetables and fruit in your diet. With an ample supply of fresh fruit and vegetables, you won't lack the *minerals* and *trace elements* you need to build up muscles and bones. You

Vitamin Content of Selected Vegetables

Vegetable	Vitamin A	Vitamin B₁	Vitamin C
Asparagus	●	●●●	●●
Beets	●	●	●●
Belgian Endive	●●	●●	●●
Blackberries	●	●●	●●
Broccoli	●●	●●●	●●●●
Brussels Sprouts	●●	●●●	●●●●
Bush Beans	●●	●●	●●
Carrots	●●●●●	●●	●
Cauliflower	●	●●●	●●●
Celery	●	●●	●●
Chinese Cabbage	●	●	●●
Chives	●●	●●●	●●●
Corn	-	●●●	●●
Cucumbers	●	●●	●●
Currants, Black	●	●●	●●●●●
Currants, Light	-	●●●	●●●
Currants, Red	●	●●	●●●
Eggplant	●	●●	●●
Endive	●●	●●	●●
Fennel	●●●	●●●●	●●●●
Garlic	-	●●●●	●●
Kale	●●●	●●●	●●●●
Kohlrabi	●	●●	●●●
Lamb's Lettuce	●●●	●●	●●●
Leeks	-	●●●	●●●
Lettuce	●●	●●	●●
Onion	●	●	●●
Parsley	●●●●	●●●	●●●●●
Parsnips	●	●●	●●
Peas	●●	●●●●	●●
Potatoes	●	●●●	●●
Pumpkin	●●	●●	●●
Radishes	●	●	●●●
Raspberries	●	●●	●●
Red Cabbage	●	●●	●●●
Rhubarb	●	●●	●●
Savoy	●	●●	●●●
Shallots	●	●	●●
Spinach	●●●	●●●	●●●
Squash	●●	●	●
Strawberries	●	●●	●●●●
Sweet Pepper	●●●	●●●	●●●
Swiss Chard	●	●●	●●●●●
Tomatoes	●●	●●	●●
White Cabbage	●	●●	●●
Zucchini	●●	●●●	●●

Not Present: -   Small Amount: ●●   High Amount: ●●●●
Present: ●   Medium Amount: ●●●   Very High Amount: ●●●●●

will also have enough *roughage*, which stimulates the movement of the intestines (peristalsis) and aids digestion.

It isn't enough just to drink fruit juices. Commercially canned vegetables, laden with salt and preservatives, are not always in your best interest. For your health's sake, you should eat and enjoy freshly harvested, whole fruits and vegetables.

Our food consists of substances that supply energy—fat, protein and carbohydrates—and of substances that guarantee a smooth metabolism: vitamins, minerals, trace elements, roughage and water.

With a few exceptions, *fat* and *proteins* are only found in small amounts in fruits and vegetables. We acquire these substances mainly from animal products, which supply protein with high biological value. This source supplies protein building blocks that our bodies cannot produce and is more complete than protein found in plants.

Carbohydrates are sugar, starch and cellulose. The human stomach can only digest sugar and starch. Cellulose is necessary because it adds roughage (or fiber) to the diet.

The carbohydrates in fruit (fructose and dextrose) can pass directly into the blood and act quickly and effectively to release energy. There is relatively little digestible carbohydrate in vegetables. They distinguish themselves mainly through their vitamin, mineral, and roughage content.

Vitamins are found in all types of fruits and vegetables. They guard against disease and prevent metabolic problems. The vitamins A, B group, C, and D are of special importance.

Vitamin A (Retinol) is formed from carrots and related vegetables. It's important for the skin, hair and eyes. A deficiency of Vitamin A can lead to night blindness. Adults require 0.9 mg daily.

Vitamin B₁ (Thiamine) is mainly found in cereal (grain) products. Commercial processing affects Vitamin B₁ content in grains—slightly ground, light-colored flour contains less thiamine than dark flour. This vitamin is important for proper nerve function. Large deficiencies can lead to nerve inflammation, convulsions, and to the paralysis of beri-beri. Adults require 1.5 mg daily.

Vitamin C (Ascorbic acid) is important for the health of connective tissues and blood, and as a protection against infection. A pronounced lack of vitamin C can lead to scurvy, which occurred on sea voyages long ago, when crews and passengers had to do without fresh fruits and vegetables. Foods rich in Vitamin C help fight spring lassitude and colds. Adults require 75 mg daily.

Storage

A good proportion of your root crops, and many kinds of unripened vegetables, can be stored after they are harvested without any special treatment. These are set out on trays, or

To store leeks, embed them in the soil in one corner of the garden.

buried in peat or sand in storage boxes. Any vegetable that you store should be ripe, healthy, undamaged and dry. Crops stored on trays must be stored

Root vegetables and tubers keep fresh for several weeks embedded in damp sand.

where they can be seen, so that you can immediately sort out any fruits that begin to decay.

A well-ventilated basement with a temperature of about 35-40 degrees Farenheit and a high humidity is an ideal place for storage. Some homeowners construct simple shelved areas to keep their crop.

Root vegetables and tubers are especially suitable for long storage. They keep well when embedded in damp sand, in cool, ventilated areas.

Salting

Besides simple storage, preservation has a major role in saving your crops for the winter. The oldest methods for this are *salting* and *drying*.

When you salt a crop, the salt draws moisture out of the vegetables, which inhibits the activity of organisms that could cause

Use special earthenware preserving jars for successful salting. After cleaning and curing beans, they are mixed with salt, put into the pot and pressed down firmly. Then set the lid in place and fill the rim of the container with water. This seals the contents air-tight, while allowing the bubbles formed during fermentation to escape.

Even home-salted sauerkraut (pickled cabbage) is a delicacy that you can easily make. All that's needed is white cabbage out of the garden, salt, a large container—and a little patience. Finely grate the white cabbage, then layer with salt in a clean, fat-free earthenware pot (about 3 ounces of salt to 10 pounds of white cabbage). Press the contents down so firmly that the juice that is formed rises above the level of the cabbage. Finally, cover the cabbage with a clean cloth, lay a slab of wood over it, and weight it with a clean stone. The sauerkraut will be ready after four to six weeks. For a special taste treat, add layers of juniper berries or apples (a little less than 1 pound to 10 pounds of cabbage).

spoilage. High salt concentrations are also injurious to bacteria.

Pole beans are the most suitable for salting, and salted beans almost taste better than ones that are frozen. And, of course, sauerkraut is actually white cabbage that has been salted.

To salt a vegetable, layer the clean vegetable with salt in a suitable container, press the mixture firmly, cover it, and store in a cool place.

The liquid created by this process should be kept in place, not thrown away. In time, a scum

Drying

Drying draws so much moisture out of the fruit that any damaging organisms cannot remain active. Practically all types of fruit, plus all herbs, beans and peas are suitable for drying.

Before you dry fruit, cut it up, then blanch it for about 1 minute by dipping it in boiling water. Then dry it at a low temperature in the oven or on a special drying device.

To dry herbs, simply tie them in bunches and hang them with their leaves downwards in an airy place.

Store dried herbs in jars away from light so they keep their full color and aroma.

To dry crops from your harvest, use a simply-made wooden frame with a drying surface made of muslin or netting wire.

will appear on the surface, and this should be skimmed away occasionally. Then, remove the vegetable as needed, wash it, and prepare it as you wish (see Recipe Section).

Freezing

When you freeze fruits or vegetables, remember: everything must be freshly harvested, undamaged, very clean and as dry as possible.

Most vegetables are blanched before freezing, to kill any bacteria that may be present, then are put into suitable containers. Fruit can be frozen with or without sugar, according to how you intend to use it.

The Garden in Winter

Harvesting winter
crops and planning for
spring.

Your most important job in a winter vegetable garden is to institute frost-protection measures for the plants remaining in the garden through the winter. Among these vegetables are kale, Brussels sprouts, parsnips and leeks. Before the first frost, heap soil up around the plants. Cover them with brushwood or hay when you expect snow. (That also makes them easier to find, once snow comes....) Plants covered in this way can provide fresh produce well into the winter in the coldest zones, and throughout the winter farther south.

Apply a layer of mulch late in the fall to protect your top soil from erosion caused by wind and snow. Mulch can be made from your garden waste (as long as the plants were healthy), such as the nutrient-rich leaves from harvested cabbages, and vines from tomatoes or cucumbers. You can also use leaves raked from the lawn. If you live near a farming area, spoiled hay is often inexpensive and makes a good mulch.

You also will need to cover your perennial plants, such as rhubarb, asparagus, strawberry plants, and berry bushes. Well-rotted manure, especially from stables, with its mixture of straw, is excellent mulch around heavy feeders like rhubarb.

Protect the compost heap from winter rain and snow by covering it with dark plastic film. When the weather allows, turn the heap, or move it to another place. By mixing the materials, you renew the decay cycle, and accelerate its rate of decomposition.

Winter is the time to do the work that will save you time and effort in the spring: cleaning tools and appliances, repairing or buying new ones, tidying up, sterilizing potting soil and containers, building a shed, or laying out new paths. Branches that you want to use for peas and beans can be cut now—an easier job when trees and shrubs don't have any leaves.

Winter is also the right time to work out a new garden plan and to begin collecting suitable plant varieties for planting in the spring. Assess your successes and your failures, and decide on new strategies.

It's fun, on cold winter evenings, to sit comfortably at home, leafing through a garden catalog and dreaming about what the coming gardening year will bring in the way of delicacies.

Winter is also the time to lie back a little. Relax and be happy about the success of your past gardening year. Spring comes faster than you think, and with it comes hard work, the kind that can give you much pleasure.

Planting Advisor

The second section of our book reviews the types of vegetables generally grown in American gardens, and gives you detailed information about seeds, plants and harvests. Each chapter follows the same organizational pattern, to help you find your way quickly and easily through the information.

The chapters are organized according to plant families, or by use. For instance, all root vegetables are discussed together, as are cabbage varieties and lettuce varieties. Each chapter is organized in the same way. You will find information on special characteristics, such as growth and appearance, growing characteristics, and so forth. There also are detailed growing instructions, so that you will know each plant's specific needs—on the weather, soil and nutrients—as well as full information about cultivation, care and harvesting. When necessary, there are sections about pests and diseases that affect a particular plant.

Photographs and drawings, along with helpful hints about special cases, illustrate each chapter and help clarify the text.

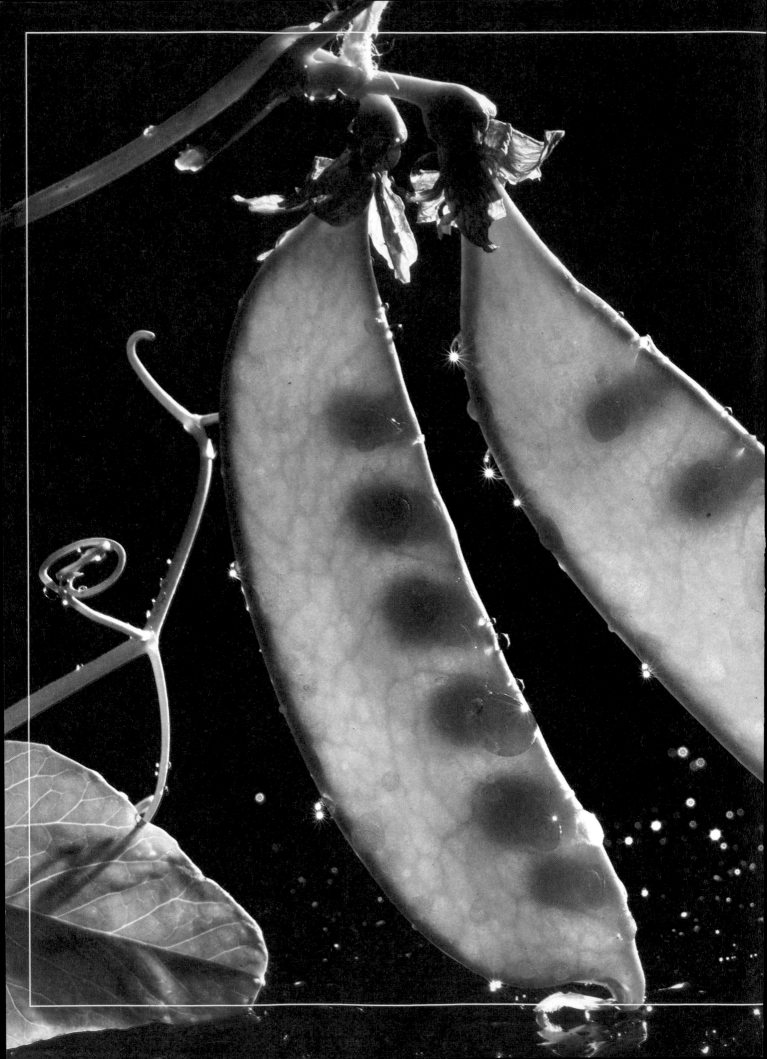

Legumes
In fullness and plenty

Legumes (Pod Fruits)

Peas and beans belong to the large legume family. Both are closely related to many ornamental plants, such as the sweet pea; soybeans and peanuts also belong to this family. Because of their relatively high protein content, legumes are the most important plant family. In many cases, both pod and seed are edible. (Actually, the term "pod" isn't botanically correct. Real pods are divided into two halves by what is called a septum. It is somewhat hard and cannot be eaten.)

The origin of the pea is a little obscure. Archaeologists have found no Greek, Roman or Egyptian drawings that indicate anything was known about it. Beans, on the other hand, originated on the American continent. Like many other vegetables, they were then taken to ancient Europe by the Spaniards.

Legumes are unique plants because of their small root nodules. In these nodules are microorganisms that can take nitrogen from the air and change it into a form plants can use. When the microorganisms die, the nitrogen is released and becomes available to the host plant. (See also the discussion of legumes in the section "Green Fertilizers".)

Today legume varieties are developed especially to give good yields and excellent flavor. Growing them is relatively problem-free, mainly because they can, so to speak, provide themselves with their own food.

Peas

Weather, Soil and Nutrients

Although peas do like warmth, they germinate well in cool weather, so plant them as soon as you can work the soil. Light frost won't bother the seedlings, although it can harm blossoms. If your climate is particularly warm, grow peas in very early spring or late fall. Peas feel at home in almost any soil, although they do especially well in earth that's light, loose and has an ample supply of humus.

Before sowing, dig in about 1 ½ ounces of universal vegetable fertilizer per square yard. Even though the peas build up sufficient nitrogen as they grow, quick development of the young plant requires an early supply (together with the other important nutrients and trace elements).

Cultivation and Care

Plant pea seeds about $1^1/2$ to $2^1/2$ inches deep and about $1^1/2$ inches apart. The distance between rows should be about 20 inches. To support the tendrils, stretch chicken wire on poles or lay brush between the rows. Any support should be about 3 feet high. As soon as the plants are hand high, mound the earth up around the stems. This is called *earthing up*, and gives the plants a better hold. Some low-growing varieties support themselves. You can plant your whole bed at once, or, if you wish to have fresh peas over a long period, sow seeds at weekly intervals for about 4 to 6 weeks. As they grow, be sure to provide enough moisture.

Harvesting

Peas taste best when they are harvested young. What's more, frequent and early harvests increase the number of fruit buds and the total yield, so don't wait until the pods are bulging or beginning to dry out. Pick them once or twice a week. Always use both hands to pull the pod from the vine so you don't damage the plants.

Position in Crop Rotation

Because pea root nodules improve the soil, and because the plants protect the soil during early spring rains, peas are especially valuable as first crops.

Special Cultivation Tips

Garden Peas

Garden peas have large, smooth seeds. When fully ripe, they look slightly floury because they have stored a large proportion of their carbohydrate as starch.

Sow the seeds in the garden as soon as the soil can be worked

and continue sowing until the weather is very warm. Harvest peas before the pods turn yellow.

When mature, garden peas are especially suitable for canning and freezing.

Sugar Peas

Sugar peas are especially delicious and can be eaten pod and all. They don't have the parchment-like inner skin that lines other pea varieties, and when harvested early they don't produce fibers.

Sow sugar peas just like any other variety, and harvest the pods before the peas inside are clearly visible—the earlier the better!

Bush Beans

Weather, Soil and Nutrients

Bush beans are cold-sensitive, so don't plant them until all chance of frost is past. They prefer a light, loose soil with an ample supply of humus. Thin out very heavy soils with compost or other soil conditioners (see General Section). Before sowing, dig in about 2 ounces per square yard of universal vegetable fertilizer, to provide the young plants with sufficient nutrients as soon as possible.

Cultivation and Care

Plant beans in rows about 16 inches apart, either singly or in hills. For single-seed sowings place a seed every 2¹/₂ to 3 inches. When sowing in hills, set 4 or 5 beans every 8 to 10 inches. In either case, bury the seeds about 1¹/₂ to 2 inches deep. To ensure several harvests, sow the seeds at weekly intervals, and plant varieties with staggered maturity dates.

Beans require the same care as peas. Earth up the plants several times until they begin to flower, and be sure to provide sufficient water. If the bed dries out the plants may shed their flowers, causing a low yield.

Harvesting

Harvest bush beans from the time that the pods are about 3 to 4 inches long. Many people prefer the very young pods to older ones. It's important to pick the first beans early in order to advance the formation of new pods. Usually, you'll harvest the unripe pods, but you may also harvest the fully ripened seeds. Then split the pods, remove the seeds and dry them in the air.

Position in Crop Rotation

Bush beans, like peas, are an excellent first crop. They enrich the soil with nitrogen and encourage soil mellowness.

Special Cultivation Tips

Climbing Beans

Climbing beans are very popular. New varieties are fiberless and especially tasty. They are resistant to some fungus diseases and have a heavier yield than bush varieties.

Haricot Vert

Haricot Vert is a French bean variety that's available from many specialty seed catalogs in this country. (Some seed companies have developed their own varieties to resemble Haricot Vert in size and flavor.) Haricot Vert has a delicate bean flavor prized by gourmet cooks. If you don't want to grow a special planting of haricot vert, substitute very young pods of other bean varieties.

Haricot vert is a tender vegetable that must be harvested when it's very immature (no longer than 3 to 4 inches), because it forms fibers as it matures. Pick the pods 2 to 3 times a week.

Wax Beans

Wax beans are yellow bush beans that are especially attractive in salads because of their lovely color. New varieties bear especially high yields.

82

Pole Beans

Weather, Soil, and Nutrients

Pole beans are just as sensitive to frost as bush beans and must be set out only after the last frost, when the soil is well warmed. Their soil, nutrient and weather requirements are the same as those of bush beans—a light, loose, warm soil with an ample supply of humus. Before planting, dig in about 2 ounces of universal vegetable fertilizer per square yard to supply young plants with sufficient nutrients right away.

Cultivation and Care

Plant pole beans approximately 1¹/₂ inches deep, in hills of about 5 seeds each. Space the hills 24 by 16 inches apart. To advance the harvest by 14 days, begin them indoors, 4 or 5 seeds to a plant pot.

Before you sow pole beans, set out poles to support the plants. You can provide one vertical pole for each hill, or set up two from every second hill and lay one horizontally across the top of the vertical poles. You can also use several poles to create a tent-shaped formation.

Beans tend to sprawl if allowed to go their own way, so you'll have to train them by tying them to the poles. Do this gently to protect the growing vines. Pole beans also need a lot of moisture, so water them during dry periods or they will shed their blossoms.

It's best to position pole beans at the north end of your garden so that their tall plants won't shade other vegetables. Or, take advantage of their dense growth by using them as a natural landscaping screen. If you have limited space, train pole beans up a south-facing wall.

Pole beans require the same earthing up, weeding, and harvesting as bush beans and are just as valuable as an early crop in a rotation plan.

Harvesting

Pole beans that are harvested early are especially tender and tasty, so pick them twice a week. Use the same care as when you harvest peas: use both hands so that you don't damage or tear off the developing tendrils.

Pole beans have a higher yield than bush beans. Frequent picking encourages new flower buds to form until well into late summer.

Scarlet Runners

The scarlet runner is a special pole bean. Its plants are much more robust than those of other pole beans, so they will bear heavily even in high, raw locations. With their long red or white flower clusters and vines that grow as long as 10 to 12 feet, scarlet runners are very attractive and work well as a green covering for garden sheds and walls. They can also be trained up a bamboo trellis on a balcony and quickly create an attractive privacy screen.

Scarlet runner beans develop a thick, rough-textured pod, but the beans are tender and tasty, nonetheless.

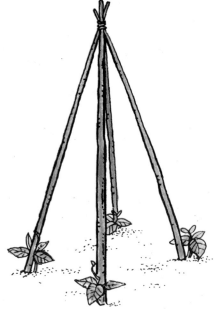

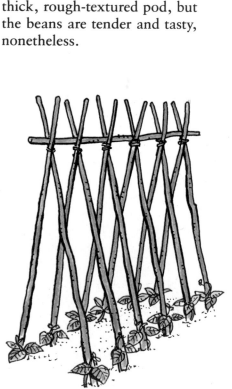

Pole beans and scarlet runners require support. For this, before planting, place 3-foot-long poles made of wood, metal or sturdy

plastic in the soil. You can arrange them in squares, with the poles tied together in the shape of a tent, or in double rows with every second stick tied together

and with another pole laid horizontally across the tops. Wire netting, standing free between pegs or in front of a wall, can also serve as a support.

Broad Beans

Broad beans are also known as Fava beans, English broad beans or horse beans. They are primarily grown to be shucked like limas, but have a milder flavor. *Don't* eat uncooked broad beans. They contain a natural chemical that can cause nausea. The cooked beans make fine eating.

Weather, Soil and Nutrients

Broad beans tolerate temperatures up to 20 degrees F., so they can be among the first plants in your garden. They prefer a medium to heavy soil with sufficient moisture. If your soil is light, work in compost or a green fertilizer before planting. Before you sow, dig in 2 ounces of universal vegetable fertilizer per square yard. If your soil is light, fertilize again with 1 ½ ounces per square yard at the beginning of the flowering period.

Cultivation and Care

Plant broad bean seeds 2 inches deep, and 3 to 4 inches apart. The rows should be about 24 inches apart. Sow the seeds as soon as you can, since the plants aren't frost-sensitive. They require no support.

Cultivation measures, harvesting, and crop rotation are the same as for peas.

Pests and Diseases

All bean varieties are attacked frequently by the black bean louse. Spraying the leaves and stalks with a heavy stream of water helps in only rare cases. If you have problems, spray early and repeatedly with an organic, biodegradable insecticide before harvesting. (Warning: take note of the waiting time!)

By the way...

To improve the flavor of broad beans, remove the stalk-like stem that attaches each seed to the pod.

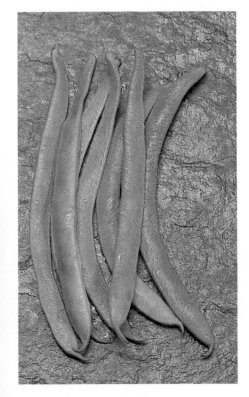

Fruit-bearing Vegetables, Fennel and Rhubarb
The big harvest

Fruit-Bearing Vegetables

Any plant grown for its fruit rather than its leaves, roots or tubers, is counted among the fruit-bearing vegetables. Among these are all squash and pumpkin plants, sweet peppers, and corn. (Tomatoes also belong here but because of their special importance, they have their own chapter.)

Strictly speaking, fennel and rhubarb don't belong with the fruit-bearing vegetables. You don't harvest the leaves, roots or fruit—only the thickened leaf stalks. Despite this, they have been included with these vegetables because most cooks prepare them all in the same way.

Cucumbers, Zucchini, and Pumpkin

Cucumbers, zucchini and pumpkin belong to the squash family (Cucurbitaceae)—a family full of juice and strength. Experts still disagree about the cucurbits' origins, but there is little doubt that they originally came from a warm Asiatic region.

No gardener should forego the easily prepared, pleasant summer dishes made from cucumbers, zucchini, or any of the preserves made from these vegetables.

Cucurbits aren't difficult to grow. By observing a few basic rules, you can bring their original tropical lusciousness into your own garden.

Weather, Soil and Nutrients

Because of their tropical beginnings, cucurbit plants require plenty of warmth and, with the exception of pumpkin, love a sunny place. They prefer a well-drained, loose soil with a rich supply of nutrients and humus. Although they require a lot of moisture, good drainage is also essential—they don't like cold or wet "feet." If you have clay or heavy loam soil, it needs to be loosened and thinned.

Because of cucurbits' high nutrient requirements, dig manure, green fertilizer or other organic fertilizers into the soil before you plant. This is best done in the autumn. Before planting, or about 14 days afterwards, add 1 1/2 ounces of universal vegetable fertilizer per square yard. Then add the same amount 1 or 2 more times, at 4 to 6-week intervals.

Cultivation and Care

Sow frost-sensitive cucurbits only after you're sure there's no further danger of frost, and the soil is well-warmed. If your growing season is particularly short, start your seeds early, in pots or in flats, and transplant when the soil is warm. You can mulch cucurbits with black plastic, or grow the seedlings under plastic cloches. The latter will give you much earlier growth and harvest. (If you use a cloche, be sure that the air can circulate inside). A black plastic mulch is also valuable, since its dark color absorbs the sun's heat and warms the soil more quickly than if it were uncovered.

Harvesting

You can harvest cucurbits as soon as the fruits are large enough to be useful, and continue harvesting until fall.

Place in Crop Rotation

All cucurbits have high nutrient requirements, so don't plant them after heavy feeders.

Special Cultivation Tips

Gherkins

Gherkins are a small cucumber variety grown mainly for pickles. They require the same cultivation, care and feeding as other

Unlike many plants, curcurbits have single-sex flowers. The ovules and pollen are not together in one flower (as, for example, in apples). Instead curcurbits have male flowers (which carry pollen) and female flowers (ovules, the fruit-forming bodies). You can recognize the female flower by the small, gourd-like thickening at the base. (See upper photograph for female flower, see lower photograph for male flower).

cucumbers. However, pinch off the main shoot when about 3 leaves have fully formed. This forces the development of side shoots, which are more fruitful than the main stem and bear a rich yield.

Cultivation and Care

Sow in the open only after the soil is well warmed. Plant 5 or 6 seeds in hills set 16 to 24 inches apart. After the second pair of leaves forms, thin each hill to the two strongest plants. Young cucumbers are especially tasty because their seed core is only slightly developed. Pickle larger overripe fruits in vinegar or mustard (see Gardener's Cookbook Section).

Cucumbers

Cucumbers do especially well when you train them on a trellis, since they are climbing plants by nature. Trellis-trained plants also take up less space in your garden, damp soil doesn't rot the fruits and they are kept clean and safe from slugs. You can build a special climbing frame or a temporary structure of wire netting or twine.

Sow cucumbers as you do gherkins. As with pickling gherkins, pinch off the main shoot.

Begin harvesting cucumbers when they are a maximum of $4^1/2$ to 5 inches long and are still small and firm, since that size tastes best. Frequent picking encourages the plants to flower again and will increase your yield.

Zucchini

Zucchini grows quickly and needs a lot of room. Plan on just about 1 square yard for each plant. Only small zucchini taste good raw, so for salads and raw relishes pick fruits that are no longer than 5 to 8 inches. Larger ones taste best after they are cooked.

Some of today's varieties bear fruit very early and continue to yield for two or three months. The fruits are as tender as butter and have thin, soft skins. Some varieties have open, bushy shapes and are non-climbing. Other varieties produce plants that have predominantly female flowers (only the female flowers bear fruit).

Pumpkins

Pumpkins are like all cucurbits—they develop luxurious growth and demand regular fertilizing and plenty of water. Some gardeners have found one effective way to deal with pumpkins' heavy appetites and at the same time solve a persistent garden management problem.

The management problem is that of supplying a compost heap

Zucchini will grow rather large if you allow them to grow to their full size. As long as you peel them and remove the seed core, they taste good stewed or boiled, with or without stuffing.

To promote fertilization in greenhouses or in beds that receive little wind, use a paintbrush to transfer some of the pollen from the male to the female flowers.

with shade to keep from drying out. The solution is to plant pumpkin seeds right in the heap. The growing plants are well fed, and their vines shade the heap. An alternative plan is to start the seeds indoors, in pots, and plant them later on beside the heap. Then train the vines over it. The plants benefit from the heap's nutrients without depleting them. If you employ the second method, add 1 1/2 to 2 ounces per square yard of universal vegetable fertilizer twice during the plants' growth period.

If you plant your seeds in the garden, allow 80 by 80 inches between each hill and insert 4 to 6 seeds per hill. Once the seedlings have 2 or 3 pairs of true leaves, thin them to 1 or 2 plants per hill.

Once the first frost destroys the vines' foliage, harvest your pumpkins. They will keep for weeks in a cool, well-ventilated place.

Pumpkins are used in a number of ways in different countries. If you only know pumpkin as a sweet-sour side dish or something that makes great pie, then try out the new recipes in the Gardener's Cookbook section.

Dried pumpkin seeds are a marvelous, nutritious snack, both for people and birds.

Eggplants and Sweet Peppers

Eggplants and sweet peppers are members of the nightshade family (Solanaceae). Most species of this family (potatoes and tomatoes are also members) come from the tropics. In the 17th century the Portuguese brought eggplants to Europe from Asia. Even earlier, at the beginning of the 16th century, the Spaniards brought sweet peppers to the Old World, probably from South America.

Weather, Soil and Nutrients

Like all tropical plants, eggplants and sweet peppers require a lot of warmth, so don't set them out in the garden until all chance of frost is past and the soil is well warmed. Both prefer a nutrient-rich soil with an ample supply of humus. Before sowing, add 1 1/2 to 2 ounces per square yard of universal vegetable fertilizer. Add a comparable amount when the fruits first form, to enhance the size and quality of the yield.

Cultivation and Care

Eggplants and sweet peppers require a fairly long warm season, so are relatively difficult to grow in northern zones. In northernmost areas you may have to grow them in a greenhouse or under high plastic cloches.

Start the seedlings indoors, in flats, about 4 to 8 weeks before the final frost, and keep the air temperature at 70 to 80 degrees. (You can keep the flat in a warm place, like on top of a refrigerator or a water heater, or use flats with built-in heating systems). Thin the young seedlings to about 1 inch apart after the first pair of leaves develop. Once the seedlings are about 3

inches high, transplant them in a greenhouse, or, if you plan to grow them in the garden, transfer them from flats to peat pots and keep them in a draft-free, sunny place (like on a window sill) until you're ready to set them, 20 by 28 inches apart, in the garden.

Don't plant seedlings in the open or under cloches until the outside temperatures have reached 60 to 70 degrees F. During the growing period, keep the soil evenly watered.

Fully grown plants can be as tall as 3 feet and produce several branches. Greenhouse plants should have all but four shoots pinched out; those in the garden should have no more than three. Those remaining will develop greater strength and bear larger fruits. If a plant produces heavily, you may have to prop up the branches.

Harvesting

Once the fruits begin to ripen, harvest them every week or two. Do *not* just pull them off. You could damage the roots or break off the whole branch, and then the plant won't bear any longer. Instead, use a knife to cut through the stem where it joins the fruit.

Special Cultivation Tips

Eggplants

The eggplant's name is as unusual as its shape and color. The name comes from the original variety, which produced white and yellow fruit in the shape and size of hen's eggs. (This unusual variety is available in some seed catalogs, if you're feeling adventurous...)

Harvesting

Harvest eggplant fruits before they are fully ripe, while they are still dark purple and shiny. Since eggplants are very frost-sensitive,

harvest all fruits before the first frost.

Keep track of where you planted eggplants, so that you don't plant them in the same soil two years in a row. If you're planting in a greenhouse, you must either change the soil or sterilize it to avoid passing on diseases.

Sweet Peppers

Harvesting

Since sweet peppers are perfect at all stages of their development, you can harvest them anytime after the fruits are well formed, whether they are green, yellow or red. Green fruits have a slightly sharp, slightly bitter, but very pleasant flavor. Ripe red or yellow fruits are slightly sweet. The riper the fruit, the higher the Vitamin C content. (Don't confuse red sweet peppers with red hot peppers. The two varieties are completely different.)

Regular harvesting will increase blossoming, and therefore increase your yield. Be sure to harvest all fruits before the first frost.

As with eggplant, don't plant

sweet peppers in the same location two years in a row.

Corn

Sweet corn is the only fruit-bearing vegetable in the richly

varied grass family. Its usefulness has been known for a long, long time, and it probably originated in Mexico. Although corn is a child of warmer regions, plant breeding, especially development of the F1 hybrid varieties, has continually expanded its range. Tailor your seed selection to your particular growing zone.

Weather, Soil and Nutrients

Sweet corn needs lots of sun and warm temperatures in order to germinate. It has no special soil requirements, but it flourishes best on a loose soil rich in nutrients and humus. Before sowing, or about 2 weeks afterwards, supply 1 1/2 to 2 ounces of universal vegetable fertilizer per square yard, and add 1 or 2 doses during the growing period.

Cultivation and Care

Corn is sown after the last frost when the soil is well warmed. Plant seeds every 2 inches, and set them 1 1/2 to 2

inches deep in rows 30 inches apart. Later, thin the seedlings to the strongest young plants, no less than 8 inches apart. Since the plants have shallow roots, be careful as you cultivate the rows.

If you plant just one row of corn, you won't have anything to harvest. Corn relies on wind currents to pollinate the forming ears, so it needs close neighbors all around. Plan for at least three rows of corn to ensure adequate pollination.

Harvesting

When the silk at the tips of the corncobs turns dark brown, the ears are ready to harvest.

The kernels should be milky and still so soft that you can split them with the light press of a fingernail. If you plan on having fresh-cooked corn for a meal, have the water boiling on the stove before you head for the garden. Nothing tastes better than corn brought straight from garden to kettle. Once the ears are picked, the sugars stored in the kernels begin to change to starches.

Fennel

Fennel is a member of the umbelliferous family of plants, as are carrots, celery and many herbs. It has a delicate taste, reminiscent of anise, and is very popular with Italian cooks who sometimes call the vegetable sweet fennel or Florence fennel.

Only the thickened leaf stalk, which is sometimes called a "sham tuber," is harvested. You can eat fennel raw or cooked. It's especially good in diets for people with sensitive stomachs. (Don't confuse this plant with the herb fennel—the two are separate plants.)

Weather, Soil and Nutrients

Fennel can withstand light frosts (up to about 26 degrees F.) without harm. It requires a loose humus soil and plenty of water in order to be able to form large tubers. Before planting, dig 1 1/2 ounces universal vegetable fertilizer evenly into the soil, and add another 1 1/2 ounces about 4 to 6 weeks later.

Cultivation and Care

Sow fennel seed in the open

about 1 inch deep in rows 16 inches apart, and thin the seedlings to about 6 inches apart.

Check the description of the variety you intend to plant. Older ones must be planted quite late or they will *bolt* (form a flower stalk), and then the plant can't be used as a vegetable. Some newer varieties no longer have this problem and will produce a full yield even if sown as late as mid-July.

Fennel requires no special treatment outside of regular watering and shallow hoeing. When the tubers begin to form, earth up the rows lightly. The soil around the stalks will *blanch* the tubers, (keep the tubers light and tender).

Harvesting

You can harvest fennel from mid-August until mid-October. Although fennel can withstand light frost, it's better to harvest it earlier and store the tubers.

When you embed fennel tubers in damp sand or peat and keep them in a cool cellar or a cold frame, they will remain fresh for some weeks. Before you place them in the container, trim away all the green parts of the plants.

Rhubarb

Weather, Soil and Nutrients

Rhubarb is a perennial and is one of the first plants to nose up through the soil in the spring. And although it makes no special demands on the weather since it's a hardy plant, it doesn't do well in zones that don't experience a long cold winter. Like many perennials, it needs that dormant period in order to grow as it should. On the other hand, in zones with particularly severe winters, you need to mulch the plant's *crown*, or head, with hay or straw to protect it from extreme temperatures.

Since rhubarb is a perennial and a heavy feeder, it's worth your while to spend some time preparing the bed before planting. To accommodate its deep roots, loosen the soil to at least a spade's depth. To meet its nutrient needs, especially during the first year, dig in plenty of farmyard manure. (Some gardeners plant rhubarb near the compost heap.) Once the plants are in, they need about $3^{1}/_{2}$ to $5^{1}/_{2}$ ounces of universal vegetable fertilizer (divided between 2 fur rows) in addition to organic fertilizer. Add this right after harvesting, and once again in late summer.

Cultivation and Care

It isn't necessary to grow rhubarb from seed. Instead, new plants are started from pieces split from the roots of existing plants. This is called *root stock*.

To split a rhubarb root, dig up the plant after the leaves have died usually about the beginning of August. Then divide the root into pieces with a spade or a sharp knife. Each piece must have at least 3 well-developed buds. Set the pieces out in a cool, well-ventilated place for a

few days, long enough to *cure* (dry) them, so they don't rot when planted. Once the cut surfaces are well dried, plant the pieces about 40 by 40 inches apart. Bury the plants so that the buds are just hidden.

Harvesting

In order to ensure a good rhubarb harvest for many years, don't pick any stalks the first year. In the second year you can pick some, but take only the thickest ones. By the third year, the rhubarb's crown will be fully developed, and you can pick as much as you want.

To harvest rhubarb stalks, grasp them near the base and twist them loose. They will break away at a node that connects the stalk to the crown of the plant. Never cut rhubarb stalks—cut places begin to rot the plant. When you harvest, never remove all the stalks at the same time because you'll retard new growth. *Never* eat the leaves or the roots of a rhubarb plant—they are toxic to humans.

Since new stalks replace the ones you harvest, you can pick rhubarb again and again for up to two months. The plant will form a flower stalk in May or June, and then you should allow the plant to rest until the following spring. Remove the flower stalk to divert the plant's strength from seed formation to food storage and root development. Treat rhubarb well and it will continue to flourish year after year.

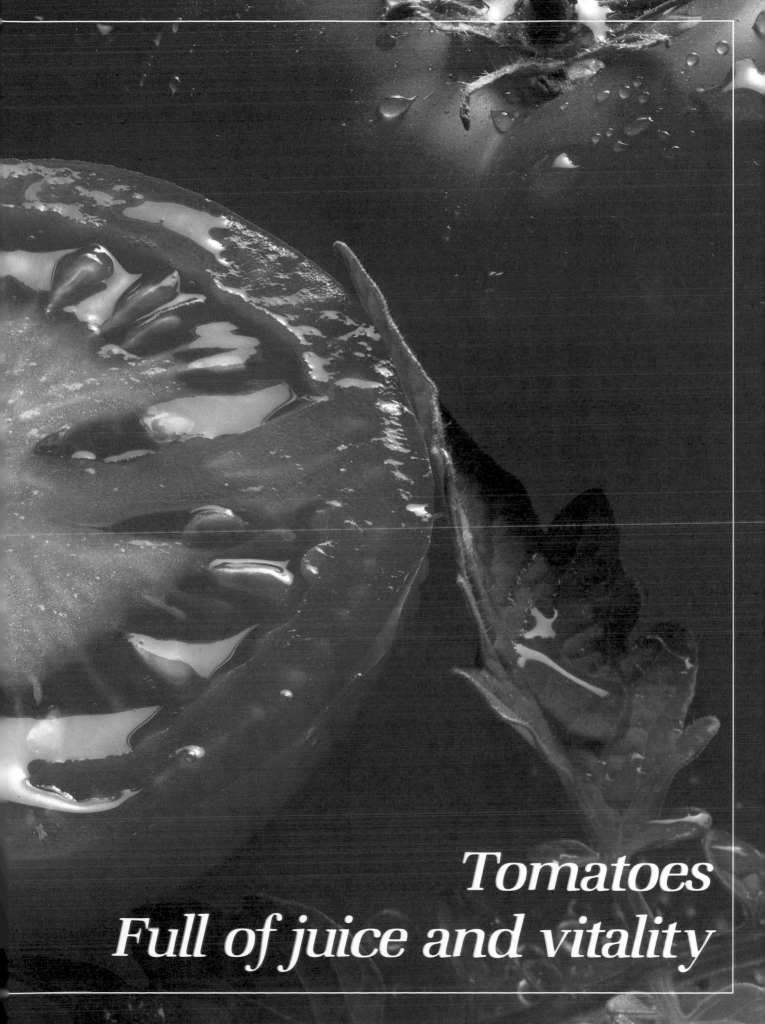

Tomatoes
Full of juice and vitality

Tomatoes

Tomatoes from your own garden taste exceptionally good. You'll really notice the difference if you've never had access to garden-fresh tomatoes. Tomatoes sold in stores are often harvested when half-green, then ripened during transport. The tomatoes from your garden, on the other hand, develop their full color and vitality from the richness of soil and sun.

Originally, tomatoes came from Peru, where they still grow wild today. We have the Aztecs to thank for both the fruit and its name—they called the plants "tumatl." Spanish conquerors brought them back to Europe as spoils of their conquests, and from there the tomato conquered the whole world. During its long history it has sometimes been given names full of fantasy— apple of paradise and love apple. At other times, its red fruits were believed to be poisonous. Today tomatoes are more versatile than any other fruit.

You will find many tomato varieties, including more than one that is particularly suited to your own growing zone. Over the years gardeners have developed a number of techniques to pamper their original "sun children." Try a few, and your rich harvest will reward your extra effort.

Weather, Soil and Nutrients

Tomatoes are very frost-sensitive, so don't sow seeds or transplant seedlings until all possibility of frost is past and the soil is well warmed. Choose a bed location that has full sunlight all day long. Plants set along a south-facing wall of your house will be protected from drafts. In contrast to most other

plants, tomatoes can be grown in the same place for many years.

Tomato plants prefer a loose, well-drained soil enriched with humus. Because their roots penetrate the soil deeply, turn the earth over at least one spade's depth the autumn before planting.

Cultivation and Care

There are two ways to plant tomatoes in your garden. You can plant them from seed, either directly in the garden or in flats indoors, or you can purchase seedlings from your local nursery or other outlet. The way that's best for you will depend on your growing zone.

The advantage of starting seeds indoors is that you can grow the specific variety that you want—and once you begin to peruse the seed catalogs, you'll see what an advantage that is. Starting seeds lets you control the length of the growing season as well as the type of tomato you want.

To start your own seedlings, divide the growing time into two stages. The first stage begins 6 to 8 weeks before planting in the garden. Sow the seeds in flats, and after they have their first set of true leaves, thin them out to about 1 inch apart. When the seedlings have developed 4 leaves,

which will take about 2 to 3 weeks, separate them into individual peat pots to help them develop strong, compact root balls. After the seedlings have 8 leaves, harden them off and put them in the garden.

You can also purchase seedlings from a nursery or other plant outlet. These plants will already be hardened off and ready for transplanting. You'll have fewer varieties at your disposal, but the convenience is sometimes worth the sacrifice.

In the garden plant seedlings 16 by 32 inches apart. Don't just position the root ball under the soil, instead, dig a trench about 2^1/$_2$ inches deep, and lay the plant in sideways. Cover the root ball and most of the stem, up to the newest set of leaves. Firm the soil and water well. The buried stem will develop roots, increasing the strength of the entire plant.

Apart from shrub tomatoes, most varieties require support (although some gardeners just let the vines sprawl over the ground, if they have enough room.) To create supports, use sturdy metal or wooden poles, or trellises

made of coarse netting or plastic poles. Metal and plastic materials are more expensive but that's offset by the fact that they'll last

practically forever. On the other hand, wooden poles are more natural-looking and attractive.

After you stake out tomatoes, tie up the plants repeatedly as they grow. Make all the ties

By the way...

Tomatoes need a lot of water to produce fruits. One way to supply it is to set large empty plant pots into the earth next to each plant. Fill these with water repeatedly, so that the tomato's roots can take it in directly.

ers during daylight hours). When you know you're in for a heavy killing frost, pick all the remaining fruits, green as well as red. In a cool, dark room, green tomatoes will ripen well, if you wrap them individually in sheets of newspaper. Lay smaller ones in egg cartons.

Pests and Diseases

In all growing zones, be sure to grow tomatoes that are resistant to verticulum wilt, and if possible, fusarium wilt. These two diseases are problems in almost all parts of the country, and they can destroy your entire crop.

When tomatoes are too damp or grow too closely together, they will often suffer from botytis (grey horse mildew) and brown rot. To prevent this disease, take care that the plants get plenty of light and air and choose resistant varieties.

Slicing Tomatoes

Slicing tomatoes are quite large (some weigh 2 pounds or more), and their shapes are often slightly ribbed or fluted. As a result, the fruits are especially meaty and tasty. Proven varieties have few

fairly loose—the flesh of the plant shouldn't grow into the twine.

Tomato plants develop side shoots that grow from the joint where the leaves join the stem. Many gardeners regularly remove these shoots in order to divert the plant's strength to the fruits developing on the main stem and branches, feeling that these will form a sufficient number of fruits.

If you decide to trim away the shoots, don't remove any after you're about a month away from the first frost. At that time, leave a maximum of 5 blossoms on each plant—no more ripe fruits will be able to develop, and any that start to will divert necessary

nutrients from those already ripening.

To promote pollination of the flowers (especially when the plants are located in wind-sheltered places), shake the plants vigorously once a day at noon.

Harvesting

Harvest tomatoes as soon as they become red. Early varieties will be ready in 50 to 70 days. Older varieties can take 90 days or even longer. To pick the fruits, bend them upwards a little to loosen them easily from the stalk. If you pull them away too roughly, you can damage the vines.

Cloth or tarp covers will protect ripening tomatoes from early frosts (be sure to remove the cov-

Plum or Paste Tomatoes

Plum or paste tomatoes are sometimes called "Italian tomatoes," because of their popularity in Italian cuisine. This variety is grown predominantly for use in sauces and soups. The fruit is pear-shaped rather than round, and it has firm flesh and few seeds. Plum tomatoes are also suitable for freezing.

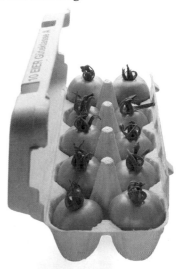

seeds and although they are soft-skinned, they are firm bodied.

Because slicing tomatoes are so large, they are suitable for salads, for grilling, and for eating raw.

Cherry Tomatoes

Cherry tomatoes are especially good as garnishes for cold dishes and salads. They are too much of a delicacy to cook. The fruits usually grow in bunches, and each one grows no more than $3/4$ to $1^{1}/_{2}$ inches in diameter. Their flavor is pleasant and slightly sweet.

Cherry tomatoes are very productive and easy to grow. They also do well as potted plants—some varieties are even bred especially to grow in hanging pots all year round.

By the way...

Small green tomatoes that are picked before the first frost ripen well when they're placed in egg cartons and stored in a cool place.

99

Potatoes
Treasure of the earth

Potatoes

The mountain highlands stretching from Bolivia to Chili is the homeland of the potato. This vegetable, with a history that goes back to the Incas, is at least 2000 years old. As with so many of our now-common vegetables, Spanish explorers introduced them to the world.

Getting farmers to grow potatoes did take a while, however. Many were astounded that the tubers under the earth, not the berries above the ground, were the edible parts of the plant. Their distrust of this strange vegetable was so great that they could only be brought, little by little, to grow it in their fields.

Today most of us can't imagine our daily diets without the potato. Its popularity has grown as people have discovered more and more ways to serve it, and it is no longer tied to just being boiled in salt water.

Weather, Soil and Nutrients

Potatoes need plenty of warmth. The soil temperature should be at least 45 degrees F. when planting them.

Potatoes prefer a light to medium heavy soil that is very loose. Heavy soils are unsuitable for potatoes—the tubers don't develop well, and you'll have a lot of trouble when you try to dig them up. Since potatoes are heavy feeders, they need well-fertilized soil. Before setting out the seed potatoes, add $1^1/_2$ to $2^1/_2$ ounces of universal vegetable fertilizer. If you fertilize with manure, it should be well rotted or soil insects will damage the tubers.

Cultivation and Care

Potatoes are very susceptible to viruses, and most gardeners lack the experience and the opportunity to grow their own healthy plants, so every year you should buy new, healthy, disease-resistant seed potatoes. That's the best guarantee for a certain yield and

healthy, tasty potatoes.

When you purchase seed potatoes you'll get either whole seed tubers or cut pieces, depending on your source. You must prepare whole tubers before you plant them. Cut them in pieces so that each piece has at least two eyes and a substantial portion of the flesh of the potato. Let the pieces cure for twenty-four hours before you plant. Otherwise the cut sides could rot.

There are three main types of potatoes, based on maturity dates—early, midseason and late. Which variety is best will depend in part on your growing zone. If you live in a southern growing zone, select varieties especially designed for warm weather and plan on potatoes as a late rather than an early crop. In moderate to short zones, grow potatoes as a spring crop, harvest early, and use the bed for a second crop. If

your season is long enough, try midseason and late potatoes. These are especially suitable for storage.

Prepare the soil bed. In autumn dig deeply, and thoroughly loosen it with a grubber in the spring. If you plan to use manure or other organic materials, such as compost, dig it in during the fall, or, at the latest, early spring. The same applies to green fertilizer—if you plan to use it as an interim crop, grow it and turn it under the previous fall.

Plant potatoes in rows, each seed potato 4 inches deep and 12 inches apart. Place the cut side facing down. The tubers will develop above the seed. Individual rows should be 30 inches apart. When the foliage reaches a height of 4 to 6 inches, earth up the plants to the top set of leaves. Earthing up loosens the soil, destroys germinating weeds, and above all, encourages the development of the growing tu-

bers. Repeat this process several times until the vines develop buds. Before earthing up the plants for the final time, apply

one last dose of fertilizer, about 1¹/₂ oz. per square yard.

Harvesting

Begin harvesting your potatoes a week or so after the vines flower. Pull away the soil carefully and try not to disturb the roots. Remove only as many tubers as you need each day, so the others can continue to develop.

Once the foliage dies down, harvest the entire plant. Carefully lift out the entire root system with a garden fork or pitchfork. You'll be astonished at how many potatoes have grown from one single tuber.

The unsurpassable flavor will also surprise you. Freshly harvested and prepared potatoes from your own garden are much more flavorful than those you buy at a store because storage definitely affects their taste. Later, you can plant the land with a second crop (usually lettuce) or a green fertilizer.

Brassicas
Grandeur in the garden

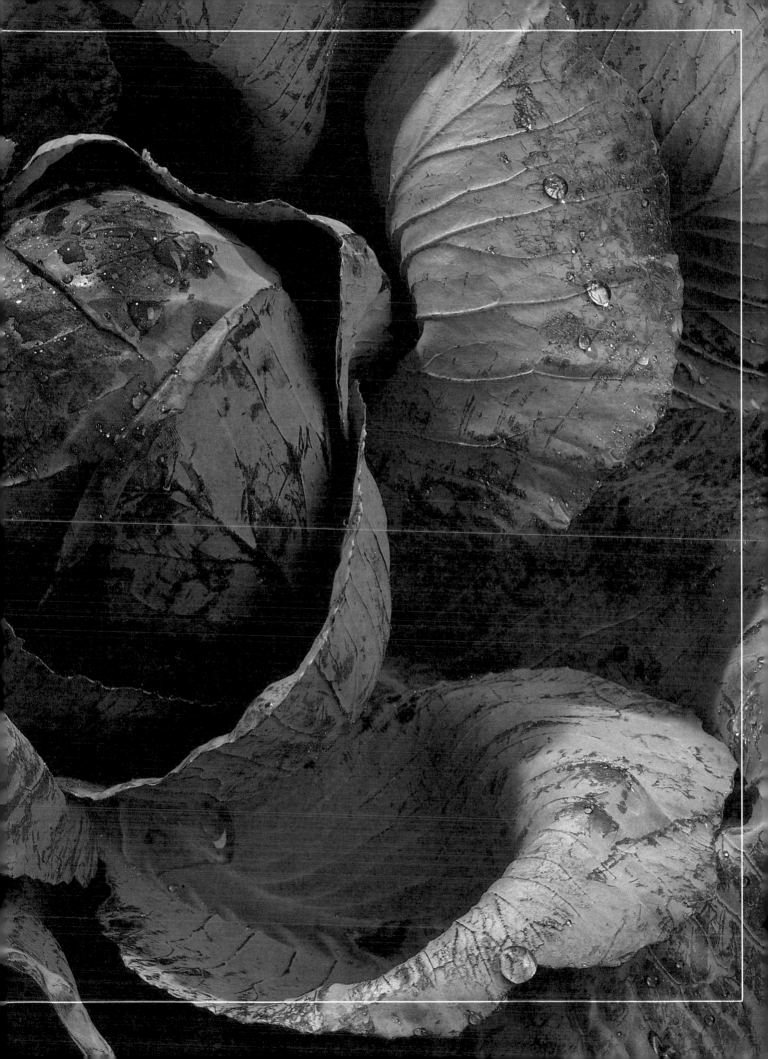

Brassicas (Brassicaceae)

Cauliflower, broccoli, Chinese cabbage, kale, kohlrabi, Brussels sprouts and cabbages are all members of one of the most important plant families—the Brassicas (Brassicaceae).

Most brassicas are biannuals, so they store abundant nutrients during their first year, and use them to produce flowers in the second. To take advantage of this rich store of vitamins and minerals, harvest brassicas in their first year, before they flower.

You should, however, allow yourself the pleasure, just once, of letting a cabbage plant come into bloom. You'll be amazed at how much more is hidden in a cabbage than just a hearty winter meal.

Raw cabbage is important in people's diets because of its nu-

tritional value and its beneficial effect on the liver, intestines, and indeed the whole metabolism.

Cauliflower and Broccoli

Weather, Soil and Nutrients
Cauliflower and broccoli are cool weather plants, so your planting should be done either in leaves. These are tied in place. the spring or late summer. Since both varieties have better flavor after being exposed to frost, they make an excellent second crop. Locate the beds in a sunny spot, and keep the soil well watered.

These two plants flourish best on medium heavy soils that have a large supply of organic substances. Their flavor is improved through regular, harmonious fertilizing. Before planting, apply 2 ounces of universal vegetable fertilizer per square yard. About 3 weeks later, supply $1^1/_2$ ounces per square yard, and the same amount again when the heads begin to form.

Cultivation and Care
You can set out spring seedlings from 4 weeks before to 2 weeks after the final frost date, so start your seeds indoors about 4 weeks before you want to plant. When the *cotyledons* (or initial false leaves) are well developed, separate the seedlings into $2^1/_2$ to 3-inch peat pots. Move the seedlings to their final location when they have developed 4 or 5 leaves.

If your season is short, start summer cauliflower or broccoli indoors. Then move the seedlings to a cold frame or an outside nursery bed from the end of March until June, when they are set directly into their permanent bed.

For autumn harvest, sow both cauliflower and broccoli in outside nursery beds around mid-season. About 5 weeks after sowing, discard any sickly plants, moisten the seedling root balls well, and set them in their final location.

Early cauliflower plants should be 20 to 24 inches apart; fall plantings should be 24 to 32 inches apart. Space broccoli 20 by 20 inches apart.

To grow either of these vegeta- bles successfully, you must water them regularly. Without plenty of water, the heads will be misshapen, or the plant may bolt. When this happens, the plant is useless. Cultivate often to keep the surface soil loose and weed-free.

Position in Crop Rotation
Never follow one brassica variety with another. Plan your plantings so that you only grow brassicas in the same soil bed every 4 years.

Special Cultivation Tips

Cauliflower

Cauliflower is one of the most popular garden vegetables. It's flavor is excellent, and the plant is easily digestible.

Harvesting
The small "flowerets" of a formed cauliflower head are called the *curd*. Most people believe that curd must be white to be flavorful. Actually, in terms of quality and flavor, it makes no difference whether the color is white or off-white. If you want very white heads, you'll have to blanch them, a process that takes 2 to 3 weeks. To blanch, you must protect the heads from the sun's rays by crossing the just-formed curd with the outer

During the blanching period, check the curd regularly to make sure that it's still tight and well-formed. Once the curd begins to spread, or become less tight, the flavor will be lost.

Don't harvest cauliflower until the head loosens slightly on the outside. Be alert, however; if you wait too long, the head may soon lose its round shape and its delicate flavor.

Broccoli

Since broccoli is never blanched, it is easier to grow than cauliflower, and like cauliflower, it's picked before it's fully developed. It has a more delicate flavor than cauliflower—some even say it tastes a little like asparagus. Broccoli contains more vitamins than cauliflower, and its stalks are considered a delicacy.

Harvesting

Harvest broccoli when the head is well developed but is still tightly closed. If you don't plan to harvest right away, watch the plants carefully once the head has formed. When the green buds open their yellow blossoms, and that can happen very quickly, broccoli is worthless as a vegetable. It's most valuable when it's freshly harvested—it can wither after only a few hours.

After you harvest the main head, the main stem will form numerous small side shoots, which you can harvest for several weeks.

Kohlrabi

Kohlrabi is a plant grown not for its leaves, but for the swollen bulb that develops along its stem. Most varieties mature within about 60 to 70 days, and the vegetable can be eaten raw or cooked.

Weather, Soil and Nutrients

In most zones, you can sow kohlrabi directly into the garden around the final frost date. Those in short-season zones should begin seeds indoors and transplant them when the seedlings form 3 or 4 true leaves.

Kohlrabi flourishes trouble-free on practically all soils. It grows especially well, however, on light humus soils that warm up quickly. If your soil is light and sandy, be sure to provide the plants with sufficient water.

An addition of organic fertilizer will enhance production. As always, turn manure under in the autumn, although you can add compost directly before cultivation. Before planting, apply 2 ounces of a universal vegetable fertilizer per square yard, and add a second dose of 1 1/2 ounces per square yard about 2 weeks later.

Cultivation and Care

In short-season zones, sow kohlrabi seeds indoors about a month before you intend to plant outdoors. When the cotyledons are well developed, separate the seedlings into $2^1/2$ to 3-inch pots. After about 4 weeks, when the plants have formed 3 to 4 leaves, transplant them out in the open. If you plant directly in the garden, thin the growing seedlings as they develop. Kohlrabi should stand about 10 inches apart, in rows 12 inches apart

As the plants grow, water them regularly. If they become too dry, the bulbs will become woody (fibrous), and a sudden heavy rain can cause them to burst.

Harvesting

Although kohlrabi is a cool weather plant, like cauliflower and broccoli, it can't tolerate frost or freeze, which cause it to bolt—the stem bulb doesn't develop, and the plant is useless.

Harvest kohlrabi at an early stage, when the bulb has reached a diameter of about $2^1/2$ to 3 inches.

Savoys, Red Cabbage and White Cabbage

Weather, Soil and Nutrients

Cabbages are a cool weather crop, and they don't do well in very warm zones unless they're grown as an early spring or a fall crop. There are three types: early, midseason and late, depending upon maturity dates. Early varieties like light soils; midseason and late varieties grow better in heavy soils.

Before planting, apply about 2 ounces of universal vegetable fertilizer per square yard. Three weeks later apply another 2 ounces per square yard, and add a final dose of 2 ounces per square yard when the heads begin to form. Simply spread the fertilizer around the plants and work it shallowly into the soil.

Cultivation and Care

For early spring planting, sow the seeds indoors or in a cold frame about a month before the final frost. You can transplant the hardened seedlings to their final bed after about 6 weeks. Set the plants 20 by 16 inches apart.

If you have a large garden and want to raise late cabbages, sow the seeds in a nursery bed in early summer. Thin the plants to 1 inch apart to prevent overcrowding. Move them to their permanent bed when the seedlings have 4 to 6 leaves. Space these plants 20 by 20 inches apart.

No matter when you plant, be sure to water the plants regularly and evenly. Otherwise, a sudden soaking can split the heads, and you'll lose your crop.

Harvesting

You can harvest cabbages as soon as the heads are solid to the touch. Rather than just pulling the head loose, cut through the

root stem below the head with a sharp knife. For a while, the root stem will produce small secondary heads that are scrumptious eating.

Spring cabbages don't store well, so only grow as many as you can use in about 4 weeks.

Harvest midseason and late cabbages before the onset of heavy frost. Cabbages flourish in cool and damp weather and can withstand temperatures to 25 degrees F.

After you've harvested the cabbages, remove the root stalks from the ground and dispose of them in the garbage. Don't put the stalks and root balls onto the compost heap, or you may spread cabbage clubroot disease, sometimes called cabbage hernia.

Brussels Sprouts

The German name for Brussels sprouts is Rosenkohl—little rosettes that grow like tiny cabbage heads in the joint where the leaves meet the stem. Brussels sprouts are a trouble-free crop to grow in autumn and winter and are valuable, delicate vegetables in a season when fresh vegetables are rare.

Weather, Soil and Nutrients

Brussels sprouts are an excellent late season crop because they are quite frost-hardy and, more importantly, light frost improves the flavor. That's because some of the plant's starch is changed to sugar upon freezing.

Brussels sprouts can be grown on any soil but they flourish best on loams and sandy loams.

Brussels sprouts require fewer

nutrients than other brassicas. It's sufficient to apply 2 ounces of a universal vegetable fertilizer per square yard before planting and add a second dose of 1 ½

keep it weed-free. Brussels sprout plants can grow to be 3 feet tall, depending upon the variety. If necessary, support the taller plants.

Harvesting

Harvesting begins when the lower sprouts are about 1 to 1½ inches in diameter. Always pick them from the bottom to the top, since they mature in this order. If you see any opened, loose, yellow or rotted sprouts, remove them immediately, or they will impair the growth of the others. In late autumn, break off the tops of the plants so that all their strength is diverted to the sprouts.

Curly Kale

Kale is a hardy plant and can withstand frost, so it's usually the last green vegetable in the garden. It has a high proportion of carotene, which together with body fat, is changed in the body into vitamin A. In addition, kale is one of the most protein-rich vegetables. Its high vitamin C content can be destroyed during cooking unless it is stewed very gently. When blanched, kale is very suitable for freezing.

Weather, Soil and Nutrients

As with many other cool weather plants, kale doesn't grow well when the temperature rises too high, so take this into consideration when planning your crop rotation. It flourishes in half-shady locations and is the least demanding of all the brassicas. However, it prefers soil that is heavy but not too compact.

Before planting, dig in about 2 ounces of a universal vegetable fertilizer per square yard. During the main growing period, add another 1 ½ to 2 ounces. Like Brussels sprouts, kale is not only frost-hardy, but its flavor becomes milder with freezing tem-

ounces about 4 weeks later. *Don't* fertilize with manure—it causes the plants to form sprouts that are too loose.

Cultivation and Care

If your growing season is short, start Brussels sprouts indoors. Otherwise, plant the seed in a nursery bed or in its permanent bed about 10 to 12 weeks before the first fall frost. Thin the plants to 24 inches apart as they develop.

If you are going to transplant, wait until the seedlings are about 5 or 6 inches high. Then plant them in rows, 24 by 24 inches apart. Loosen the soil repeatedly during the growing stage, and

peratures, because they change some of its starches into sugar.

Cultivation and Care

Sow kale seeds in the open beginning in midsummer, in rows 24 inches apart, and thin the plants to 8 inches apart.

After planting, loosen the soil regularly and keep it clear of weeds. Repeat this often until the crop is very thick. Kale needs plenty of moisture, so keep it well watered.

Harvesting

You can harvest kale from about mid-October, as soon as the leaves are well formed. Always remove any lower leaves that become yellow. Never completely clear the plant of leaves, or it will stop forming new ones.

Position in Crop Rotation

Kale is a good second crop after early peas or early potatoes.

Chinese Cabbage

Chinese cabbage is a special vegetable for the vitamin-poor autumn season, and its tender leaves have an unusual flavor. The plant forms a loose, oval-shaped head and has no stalk. A very wide-spread vegetable in China, it is enjoying ever-increasing popularity in western countries as well. If you have previously known Chinese cabbage only as a salad ingredient, then you certainly should try out the recipes in the second half of this book.

Weather, Soil and Nutrients

Chinese cabbage requires about the same conditions as all brassicas. The soil shouldn't be too light, and requires an addition of well-rotted manure or compost. Before planting, dig in about 2 ounces of a universal

vegetable fertilizer per square yard, and about 4 weeks later apply a second dose of 1 1/2 ounces.

Cultivation and Care

Sow Chinese cabbage directly in its permanent bed late in the season. Plant the seeds 1 inch deep, in rows about 14 inches apart. Later, thin the seedlings to 12 inches apart. Chinese cabbage sown earlier may bolt.

It's most important to water the young plants regularly and well. Work through the rows regularly to loosen the soil and remove weeds.

Harvesting

As soon as Chinese cabbage heads are large enough to pick, begin harvesting. The plants can remain in the bed without problems as long as the temperature doesn't fall below 20 degrees F.

To store Chinese cabbage, wrap the plants, roots and all, in newspaper and stand them vertically in a fruit box. When stored in a cool place, they will stay fresh for several weeks.

Position in Crop Rotation

Because it's sown late, Chinese cabbage is a very good second crop, for example, after bush beans.

Pests on Brassicas

Finally, just a word about special protective measures for this widely varied family.

The disease that is the most dangerous for all brassicas is clubroot, or cabbage hernia. This fungus disease is transmitted either through infected plant material or soil. There is no direct method of fighting it, apart from a relatively expensive soil sterilization process.

To control clubroot, remove the fungus from the planting area whenever it appears. Since the disease is especially a problem in acidic and badly drained soils, take special care to provide good drainage. Avoid using too much manure as fertilizer, and only plant healthy young seedlings.

Crop rotation also plays an important role in preventing the spread of clubroot. Plant brassicas in the same location only every 4 years, and sow a green fertilizer as one of the interim crops. Make sure that the seed mixture doesn't contain any crucifers, such as mustard, since cabbages also belong to this family. If you have problems with clubroot, disinfect the soil by adding a fertilizer with calcium nitrate (2 ounces per square yard).

Further enemies of the cabbage are cabbage flies and turnip fleas (flea beatles). Keeping the soil moist helps to prevent turnip fleas. The only help against cabbage flies is the timely treatment with a suitable organic, biodegradable pesticide or the timely removal of any infected plants.

Do *not* spray against caterpillars. In a small garden it's better to take the time to remove them by hand (see also the General Section, "Protecting Plants," p, 64).

Leeks, Onions and Shallots

Leek Varieties

Leeks and onions belong to the lily family (Liliaceae), which probably originated in areas of Afghanistan and Iran. Not only are ornamental plants such as tulips and lilies members of this extensive family, but also (and this isn't as easy to discern) the mild asparagus.

Plants in the lily family have been valued for centuries because they are biannuals that store food in roots during their first year of life to use during the second. By harvesting the plants in their first year, you benefit from their nutritional abundance of minerals, vitamins and many important hormones. This richness is exceeded by very few other crops. Even the ancient Egyptians used these nourishing plants as aphrodesiacs. In modern cuisine, onion varieties are used primarily as flavorings and as appetizing side vegetables. They are also important for their high nutritional content.

Onions

Onions are a very widespread group of eating and seasoning plants. Their distinctive flavor comes from their sugar content and sulphuric volatile oil, which is also what causes your eyes to water when you peel or cut into one.

Weather, Soil and Nutrients

Onions love warmth, and they need a dry autumn in which to ripen, but otherwise their demands are few. They thrive best,

Spring onions are the first onions from the garden.

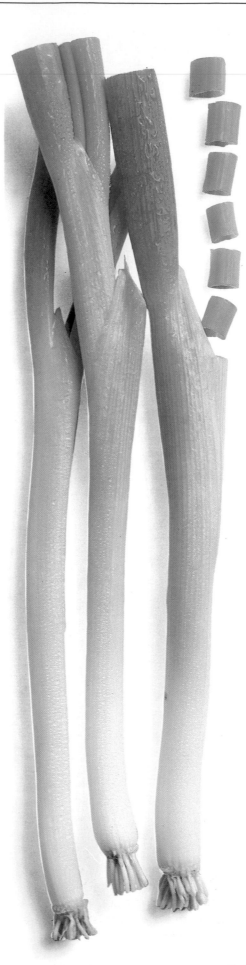

however, in light, well-fertilized soils because they have relatively shallow roots. Well-rotted compost is beneficial, since it furnishes a generous supply of minerals and at the same time loosens the soil.

Either before planting, or about 10 days afterwards, dig in approximately 1 ounce of a universal vegetable fertilizer per square yard, and add a second dose halfway through the growing period.

Cultivation and Care

You can sow onion seeds directly into the garden from four weeks before the last frost date until about two weeks after, as long as the weather remains cool. If your fall is long and cool, you can start a late crop. Onion seeds are small and should be planted no more than 1/4 inch deep, in rows 12 inches apart. In about 4 to 6 weeks, shoots will appear. At that time, thin the plants to about 2 to 6 inches apart, depending on the size you plan to grow.

You can grow onion seedlings indoors from seed, or you can purchase them from local nurseries or other outlets. Plant the seedlings outdoors from 2 weeks before the last frost until 2 weeks after. Set them about 4 inches apart in rows 12 inches apart. Harvest them as they grow, and you'll thin them at the same time.

Planting onion sets shortens the growing period, since the bulbs are already formed. Always select sets with a diameter of between 1/2 to 3/4 inches. Larger ones have a tendency to bolt. Don't plant the sets until after the danger of frost is past. Then set them 6 to 10 inches apart, in rows 10 inches apart. Be sure that they aren't too deep—the tip of the bulb should just barely be

114

exposed above the soil.

It's important to keep the bed weed-free, but hoe carefully and shallowly so you don't disturb the onions' shallow roots.

Harvesting

Pull onions throughout the summer as you need them—you'll be thinning the bed at the same time. They will be almost ready to harvest when the green tops fall over and die off (if some remain upright, break them over, but not off). Leave them in the soil until the tops are brown, usually about 2 weeks. Then, on a dry warm day, pull them up, or use a garden fork to dig them up—carefully!

Clean and carefully examine all the bulbs. Remove any damaged ones for immediate use, because they won't store well. Leave the remaining bulbs out in the sun to cure for one or two days. Then plait them together and store them in a dry, airy place.

Special Cultivation Tips

Spring Onions (Scallions)

Scallions are treasured for their mild, slightly spicy taste. They

mature very early, so you must pick them when they are small and very young. (You can also eat the green tops.) Then they are especially nourishing and the leaves are very flavorful.

Pearl Onions (Silver Skin Onions)

Pearl onions are small, very white onions designed especially for pickling. Sow the seeds about 1 inch deep, in rows 2 to 3 inches apart. Sow the seeds fairly thick and deep, and don't thin them out.

Harvest pearl onions about 10 to 12 weeks after sowing, while

they are still small. Cut off the stem and roots at once, and pickle almost all of them in vinegar.

Yellow Onions

Everyone recognizes common yellow eating onions. They have a sharper flavor than spring onions and are especially suitable for cooking and frying. The stems aren't eaten.

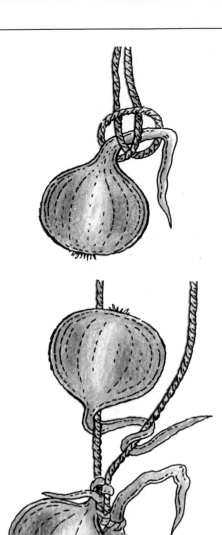

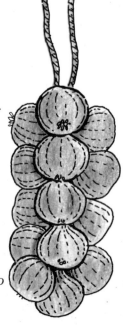

This diagram shows how plaiting is done. Place the dried foliage across a piece of string (as shown in the diagram) and pull it tight. Remove onions from the top down, and cut each loose through the stem, taking care not to cut through the string.

Red Onions

Red onions have a spicy flavor, but they aren't as hot as yellow onions and are usually eaten raw. Their intense reddish-purple color enriches the beauty of any raw vegetable salad.

A basket of shallots is a delicacy that you can only rarely buy.

Shallots

Shallots are an especially delicate onion highly prized in French cuisine. Smaller and thinner than eating onions, they are always grown from sets, but instead of developing a larger bulb, each set develops many small, offset bulbs. Because shallots ripen early, they can provide you with fresh onions until the other varieties are ready.

To grow shallots, plant them as you would standard onion sets, at intervals of 6 by 12 inches. Set each set shallowly in the earth so that its top is just above the surface. As they grow, use the young shallot leaves like chives.

Garlic

Garlic is another vegetable that cannot be started from seed. Instead you plant cloves from a bulb grown the year before.

Garlic is an onion variety that comes from the Orient. Its value lies in its high concentration of volatile oil and in its effective anti-bacterial substances. When you plant single cloves alongside tomatoes or cabbages, garlic has a bactericidal and fungicidal effect, and it also repels pests. It also has many applications in herbal medications, and is said to stimulate the appetite and aid digestion. Most of us know it as a flavoring in many dishes.

Cultivation

There are two varieties of garlic, the winter (or white) and the spring (or red). In both cases, the outer, small cloves are separated

from a mature garlic bulb and are planted at intervals of 6 by 12 inches. In warm zones, plant garlic in October or November. It's better to wait until March or April in colder regions.

Leeks

Leeks are a distinctive variety of onion, with tall pale stems that can grow to be thicker than 2 inches around. Gourmets prize its delicate flavor, raw or cooked, alone or with other ingredients. Leeks benefit the garden because after they are harvested, their large mass of fine roots leave behind a healthy, loose soil.

Weather, Soil and Nutrients

Leeks grow best in cooler weather, so in warm zones consider them as a fall crop rather than a spring one. Although they aren't demanding, they grow especially well on a soil that is rich with humus and well supplied with water. You must loosen soils with a high clay content to a depth of one spade blade. Before planting, dig in about 2 ounces of universal vegetable fertilizer per square yard and about 4 to 6 weeks after planting apply a second dose of 1 1/2 to 2 ounces.

Cultivation and Care

Leeks are a long-season crop and can take as many as 150 days to go from seedling to fully mature plant. In most zones you should start seeds indoors about 4 to 8 weeks before the last frost. You can set seedlings out 2 or 3 weeks before or after the last frost. Before you transplant, trim plant tips and roots a little. Plant them 4 inches deep and 6 inches apart; the distance between the rows should be 16 inches.

In long-season zones sow the seed directly in the garden, 1/2 inch deep in rows 16 inches

apart. Later, thin the plants so they are 6 inches apart.

During the growing season, keep the rows weed-free and the soil loose. As you work the rows, earth up the growing stalks to blanch the stems. Always water well—leeks need more moisture than onions.

Harvesting

You can harvest leeks all summer long, but they require a lot time to achieve their fully ripened, thick stem. When you dig them up, don't cut off too much of the green leaves because they contain most of the vegetable's valuable vitamin A.

You can store leeks indoors during the winter, but in most places they can overwinter right in the garden. Simply cover the

By the way...

rows with brush, straw or some other thick mulch, and dig the leeks up as you need them. You will be able to harvest them far into the next year.

You can also grow pearl onions from leeks. Rather than harvest overwintered leeks, leave them in the bed. As soon as flower buds appear, break them off, whereupon each plant will form small white onion bulbs. Harvest these in autumn and immediately replant those that are not used. Over the winter you can harvest green leaves to use like chives. The next year, you will be able to harvest a whole cluster of pearl onions.

Lettuces and Greens Colorful and full of vitamins

Lettuce and Greens

Is there anything as refreshing as a colorful salad out of your own garden, anything more delicious than tender greens, freshly harvested, full of vitamins, rich in minerals, and unsurpassed in flavor? Fresh lettuce and greens the whole year round, from winter until well into late autumn—with our directions for an optimal yield this enjoyment will be trouble-free.

It doesn't matter whether you want to enjoy a simple, freshly picked green salad or one that is elaborate and full of color—make use of the whole variety your garden can offer. And when you prefer it hot, then look carefully in the Gardener's Cookbook section. You may discover that many vegetables you use only in salads can also be enjoyed as cooked vegetables.

Head Lettuce, Butterhead Lettuce, Leaf Lettuce and Cos (Romaine)

Weather, Soil and Nutrients
Lettuces thrive best in temperate climates. Choose a sunny place to plant early and late varieties—lettuce will flourish especially well in such a setting. Varieties bred to flourish during the heat of summer will even grow well in half-shade.

All four lettuce varieties can be grown in any garden soil, except one that is light sand, and since it cannot hold moisture, a regular water supply is a prerequisite for successful lettuce. They lose a lot of water from their large leaf surfaces, and their shallow roots need a ready supply to replace it.

Be very careful how you fertilize lettuce. If the plant grows too quickly and luxuriously, it will be more susceptible to drought. An application of well-decayed manure before a fall planting can prove valuable, and before planting, dig in 1 1/2 ounces of a universal vegetable fertilizer per square yard.

Pests and Diseases
When lettuce leaves become discolored around the edges, it doesn't necessarily mean that the plant is diseased. More often it's a sign of a problem with watering.

Lettuce rot in leaves and the root stalk is caused by various fungi and bacteria. To combat

them remove the affected leaves and keep the soil permanently loose. That means you have to provide the optimal amount of water and keep the bed well hoed. This condition will keep the humidity level around the plants down.

Birds can cause a lot of damage to lettuce, especially when the early plants are the only green things in the garden. Nets and plastic coverings can help. If you notice aphids, attack the problem as quickly as possible because they carry virus diseases. Either remove affected plants before the pests can spread to others, or spray early with an organic, biouegradable pesticide. (Take note of the waiting time.) It's best to pick slugs by hand off the growing plants—it doesn't pay to use slug poison in small gardens.

The best way to avoid diseases is to choose varieties that are resistant to blight and virus diseases.

Special Cultivation Tips

Head Lettuce

The most common lettuce is tender head lettuce. It's only eaten raw and can be harvested the whole year round.

Cultivation and Care
For spring cultivation, start the seeds indoors 4 weeks before the last frost. As soon as the first pair of true leaves have formed, thin the plants to about 1 inch apart. Transplant them in the open after the soil has warmed up, at intervals of 10 by 12 inches. Moisten the root ball before planting. Don't set the seedlings too deeply in the ground—the leaves must remain above the surface of the soil—and water lightly after planting. A black plastic mulch around lettuce plants can advance the harvest by up to 2 weeks.

After you transplant the seedlings, begin to sow directly in the garden every 2 weeks, so that you always have fresh lettuce on hand. Sow the seeds in rows about 12 inches apart, and thin the young plants until they are 10 to 12 inches apart.

Harvesting

Harvesting occurs, on average, about 8 to 10 weeks after sowing. Harvest head lettuce when the head is well-formed, firm and closed.

Butterhead Lettuce

This lettuce is also known as Boston or bibb lettuce. Many people feel it is better tasting than the traditional head lettuce, but it isn't grown as often nor seen as often in grocery stores. The outer leaves are a rich, dark green, and the inner leaves form a compact head that isn't as solid as that of a head lettuce. The brittle leaves and leaf ribs crackle stiffly when eaten.

Cultivation and Care

Butterhead lettuce requires the same care as head lettuce. However, set the plants 12 by 12 inches apart.

Leaf Lettuce

Leaf lettuce doesn't form a heart. It can be used as a raw fresh lettuce, or it can be cooked. You simply cut away the outer leaves (don't cut it down too low), and it will continue to form leaves. There are various varieties featuring numerous leaf shapes—some are even red.

Cultivation and Care

Sow leaf lettuce in the open from the time of the last frost, in rows 6 inches apart. Make additional sowings every 2 weeks, in order to have a continuous harvest.

Harvesting

Begin to harvest leaf lettuce as soon as the leaves are well-formed—in fact as you thin the beds, use even the smallest leaves for an early spring treat. If you cut the leaves too low on the stem, you'll damage the young stipules—the "heart" leaves. Always pick only the outer leaves (these are the oldest) so that the plant will continue producing.

Cos or Romaine Lettuce

Cos lettuce is somewhat more flavorful than the other lettuces and tastes a bit like endive. It can be eaten raw or cooked. Some plants may begin to form heads that are too open. In such cases, simply bind the leaves together lightly with twine. This will improve the head's formation, and the the inner leaves will remain light and tender.

Cultivation and Care

Cos lettuce is definitely a cool-weather crop. Begin the seeds indoors about 4 weeks before the last frost date, and later in a cold frame. Transplant the seedlings in the garden 12 by 12 inches apart. Grow this lettuce early because the danger of its wilting in the summer is very great.

Harvesting

Harvest cos lettuce about 6 to 8 weeks after planting. When the heart leaves begin to open you cannot wait much longer with the harvest because the plants then begin to bolt.

121

Endive

The flavor of endive can sometimes be slightly bitter. Blanching can help solve that problem. Endive is, almost without exception, eaten raw and is prepared much like head lettuce.

Weather, Soil and Nutrients

Endive is less sensitive to frost than head lettuce, and it doesn't make any special demands on the weather. Although endive can grow on all garden soils, it gives the best yield on humus soils. It needs more nutrients than head lettuce. Supplement any organic fertilizer, such as manure, with 2 ounces of universal vegetable fertilizer per square yard. Because endive has a long taproot, it isn't as sensitive to drought as other lettuces.

Cultivation and Care

Endive will bolt if it grows during the long days of summer but is an excellent spring and fall crop. You can transplant seedlings into the garden as early as 2 weeks before the last frost date. Or, sow the seeds in their permanent bed about 15 weeks before the first frost in the fall. Growing plants should be spaced 12 by 12 inches apart. After planting, it's

especially important to provide them with plenty of water and keep the soil hoed and weed-free.

Endive can be somewhat bitter, but that can be modified with blanching. (This isn't necessary with some of today's varieties, which develop self-blanching hearts—that is, their younger leaves produce no chlorophyll.) Tie the leaves of endive together carefully with twine to bleach the centers, or invert a large clay flower pot over the growing plant. If endive plants grow close together, the leaves often blanch automatically.

Harvesting

Harvest endive when the inner heart is well developed. In mild areas this plant can stay in the garden until well into the winter. When there is a danger of frost, remove the whole plant, roots and all, and set it in a box of moistened sand. If you keep the roots moist and the leaves dry, the plants will keep for some time.

Position in Crop Rotation

Endive is especially suited for a second crop, but be sure to rotate crops carefully—never plant lettuce after lettuce.

Lamb's Lettuce (Rapunzel)

With an Old World name that reflects the fairy tale featuring a young woman with very long hair, Rapunzel, or lamb's lettuce, is the only lettuce member of the Valerian plant family. It still grows wild in some areas and is a fairly hardy plant that makes an excellent second crop. Lamb's lettuce has the largest vitamin C content of all the lettuces.

Soil, Nutrition and Weather

Lamb's lettuce can withstand slight frosts, but should be protected with a mulch cover of brush or straw in the winter. It thrives well in all soils, but prefers a medium-heavy, weed-free soil. Before sowing, dig in about 2 ounces of a universal vegetable fertilizer per square yard.

Cultivation and Care

Lamb's lettuce is usually sown as a second crop, although it can be sown in early spring after the last frost. Plant the seeds thickly in rows 6 to 8 inches apart. If you're sure your bed is weed-free, you can broadcast the seed (see p. 44). As soon as the seedlings sprout, loosen the soil between the rows again, but try not to get loose earth on the plants.

In short season zones, a fall crop of lamb's lettuce can be sown in a cold frame where it will remain until it's harvested.

Harvesting

Harvest lamb's lettuce as soon as the leaves are well formed. Always cut the whole leaf rosette off with a sharp knife. In zones with mild winters, cover the plants with brush, straw or some other covering, and you'll be able to harvest until spring.

Sugarloaf (Leaf Chicory), Belgian Endive and Radicchio

Drive down country roads in the summer, or let a city lot go to seed, and probably one plant that will spring up is tall, slender, and bears twenty or more daisy-like blue flowers. This is one variety of chicory, and its roots, when roasted and ground, have long been used as a coffee substitute. The chicory varieties that you will most likely want in your garden are the salad succory (better known as Belgian endive), sugarloaf and radicchio.

Weather, Soil and Nutrients

All members of the chicory family can withstand light night

frost, as well as short periods of drought. Sugarloaf and radicchio can be grown on almost any type of soil. The only unsuitable ones are stony soils and ones that have been fertilized with fresh manure.

To prepare the bed for planting, dig in about 1 1/2 ounces of a universal vegetable fertilizer per square yard. Then, 4 to 5 weeks after planting, supply an additional 1 to 1 1/2 ounces per square yard.

Sugarloaf (Leaf Chicory)

Sow the seeds for sugarloaf in midsummer. If you plant too early, the plants may bolt, and later plantings are less productive. Sow the seeds sparsely in rows about 16 inches apart. When the plants are about 4 inches high, thin them out to 12 inches apart. Hoe often to keep the soil loose and weed-free dur-

ing the growing period.

If your variety isn't self-blanching, about 3 weeks before you plan to harvest, cover the plants with black plastic or an inverted flower pot, or tie the leaves around the forming head to blanch the leaves before picking.

Harvesting

Pick sugarloaf leaves as they mature, and harvest the plants when they have formed a firm, closed heart. You can keep sugarloaf until the following spring if you carefully dig the plants *with their roots* before the first frost and store them in a cool place. (They do well if you hang them by the roots in a basement.)

Radicchio

Radicchio is known mainly as an ingredient in fresh Italian salads, but its fame is becoming more widespread all the time. Its brilliant red leaves contrast with the usual green of other lettuces, and makes it a welcome addition to any salad.

Cultivation and Care

Sow radicchio in the open from mid-July to mid-August, in rows 16 inches apart. When the plants are about hand high, thin them to 4 inches apart. Hoe often to aerate the soil and combat weeds; water as often as is necessary.

Harvesting

Some radicchio varieties build heads in autumn. You can harvest these from the time they begin to form. Don't cut them off too far down on the root stalk because plants protected during the winter can develop small heads again in the spring.

The leaves of other varieties only form loose rosettes. Cut off these leaves in the autumn, but do not use them. Instead protect the plants with a thick mulch of brush or straw, and in the spring you'll be able to harvest the small heads that form.

Belgian Endive

Belgian endive (which is sometimes called French endive) is a delicacy that takes time to grow, but it's worth the effort. What's more, the techniques aren't as difficult as is generally thought. Generally speaking, you grow the plants for the roots, not the leaves. You then dig the roots in the fall, sprout them under very specific conditions and harvest the tall, oval plant that develops. You can prepare Belgian endive in a myriad of ways, and it is just as fine in uncooked as cooked dishes.

Weather, Soil and Nutrients

Belgian endive has the same demands as its relatives radicchio and sugarloaf, but requires deep, well-loosened soils. Before planting, dig in 1½ ounces of universal vegetable fertilizer per square

yard, and apply a second dose of 2 ounces about midway through the summer. The second fertilizing is especially important for strong root formation.

Cultivation and Care

Sow the seeds thinly in rows 12 inches apart as soon as the soil is well warmed in the spring. When the plants have 3 leaves, thin them out to about 6 inches between each plant. Before the first frost, dig up the plants, roots and all.

Forcing the Roots

You must now *force* the roots to produce Belgian endive. Forcing is a method of making a plant grow under conditions that are unusual or abnormal.

Sort through the roots, and discard all but those having a minimum diameter of 1½ to 2 inches. Then, take the selected roots and cut off the leaves 1¼ inches above the beginning of the roots.

Set some of the prepared roots into a container full of damp peat. The roots must *not* touch each other, and the peat must *not* cover the leaf base. Cover the container with a piece of black plastic large enough to accommodate the growing plant without allowing any light to enter inside. If possible, place the container in a warm dark room, and keep the peat moist at all times.

You should store the roots you don't use right away in a cool place. Then at two-week intervals, prepare another container of roots. This will ensure a supply of fresh Belgian endive until well into March and April.

Harvesting

Depending upon your storage area's temperature, the bleached Belgian endive form after 3 to 4 weeks and can then be harvested.

Forcing Belgian Endive

1. *Belgian endive in the garden.*
2. *Before or after removing the roots, cut off the leaves.*
3. *Clean and gently scrape the roots.*
4. *The leaf base should extend about 1¼ inches above the root shoulder.*
5. *Store any roots that you don't plan to use immediately in a cool dry place.*
6. *Cut off the tip of the root and side roots from the roots to be forced.*
7. *Fill a container such as a bucket with peat or humus, and bury each root almost up to its shoulder; water well.*
8. *Here you can see about how high the water should stand in the container.*
9. *Cover the bucket with black plastic and put it in a dark place. The ideal temperature is about 70° F.*
10. *The leaf shoots begin to sprout after a week.*
11. *The endive is ready to harvest after about 3 weeks.*

Garden Cress

Garden cress comes from the Mediterranean area, and it's also found growing wild in southwest Asia. It's a very old vegetable plant that was known to the ancient Greeks, Romans and Egyptians.

Weather, Soil and Nutrients

Cress makes no special demands on soil and weather. Because of its short growing period, it requires no fertilizer.

Cress can also grow successfully on the window sill the whole year round. Fill a window box with peat or any commercial potting soil, sprinkle the cress seeds over the soil, then cover them lightly and gently moisten the box. Put a dark cover over the box for the first 2 days, until the seeds begin to germinate. Then remove the cover.

Cultivation and Care

Sow garden cress in the open from April until September. The distance between rows doesn't need to be more than 4 inches. The soil should be kept moist.

Harvesting

Harvest cress grown outside after 2 to 4 weeks, depending upon the weather. It's still very flavorful even when it has grown to a height of 4 to 6 inches. Cut indoor cress after about 1 week in the summer and after about 2 weeks in the winter, when the plants are 2 inches high.

Sorrel

Sorrel (like rhubarb) is a member of the knot-grass family and is a perennial. You can grow it just as easily from seed as from root stock. The large leaves taste a little bitter because of their high acid content, but the young tender leaves are especially tasty and are considered a delicacy. Sorrel can be used in soups, cooked like spinach, or served as a side dish with omelets, meat, fish and salads.

Weather, Soil and Nutrients

Sorrel is not exacting and grows everywhere, even on soils with few nutrients and little direct sunlight. Naturally, humus soils and a little sun give better yields.

Cultivation and Care

Growing sorrel is simple. As soon as the soil can be worked, sow the seed thickly in rows 10 to 12 inches apart. You don't need to thin sorrel.

Harvesting

Pick the leaves when they are young, no more than 2 to 4 inches long. Cut them about 1 to 1 1/4 inches above the soil. Leave the stalks in place and the plants will continue to grow new leaves.

Spinach

Spinach is one of the pigweeds and is closely related to Swiss chard. Sugar beet, turnips and beets are also members of the same family. Spinach is a popular plant—it can used raw in a salad, cooked as a side dish and is well suited for freezing.

Weather, Soil and Nutrients

Spinach is a cool-weather plant that will bolt if it is grown during the long days of summer. Sow the seeds directly in the garden as early as 4 weeks before the final frost. Spinach also makes a fine fall crop because of its winter-hardiness. In zones with mild winters, sow it in autumn and it will overwinter in the garden.

Spinach grows best in light, humus soil that retains water well. If the soil is heavy and has a clay content that becomes crusted and solid in times of drought, spinach will grow very slowly, form only a few leaves. and bolt very quickly.

Spinach grows quickly and therefore makes heavy demands on the soil and its nutrient reserves. Before sowing, dig in

2 ounces of universal vegetable fertilizer per square yard.

Cultivation and Care

Once spinach has formed flowers it can no longer be used as a vegetable. Since long days encourage this, plant spinach in a season with relatively short days. In spring or autumn, sow the seeds thinly in rows about 6 to 8 inches apart. Water the plants regularly during dry periods, and alwa, s keep the soil loose and free of weeds.

Harvesting

Begin to pick spinach leaves as soon as they are large enough to be used. When the plants are fully grown, cut them off at the neck of the root. The autumn sowing will yield about one full harvest before the first frost, and in mild zones, protected plants can be picked again in early spring. After the final harvest, chop down any remaining spinach stubble and discard it. This waste should not go in the compost heap.

Position in Crop Rotation

Root fly maggots sometimes infest spinach roots, and these maggots then may attack the next crops planted in that bed. As a result, you should never follow spinach with bush beans, or vice versa.

New Zealand Spinach

If you love spinach and don't want to do without it during the long days of summer, or if you have difficulty supplying spinach with as much water as it needs, then make way for New Zealand spinach.

Weather, Soil and Nutrients

Young New Zealand spinach plants are sensitive to frost, so

they are almost always grown as a summer crop. Although it grows well on soils that are too dry for spinach, you'll have a richer yield from loose, nutrient-rich soils that warm up quickly and aren't too dry.

Before planting, dig in about 2 ounces of universal vegetable fertilizer per square yard. After 6 to 8 weeks, fertilize again with 1½ ounces.

Cultivation and Care
New Zealand spinach seeds require a long time to germinate—as much as 6 weeks—so they are started indoors, even though the plants themselves have a relatively short growing period. Soak the seeds in water for 24 hours before you plant them in flats, and keep them warm and moist until they germinate. Thin them out as needed to prevent overcrowding.

Once all chances of frost are past and the soil is well warmed, select the strongest plants to transplant into the garden. New Zealand spinach plants grow quite large, so space the seedlings far apart—no less than 32 by 32 inches. Because there is so much open space between plants, keep the uncovered soil well weeded until the plants are large enough to shade the area.

Harvesting
Begin harvesting New Zealand spinach as soon as the leaves are large enough to be eaten. If you always leave at least half of the leaves on all the plants, they will keep producing until they form seed stalks or the weather gets too cold. Don't pick the shoots until the last harvest.

Swiss Chard

There are two basic types of Swiss chard, leafy and rib. Leafy Swiss chard is similar to spinach, and rib Swiss chard has a flavor that is reminiscent of asparagus.

Weather, Soil, and Nutrients
Swiss chard is unusual because

it does well in all kinds of weather. Not only does it like fairly warm weather, it's also frost-hardy. Only very cold winters can damage it. In most areas in the country, Swiss chard beds that are protected over the winter with a heavy mulch will produce a second crop in the early spring.

Swiss Chard makes no special soil demands but produces its best yields on soils rich with humus. In order to ensure an adequate supply of nutrients, apply 2 ounces of universal vegetable fertilizer per square yard. After the first harvest, supply an additional dose of 1 ounce.

Cultivation and Care
Since Swiss chard is a biannual and doesn't flower until its second year, it is an easier crop to grow than spinach. You can plant in the open 2 weeks before the last frost date. Sow thinly in rows 12 inches apart. After the seeds sprout, thin the plants until they are 12 inches apart.

Harvesting
Swiss chard grows quickly, so you should be able to begin harvesting as early as 40 days after sowing. Leafy Swiss chard is cut like spinach when the leaves are about 4 to 6 inches high. Leave the stubble in the ground so that the plant can grow again.

Young Root Vegetables

Root Vegetables

Roots seem to be the most insignificant part of a plant when compared with flowers, fruits, and leaves. They're certainly the ones we think about least often, hidden as it is in the darkness of the earth. But a plant couldn't exist without roots. Through them it takes in water and nutrients, without which no plant can survive. They give the tiniest herb just as much hold as the mightiest tree.

In order to survive in unfavorable surroundings, many plant varieties have come to develop especially strong, thick or long roots, called *taproots*. Taproots store food for times when few nutrients or water are available. In their stocky roots, these plants hold vitamins, minerals and curative substances.

Even in prehistoric times our ancestors recognized the importance of the plant roots; however, today our survival no longer depends on searching for wild roots in the fields and woods. Wild vegetables have long since passed into the hands of experienced horticulturalists and through their efforts have not only become richer in form but also tastier.

Weather, Soil and Nutrients

Root vegetables make no special demands on the weather, so almost all of them will grow in any zone. Some types must be harvested before the ground freezes, but others can overwinter within certain limitations. All root vegetables prefer a soil deeply loosened, rich with humus and almost completely free of stones. This soil allows well-formed roots to grow. Without it, the roots remain small, form branches (a condition called *ramous*) and "leggy" vegetables like these are usually discarded. Generally speaking, you should dig in about 2 ounces of universal vegetable fertilizer per square yard before you plant root vegetables. Some crops will require more during their development (see specific Cultivation Directions). It is also important to water root vegetables evenly and regularly throughout the entire growing period.

Turnips

The turnip has been neglected in many households for a long time, because it was often the only vegetable people could afford when times were hard. And yet turnips are very tasty and rich in vitamins when properly prepared (see the Gardener's Cookbook Section), and really deserve more attention.

Cultivation and Care

Plant turnip seeds outside as soon as the soil can be worked. Sow the seeds thinly, about $1/4$-inch deep, in rows 12 inches apart. (Since they are a cool-weather crop, gardeners in warm zones usually grow turnips as a fall crop. Plan on a 9-week growing period, at least, depending upon your variety.) When the first leaves form, thin the plants so they are about 6 to 8 inches apart.

To harvest the greens for salads and cooked greens, only thin the plants to 1 inch apart, then thin again as soon as the plants touch each other. Use the thinnings to supplement your meals until the

turnips are ready to harvest.

Turnips don't need to be fertilized after you plant, because of their relatively short growing period.

Harvesting
Turnips take from between 30 and 50 days to mature. Pull them while they are still quite small—not more than 3 to 5 inches in diameter.

Position in Crop Rotation
Turnips are especially well-suited to be first crops. Growing a second crop also produces a full yield because the crop is harvested so early.

Carrots and Parsnips

Weather, Soil and Nutrients
Before you plant, carrots and parsnips require an initial fertilizing with 1 ½ ounces of universal vegetable fertilizer per square yard. As soon as the foliage is about hand high, apply a second dose of 2 ounces. Spread the fertilizer evenly, and work it lightly into the soil. Be careful not to disturb the developing roots.

Cultivation and Care
Sow your first carrots and parsnips in spring as soon as the soil can be worked. Continue sowing at 2 week intervals for a harvest.

Don't water the germinating seeds too generously, since carrots don't do well if the soil is too wet. Plant the seeds ¼ to ½ inch deep, in rows 15 or 16 inches apart.

The seeds for these two vegetables germinate very slowly, so you must keep the soil weed-free until the seedlings appear. Otherwise the beds can become completely overgrown. Hoe carefully

so you don't damage the roots. Then thin the seedlings so they are 2 to 3 inches apart. Water the beds regularly until the harvest—if the soil gets too dry and then there is a heavy rainfall, the tubers can burst.

Pests
The carrot's biggest enemy is the carrot fly. It lays its eggs on the foliage, and the larvae bore into the root to spoil the crop. Infestations are relatively rare in open, windy locations, so it's best to choose a "windy corner" for carrots. Otherwise, apply a timely application of an organic, biodegradable pesticide. As always, note the waiting period and abide by it.

Harvesting
Harvest carrots and parsnips as soon as the roots are formed, and continue on well into fall. Young vegetables are especially tender and have the best flavor. If the soil is damp and loose, simply pull them up by the foliage. If the roots are large, loosen them first with a garden fork, so that you don't end up with a handful of greenery and no vegetable.

Special Cultivation Tips
Carrots and "Baby Carrots"

There are many different carrot varieties—from short and round to long and thin. The short-season round-oval variety ("baby carrots") take a shorter time to grow than most of the larger varieties, and are ready to harvest after about 8 to 10 weeks. The medium long varieties are mature after about 10 to 12 weeks, and the long varieties take about 20 to 24 weeks, although they do supply a higher yield. Of course, you can harvest any variety before it's fully mature. They are especially tender, tasty and juicy at this time.

By the way...

As you hoe carrots, take note of whether the uppermost part of the carrot (the shoulder) is becoming green. If so, lightly heap the earth around it, because the green part of the carrot does not taste good.

Parsnips

Because parsnips are completely winter-hardy they can overwinter in the garden, even in the coldest zones. In fact, they need frost in order to develop their full flavor. They have a long growing period, and must be planted in spring so they have time to fully develop.

The parsnip is related to the carrot, so both plants have similar soil and nutrient demands. Both are grown in the same way. Sow seeds about 1/2 inch deep in

By the way...

Carrots and parsnips germinate very slowly. Some gardeners mix these tiny seeds with those of quick-sprouting varieties such as radishes or lettuce. Gardeners then sow the mixture, and the quick-sprouting ones germinate very shortly to mark out the lo-

cation of the rows. This is a considerable help when it is time to loosen and weed the beds.

rows 12 inches apart, and after the seeds have sprouted, thin them to 4 inches apart.

Radishes

Radish varieties are distinguished less by taste than by the size and color of their roots. In contrast to most of their relatives (they are, like cabbages, members of the cruciferae), radishes are annuals not biannuals, and they have a short growing period. They have a sharp flavor and a high vitamin and mineral content.

Weather, Soil and Nutrients
Radishes make no special demands on the weather, they can even grow in early spring when it's still cold and damp. Some varieties tend to bolt during the hot summer days.

These vegetables have a relatively short growing period, so you must supply sufficient amounts of water and nutrients, especially when you grow them during the dry summer months. The ideal soil has a high organic content, since it holds water so well. To increase the harvest, apply about 2 ounces of universal vegetable fertilizer per square yard before planting.

Harvesting
Short-season radishes are harvested after 3 to 4 weeks, and the long white radish, a mid-season variety, takes 8 to 10 weeks to mature. Long-season varieties need a little longer. Check radishes as they grow so that you don't leave them in the ground too long. If this happens they will become slightly hard and woody. Radishes harvested early, on the other hand, are especially tender, tasty and vitamin rich.

Large White Radishes

Sow large white radishes outside from March until August, about 1/2 inch deep, in rows 10 inches apart. The correct spacing depends on the specific variety. White radishes require an evenly moist soil during their entire growth period. Once they sprout,

most varieties require an additional dose of 1 1/2 ounces of fertilizer.

Pests and Diseases

The radishes greatest enemy is the turnip flea (flea beetle). To prevent infestations, keep the soil moist. A timely application of an organic, biodegradable insecticide helps against strong attacks. If you must spray, remember that radishes mature very quickly—be especially careful to take notice of the waiting period.

Beets

Like spinach and Swiss chard, beets are members of the pigweed family. Most members of this family originated in coastal regions. In order to survive in their former salty surroundings,

their leaves have tough upper surfaces which prevent the loss of too much water.

Weather, Soil and Nutrients

Sow beets in spring as soon as there is no more danger of frost. Earmark your last planting for storage. Plant the seeds very thinly, 1 to 1 1/4 inches deep, in rows about 16 inches apart.

What we call beet "seeds" are actually tiny fruits of the beet, each one containing 3 or 4 seeds. After the seeds germinate, thin them out to about 6 inches apart, saving only the strongest plants. Use the beet greens from the thinnings as a cooked vegetable.

Harvesting

Harvest beets as soon as the roots are developed enough to be usable, and harvest the entire bed once they are mature, in 12 to 15 weeks. Check them as they grow, so they don't stay in the ground too long. If they do, they will become woody. When you harvest, don't cut the leaves but twist them off—otherwise the juice will bleed away.

To store beets for the winter, bury them in sand or peat and keep them in a cool place. They will keep for several months.

Special Cultivation Tips

Short-season Radishes

Cultivation and Care

Sow radishes in the open every 14 days from spring or until about a month before the first frost. Plant the seeds 1/2 inch deep, in rows 6 inches apart. Sow the seeds thinly, and thin the seedlings 1 to 1 1/4 inches apart—that will give them even-sized roots.

Celery

Celery is related to celeriac, but does not form tubers. It's harvested for its fleshy leaf stalks, and some gardeners blanch the stalks by earthing them up or enclosing them in a heavy paper bag. Some varieties are self-blanching, so they require less work to grow. Celery, a plant with marshy origins, is a challenging crop with a long growing period, but many feel that the flavor of home-grown celery is worth the effort and care.

Soil Nutrients and Weather

Frost improves the flavor of harvest-ready celery, but the seeds won't germinate unless the soil is well warmed and warm temperatures are consistent and reliable. Otherwise the plants will bolt. It's a difficult crop to grow in areas with short growing seasons.

Celery prefers soil that isn't particularly heavy, but has a good amount of humus and a constant supply of water. Before sowing, dig in 2 ounces of vegetable fertilizer per square yard, and twice more during the growing season add another

1 1/2 ounces, because celery is a heavy feeder.

Cultivation and Care

Start the seeds indoors 4 to 8 weeks before you plan to transplant. If you live in a mild zone, you can sow the seeds directly in the garden.

Set transplants 8 inches apart, in rows about 16 inches apart. (If you have direct-sowed, thin out the seedlings to the same distances.) Since celery was originally a wetlands plant, it requires ample amounts of water, so supply it regularly.

Blanched celery has fewer vitamins and minerals than unblanched, but some people prefer the flavor and quality of blanched celery. The process requires about 14 days, so begin about 2 weeks before harvesting. Earth up the stalks or wrap them in black plastic.

Harvesting

You can harvest celery as soon as the stalks are well formed, but it tastes best after the first frost.

Celeriac

Celeriac is grown because of its nutritious tuber (we leave it to you to discover if this vegetable really does "make tired men lively"...), and its leaves are also edible—they make a delicious flavoring for stews.

Weather, Soil and Nutrients

Celeriac is an adaptable crop that grows outdoors any time after the danger of heavy frost is past. In milder zones sow it directly in the rows.

Celeriac grows especially well on heavy loam soils with a relatively high humus content. Before planting, dig and turn the soil

134

deeply to loosen its structure. Since celeriac originally grew on salty, marshy soils, it needs a lot of moisture and mineral fertilizer. Before planting, dig in 2 to 2 ½ ounces of vegetable fertilizer per square yard, and supply the same amount twice more during the growing season.

Cultivation and Care

In short-season zones, start celeriac seeds indoors about 4 to 8 weeks before you plan to transplant. Move the seedlings to the garden after heavy frost danger is past. Plant the seedlings 12 by 16 inches apart in shallow soil or they will develop poor tubers. You must water celeriac regularly and keep the soil weed-free.

Harvesting

Harvest celeriac anytime after the tubers are between 2½ to 6 inches in diameter. If well-mulched, the plants can stay in the ground during the winter. They keep for a long time in damp sand or peat, but they must not touch during storage.

Position in Crop Rotation

You can use celeriac as a second crop after lettuce, radishes and other short-season vegetables, when your season is long enough.

Comfrey

Comfrey resembles asparagus in shape and flavor, and it is often also called "winter asparagus." However, the two vegetables aren't related.

Weather, Soil and Nutrients

Comfrey requires the same soil and weather conditions as all root vegetables. However, it needs soil that has been dug especially deep and carefully loosened. Before planting, dig in 2 ounces of vegetable fertilizer per square yard, and half-way through the season supply another dose of 1½ ounces. If you plan to enrich the soil with manure, dig it in the autumn before planting. During dry periods, water regularly.

Cultivation and Care

Sow the seeds in the garden 1¼ inches deep and 10 inches apart. When the seedlings are visible, thin them out so that they are 1¼ to 2½ inches apart. Loosen the soil between the rows repeatedly and clear the weeds carefully. If you damage the roots, they will "bleed" heavily.

Harvesting

Begin to harvest comfrey as soon as its foliage dies off. Since the roots break easily, loosen the earth in back of the roots with a garden fork and carefully pull them out. Broken roots are fine for eating immediately, but they cannot be stored. Undamaged roots keep fresh for a long time when you layer them with damp peat in a fruit box.

Garden-Fresh Herbs

Herbs

Almost all herbs have been highly esteemed for centuries as medicines, as well as flavorings. They have been known in the Western world since earliest civilization. Explorers brought back reports out of ancient Persia, Egypt, India, Greece, and China about their cultivation and use. We learned about those growing in our own yards and fields from our grandparents. Whether they were first used as medicines or seasonings isn't clear, but their uses in the healing arts probably grew from their use in cooking. Today they have a prominent place in our cuisine, and are still the sources of many modern medicines.

Herbs aren't difficult to grow, and once you've used them fresh from your garden you'll never be content with the dried products from the supermarket. Fresh herbs from the garden are full of aroma and flavorful oils, and they can transform your meals into a tasty adventure.

You don't need a large garden to grow herbs. They can grow anywhere—in the garden, on the patio, on the balcony or on the window sill—so fresh supplies can always be available.

Weather, Soil and Nutrients

Since most herbs came from the Mediterranean region, they need plenty of warmth, light, and loose soil. Although they were once wild, our cultivated varieties need a generous supply of nutrients. Every year you should supply an herb garden with about 1 to 1 1/2 ounces of universal vegetable fertilizer, and they will grow luxuriantly.

Choose a warm location for your herbs, one where they will get plenty of sun and will be sheltered from too much north and east wind. (Sage, thyme, basil, and lemon mint prefer such a location over any other.) Only a few herbs grow better in half-shade and need a damper soil that has a richer supply of nutrients. (See **Special Cultivation Tips** for Sorrel, Borage, Mint and Lovage).

Cultivation and Care

The plan for an herb bed or small garden should accommodate the different heights of individual varieties. Place low plants at the front, medium-high plants in the middle, and tall varieties at the back, so the tall plants don't shade the shorter ones.

You can grow almost all herbs from seeds. Begin them inside about a month before the last frost, or sow the seeds in the garden once the chances of frost are past and the soil is warm. In either case, sow the seeds thinly and cover them very lightly with soil (no more than 1/2 inch). As always, harden off seedlings before transplanting, or the plants may die.

It's best to sow the seeds so thinly that you don't have to

Fresh herbs, which you can use again and again, even flourish in flower boxes on a window sill.

worry about thinning out, but if necessary, as soon as the seedlings have formed 2 pairs of leaves, thin them out to 1 inch apart.

Herbs come in two main types: annuals and perennials. Annual herbs have a limited period of life from the year of sowing. They die with the onset of frost, so they must be replanted every year.

Perennial herbs live for more than 2 years (in fact, they often only blossom in the second year of their lives), so you don't need to sow them more than once. If old plants become too compact or too large, simply divide them up by digging them and cutting the root ball in half with a spade. Perennial herbs are propagated in the same way. The best time to do this is in autumn or spring.

By the way...

Always chop fresh herbs by hand. If you use something like a blender you'll lose too much of the valuable flavoring.

Special Cultivation Tips
Basil

Basil's slightly sweet, peppery flavor gives almost every dish a special taste. Tomato dishes especially profit from this seasoning, which should be added to the dish about 10 minutes before serving. It's often grown in the house because it is so attractive.

Cultivation and Care

Since basil is an annual, you must sow every year. Basil is very frost-sensitive, so don't plant it outside until all possibility of frost is past and the soil is well warmed. Six weeks before you

want to transplant, sow several seeds in plant pots. Set the seedlings in the garden 10 inches apart, in rows 8 inches apart. This seasoning plant requires regular watering—then the leaves grow lusciously. Break off the tips of the plants regularly to encourage branching out.

It's difficult to grow basil in years that are especially wet and cool. At such a time, grow basil on the window sill or under a cover that will shelter it from the rain.

Harvesting

You can pick young basil leaves as soon as they form, and continue until the plants flower. During that period they have the strongest flavor. You can also dry basil. Pick the leaves before the plants flower, and keep the dried leaves in containers protected from the light.

Savory

Savory, an annual that develops plants between 12 and 20 inches high, is most often used (sparingly) in bean dishes, since it intensifies their flavor. However, its slightly sharp, peppermint flavor also goes with many meat and fish dishes, strong soups, salads and potato dishes.

Cultivation and Care
In spring, after the soil is well-warmed, sow savory outside in

rows that are 8 inches apart. Cover the seeds very lightly with soil, and thin the seedlings if they grow too thickly. Plenty of sun and nutrients increases savory's pungency.

Harvesting
You should always gather fresh savory leaves before the plants flower, because then their flavor is most intense. The harvest period is from mid-summer to frost time.

To dry savory leaves, tie the plants in bunches and hang them in the shade. The leaves will retain their spiciness, even when dried.

Borage or Cucumber Herbs

Borage is an annual. Traditionally, it is used to flavor cucumbers, but its finely chopped leaves improve sauces, salads, fish dishes, cooked kohlrabi, and savoys. You can also garnish re-

freshing drinks with the blue flowers.

Be sure to pick the leaves when they are young.

Cultivation and Care
Borage is a warm-weather plant, so don't sow it until all chance of frost is past and the ground is well-warmed. Sow the seeds directly in the garden, and have the rows 12 inches apart.

Since you only use the young leaves, make several sowings, at 3 to 4 week intervals. Although borage will do well in full sunshine, it also grows in half-shade.

Harvesting
You can pick the first young leaves before the borage plants flower. With interval sowings, you'll always have tender leaves ready for picking. The older leaves are too brittle. Always pick borage leaves right before you're going to use them.

Dill

When most people hear the word dill, they think of some-

thing used to make pickles. However, dill is a very versatile spice: it's used to improve fresh salads, fish, poultry, and herb sauces.

Grow dill for its flowers as well as its delicate leaves. When preparing a dish with dill, always sprinkle it on just before serving, since only then can it release its full flavor.

Cultivation and Care
Since dill is an annual, you will have new plants every year.

Once all frost danger is past, sow dill in rows 8 inches apart at 4-week intervals. If the rows seem too crowded, simply thin them out. The plants, which grow up to 5 feet high, begin to blossom about two months after sowing. As long as they have an ample supply of water, they'll grow on practically any soil, but the location must be sheltered from the wind.

Harvesting

The green part of dill, the tender tips of the shoots, has an especially delicate flavor.

The dried flower umbels or clusters are used mainly for making pickles. Cut these early before the flowers are fully open, since they have the best flavor.

Tarragon

Tarragon is a perennial with a pleasant, almost sweet, spicy flavor that delicately improves fish sauces, soups, herb butter, salads, omelets, ragouts and meats. It also makes the popular tarragon vinegar, created when white vinegar is poured over the leaves. This herb should always have a place in your garden, since it's virtually impossible to purchase fresh supplies, and dried, though flavorful, is less marvelous and more expensive.

from the last frost date and sow the seedlings (spaced 20 by 20 inches) from late spring. You can also sow directly in the open from June, and thin the plants to the same spacing. The herb requires this much space because it forms strong runners from its roots, and these branch out extensively.

Harvesting

For your daily use, pick fresh leaves continually from early summer through the fall.

To dry tarragon, cut away whole plants, tie them in bundles, and hang them in a shady, dry place.

Chervil

Chervil is an annual herb with a sweetly delicate flavor. It is very popular as a garnish and is used to flavor white meat, cold dishes, soups, and savory milk and egg dishes.

Never add chervil while the dish is cooking. Instead, sprinkle it on before you serve, or serve it with the food at the table.

Cultivation and Care

Chervil thrives in both sun and half-shade. Make a thin sowing outside after all chance of frost is past and the ground is well warmed. The rows should be 6 to 8 inches apart. Don't transplant or thin out chervil. By making repeated sowings every 1 or 2 weeks, you can gather young plants throughout the summer.

Harvesting

Chervil is ready to gather within 3 to 4 weeks after you sow it. Harvest the plants before they blossom.

Cultivation and Care

You begin tarragon seeds inside

Lavender

Lavender is a perennial herb with many uses. It's often given a prominent place in an ornamental garden because of its tender blue flowers. And most people think of it as a scent used in perfumes and soaps, not as a spice. However, lavender's young leaf tips, when used sparingly, lend a spicy "provincial" flavor to fish dishes and sauces, soups, vegetables and meat dishes. Try a few

sprigs in your barbecue sauce. Even herb butter tastes better with lavender.

Cultivation and Care

Begin lavender indoors about 8 weeks before you intend to plant it outside. Or sow it directly into the garden at the beginning of summer. That is also when you should transplant seedlings. Cut lavender back quite short in autumn, and it will continue to grow for many years.

Harvesting

Gather only the tips of young lavender leaves, and begin this about 2 months after planting out.

Lovage

Lovage—also commonly

known as the "Magi herb"— is an annual herb that has a tangy, bitter-sweet flavor. As a result, cooks should use it sparingly. It improves stews, soups, meat, poultry and fish dishes, rice dishes, ragouts, and pies. You can cook the leaves with a dish or you can dry them, grind them very fine and add a small pinch to soups and sauces.

Cultivation and Care

Lovage's strong plants grow quickly and the leaves have a very intense flavor. Each plant can grow to a height of 6 feet, so most households can manage with only one plant. An adaptable plant, lovage can grow in full sun or half-shade.

You can start lovage indoors or in a cold frame, but it's just as simple to begin it directly outside. Sow any time after the soil can be worked, up until midsummer. Plant the seeds 1¼ inches deep. Lovage requires a lot of water.

Harvesting

Lovage leaves can be cut several times a year. Harvest them before the plant flowers, because the flowers draw strength and flavor from the leaves.

Marjoram

Marjoram is a very delicate, pungent spice with a slightly hot flavor. It's indispensable in a herb garden, and since it is an annual, you must plant every year. The young tips of the shoots improve sauces, soups, stews, beef, pork, and lamb dishes just as much as egg dishes, cheese dishes and salads. Marjoram is exquisite when mixed with thyme, and a little bunch of it should always accompany Christmas stuffings.

Cultivation and Care

Marjoram is a frost-sensitive plant so sow it outside only when you know there is no frost-danger and the ground is well-warmed. This herb grows best on loose humus soil rich in nutrients, and needs a sheltered location. Set the transplants in hills of 2 or 3 plants each, 4 by 6 inches apart.

It's best to start the seeds indoors; then cover the flat with a sheet of glass until they sprout. Keep the seedlings warm and moist. Marjoram is also often sown in plant pots.

Harvesting

Harvest marjoram leaves and stalks before the plants blossom. Pick fresh tips from the shoots continually, and cut the stalks about 2 inches above the soil. The plants will then grow new shoots for a later harvest. Cut marjoram for storage during very dry weather before the flowers open. Then dry the tips in an airy, dark room.

second year and they reduce the quality of the leaves. As a result, you should sow parsley every year.

Harvesting

As long as you don't become too enthusiastic when you harvest the leaves, parsley will continue to grow throughout the summer. Never cut all the foliage from the plant. Remove a few of the leaves, and retain the heart leaves. To keep parsley in stock you can freeze it or dry it in the oven. Heavily mulched parsley plants can be harvested throughout all but the worst winters.

Parsley

Parsley is the most well-loved and versatile seasoning plant in an herb garden. Not only is it rich with vitamins and minerals but its delicate seasoning also rounds out the flavor of almost every dish. There are two major varieties, crinkly and Italian (or smooth). While crinkly parsley is especially decorative in cold dishes, Italian parsley has a more intense flavor. There is also a root parsley used for seasoning.

Cultivation and Care

Parsley flourishes in light shade quite well, so a sunny spot isn't absolutely necessary. Because of its attractive dark green foliage, it's often sown as an edging for flower beds.

Parsley seeds germinate very slowly (they can take as long as 6 weeks), so it's best to start them indoors at least 8 weeks before you want to plant them outside. You can sow outside from the last frost onwards, but you'll have the best results if you wait until summer, since steady warmth is necessary for them to germinate. Either way, plant the seeds no deeper than $1/2$ inch in rows 12 inches apart. When full grown, the plant will reach a height of 6 to 8 inches.

Parsley needs moist, light, humus-rich soils. A single dose of fertilizer, applied before sowing, is usually sufficient.

Parsley forms flowers in its

Try a late outdoor sowing when your initial parsley planting doesn't "take" too well, because the seeds will germinate and grow very quickly in the warm soil of summer or autumn. You can't harvest the leaves in that year, but when spring comes you will have very early, hardy plants.

The beet-like roots of parsley are a component of "soup greens."

Mint

Anyone who has had a cup of tea made from fresh green mint leaves will never want to do without this herb again—whether it's grown in a balcony pot or in a herb garden. And although mint is less well-known as a seasoning, it can add new dimensions to the

flavor of sauces and remoulade, of veal, lamb or mutton, and of fresh vegetable salads and dishes.

Cultivation and Care

Mint is a perennial that is grown from seed or from divi-

sions of an existing plant. Start the seeds indoors or in a cold frame. Then transplant the young plants into their permanent bed at the beginning of summer. (Mint will flourish in half-shade, even under trees.) Mint plants send out very strong runners from their roots, so they need a lot of space. Set the new plants 16 by 20 inches apart. After a few years, the plants will become quite extensive. Then, in the fall, separate the roots and establish a new bed—or share with a willing neighbor.

Humus-rich soil, regular hoeing and a good supply of nutrients promote the strength of mint plants. In its wild state, mint grows beside streams and on damp ground, so their cultivated cousins require plenty of water.

Harvesting

You can pick fresh leaves continually. If you intend to dry the leaves, harvest them on sunny days.

Burnet

Burnet is really a wild plant, but it has won a firm place in herb gardens, flower pots, and window boxes in the past few years. It's a classical ingredient in

all herb dishes because of its mild, nutty flavor. Finely chopped, burnet also improves fricassees, fish, egg dishes, vegetables, salads, sour cream dishes, and sauces. Since it is a perennial, you will only have to sow burnet once to have it in your kitchen for keeps.

Cultivation and Care

Sow burnet indoors 4 weeks before the final frost date, and make additional plantings every two weeks. Thin out the seedlings once they have sprouted. Once all chance of frost is past and the ground is well warmed,

you can transplant the seedlings in the open in rows 8 inches apart. When the plant forms a flower stem, break it off before it blossoms, so that the plant's strength goes into the leaves.

Harvesting

Burnet leaves are only viable when they are young and fresh. Begin harvesting them within a week of transplanting. Pick only the young leaves. Dried burnet leaves lose their aroma and flavor.

Rosemary

Rosemary is a perennial herb with a sharp, bitter-savory flavor that unmistakably reminds you of the scent of a pine forest. The needle-like leaves make a fine

accompaniment for game dishes, fish, mutton or pork, barbecues, southern vegetables, and salad sauces.

Cultivation and Care

It takes 4 weeks for rosemary to germinate, so begin the seeds indoors, about the time of the last frost date. As you select its final bed, keep in mind that rosemary can't tolerate accumulated water. You can transplant the seedlings outside from the beginning of summer. Set the plants 12 by 12 inches apart. To overwinter the plants in the garden, cover them with a layer of pine branches.

Harvesting

Rosemary needs time to establish itself, so you should only pick individual leaves during the first year. From late spring to fall of the second year you can harvest the leaves continually.

Sage

Used sparingly, fresh or dried sage leaves are a popular ingredient in fish dishes, especially those including eels. Sage brings to meat, game and fried poultry the same tangy, smoky flavor that it gives to vegetable dishes and those containing sour cream and noodles. Because of its volatile oils, sage tea soothes coughs and sore throats.

Cultivation and Care

Sage is a perennial, so you need plant it only once. Start sage seeds indoors about the time of the last frost. Then, at the beginning of summer, transplant the young plants outside. Set them 12 by 12 inches apart.

Harvesting

Sage doesn't develop its full flavor until its second year, but even in the first year you can harvest the plants from late spring until summer. The rough, silvery leaves require a long time to dry. Examine them often and remove any leaves that become black or rotten.

Sage is a woody plant, so every year in late summer you must prune it, or cut it back. (Always do this early enough so the plants can develop new shoots before the winter comes). Leave stubble that is about hand-high.

Sage reaches imposing dimensions through its many years of life.

Chives

The flavor of chives' tube-shaped leaves betrays this plant's relationship to the onion family. Finely cut on bread, chives taste refreshingly delicious. They also lend just the right tang to milk and egg dishes, salads, vegetables, and sauces. A perennial, it can stay in its special spot for years.

Cultivation and Care

Chives grow best in a warm, shady place on a rich humus soil. Make your initial planting either from seeds or by dividing an already-established plant. Provide plenty of room for chives, because as they grow through the years, the plant will spread.

It takes longer to grow chives from seed than from divisions. In order to shorten the growth period, start the seeds indoors at least 4 weeks before you intend to plant outside. Transplant the young seeds to a cold frame or to individual plant pots, and finally move them to their permanent place in the open any time from the last frost date to late summer. Plant clusters of seedlings 8 by 10 inches apart. Chives need a steady supply of water as they grow.

When winter comes, you have two alternatives. You can dig up the plants, put them into pots and bring them into the house. Or you can leave them where they are, as long as you cover the plants with a mulch. In the spring the chives will sprout again, full and strong. During the second year chives form blossoms; break them off as they form.

Harvesting

After the plants have been in the garden for about 5 or 6 weeks, you can begin to cut the leaves. It's best to cut off only two-thirds of the length of the leaves so the plant will continue to grow. Cutting the leaves causes the plant to develop new leaves, so you'll have fresh supplies all summer long. Chives aren't very suitable for drying because they lose too much flavor. It's better to freeze them.

Thyme

Thyme isn't popular just as a spice—it's one of the oldest healing herbs against coughs, and is

also highly valued as a bath additive. Its sharp, tangy flavor makes thyme one of the most important herbs in French cuisine.

Cultivation and Care

Thyme develops as low-growing, woody plants and is often grown in rock gardens and as a decorative border around flower beds.

Start the seeds indoors a month before the last frost, transplant the seedlings in a cold frame or individual plant pots 4 weeks later, and transplant them to their final location from the beginning of summer onwards. Space the plants 8 by 8 inches apart. If you prefer, sow the seeds outside after the last frost. Thyme must be regularly watered.

Thyme multiplies abundantly and will continue to grow in the same spot for years.

Harvesting

To harvest, cut the stems just before the plants blossom. Tie

Wormwood

If you enjoy an occasional dish with a high fat content, you should plant a wormwood shrub, because wormwood is especially helpful in digesting fatty dishes. But be careful, wormwood has a sharp, bitter-spicy flavor, so season very sparingly, and use only the tips of the shoots.

Cultivation and Care

Start wormwood seeds indoors between the last frost day until late spring. Then transplant the seedlings in the open at the beginning of summer. When you transplant, select only the strongest plants and space them 12 by 16 inches apart. Wormwood is a perennial, so you will only have to plant once.

Harvesting

Harvest the leaves shortly before they blossom and dry them in a shady place.

the stems into bundles and dry them in a shaded, airy location. When possible, gather them at midday, since the herb has its highest concentration of volatile oils at that time.

Lemon Mint

Lemon mint is a perennial that grows into large shrub-like plants, so it's ideal for growing in large outdoor flower pots or in a herb garden. Its intense scent attracts bees which are indispensible for the pollination of other garden plants. At the same time, when the leaves are crushed and rubbed onto the skin, their sap relieves the pain of bee and insect stings.

Lemon mint has a slightly bitter flavor and is used in fresh salads, fruit salads, tangy milk dishes, and tomato dishes. Adding fresh lemon mint leaves to fish sauces, meat, game, and refreshing drinks is an aromatic winner.

Cultivation and Care

Lemon mint seeds require high temperatures to germinate so start them indoors about a month before the beginning of summer and move the seedlings to a cold frame. When the seedlings are about 4 inches tall, plant them in their permanent bed, 12 by 12 inches apart. Select a sunny spot and supply nutrient-rich soil to ensure strong leaf growth.

Harvesting

Lemon mint leaves are the strongest before the plant blossoms. Harvest the young leaves from a week after transplanting until late fall. Don't press the leaves when you pick them. In fall, cut back the plant stalks to about 12 inches above the soil.

147

Berries

The sweetest fruits

Strawberries

It takes some effort to grow strawberries, but do you want to do without the "king of the berries" for that reason? There are two basic types of strawberries: annuals, which bear fruit in June or July; and everbearing strawberries, which bear three or sometimes four times during the summer. You can grow either kind from seed, and with careful attention to the maturity dates, you'll have a good yield even in the year of sowing. However, most gardeners prefer to purchase plants, either through the mail or from a local supplier.

Weather, Soil and Nutrients

Originally, garden strawberries were forest plants. That means they have very special requirements. They need a lot of humus and still thrive on acid soils in the wild. They are suited to a cool, rather than to a hot climate. Even though they will grow in half-shade, they form more fruit in full sunlight.

You must prepare a strawberry bed thoroughly. In the fall, before planting, turn the soil, one spade blade deep, and enrich it with an ample supply of manure or compost. At the same time or before planting in the spring, dig in 2 ounces of universal vegetable fertilizer per square yard.

About 4 weeks after planting, apply a second dose of about 1¹/₂ ounces, and fertilize again at the end of September with an equal amount.

Cultivation and Care

For your first planting buy healthy plants from a garden center or a nursery. It's best to purchase plants grown in your own region—they are most likely to be resistant to the viruses that are part of the environment in your garden. This isn't as true for plants that you order from a large, national supplier.

Strawberries that you plant in the spring will bear fruit the first year, but you'll get a heavier yield if you plant in the late summer of the year before you plan your first harvest.

The point at which the leaves of the strawberry plant meet the roots is called the *crown*. Set the plants 12 inches apart in the garden so that the crown is just above the soil. The rows should be about 72 inches apart. After planting, you must keep the soil weed-free, but since the plant roots run very shallowly under the soil, don't dig between the rows—just rake very gently.

Protect the fruit from too much dirt and water by laying down a mulch of straw or black plastic. Black plastic can advance the harvest date. But keep a watchful eye out for slugs. Mulch makes a perfect hiding place for slugs, and they too love berries. After harvesting, remove the straw and clear the soil of dead leaves and unwelcome runners.

Harvesting

Always pick strawberries complete with their stems so that you don't lose any of the juice.

Pests

Several diseases and pests can affect strawberries. The best defense against diseases is to pur-

chase varieties that are certified to be resistant to rusts and blights. It's also a good idea to follow good cultivation practices—don't let weeds take over the beds, and keep the plants well-fertilized and watered.

Birds will enjoy your strawberries almost as much as you do. The best defense is to cover the plants with netting designed to keep birds away.

Position in Crop Rotation

Every year, strawberries send out what are called "runners." These are similar to long vines and at the end of each is a tiny new strawberry plant. Remove all runners the first year, but in the second year allow the two strongest to develop from each plant. Once they have rooted, remove the original plant (also called the mother plant) from the garden. You'll then have brand new plants to provide strawberries for the next year.

Strawberries are very heavy feeders and remove an excess of nutrients with their wide-ranging root systems. In order to prevent

Everbearing strawberries have a whole list of advantages: they can be harvested from late spring until the first frost, their special flavor is reminiscent of wild strawberries, and they can even be grown in plant pots.

soil fatigue, you need to change the location of the strawberry bed every 3 years. Once your runners are firmly rooted in fall, transplant them to the new bed location, and begin again.

Raspberries and Blackberries

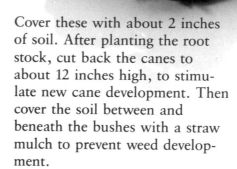

Weather, Soil and Nutrients

Raspberries and blackberries require very few special considerations, a quality that traces back to their wild forest origins. Neither makes special demands on the weather. Although both thrive in half-shade, their fruits are more flavorful when the bushes are in full sunlight.

In the spring, before they form shoots, give them about 2 1/2 ounces of vegetable fertilizer per square yard along with a plentiful supply of compost. Towards the end of the blossoming period, supply a second dose of about 1 ounce.

Harvesting

Keep a close watch on these berries as they ripen and don't pick them until they are just about ready to fall off the bushes—that's when the flavor is best.

Special Cultivation Tips

Raspberries

Cultivation and Care

Always buy your first raspberry bushes from a nursery so you are sure of having healthy resistant plants. To enlarge your berry patch later, dig out runners from your own plants and re-plant them wherever you want. Plant new raspberry bushes in autumn, 16 to 20 inches apart, in rows 10 feet apart.

Each plant you purchase will consist of a root stock (called a *rhizome*) and a cane. On the top of the rhizome you'll see several buds, called "ground buds."

Cover these with about 2 inches of soil. After planting the root stock, cut back the canes to about 12 inches high, to stimulate new cane development. Then cover the soil between and beneath the bushes with a straw mulch to prevent weed development.

Raspberries allowed to grow as they please will soon form an impenetrable tangle. One way to get around this is to train the bushes on a trellis. Pruning them is simple. Right after the harvest, cut off the old canes close to the soil and leave only about 8 to 12 young canes per plant. Fasten these to a trellis.

Pests

Raspberry twig disease is the raspberry's greatest danger. This fungus disease appears in spring as brownish spots on young twigs. To help prevent this disease, remove spent twigs immediately after the harvest, mulch your bushes regularly, and spray in the winter with green copper.

Blackberries

Cultivation and Care

Unlike raspberries, blackberries are planted in the spring. Although you can take rhizomes from established plants, it's best to buy resistant stock from a reputable nursery. Plant them just as you would raspberries. Mulching has also proven itself to be valuable for blackberries.

Pruning blackberries is as necessary as for raspberries. As you prune, keep in mind that blackberries bear fruit on *2-year-old wood*, so your bushes won't bear their first year. Once the canes are 3 to 5 feet long, cut 3 to 5 inches off the end of each one to encourage the formation of side branches. In late fall cut back all but 6 or 8 of the strongest young canes per bush, and fasten these to a wire or trellis.

The canes will bear fruit the following year and as soon as you've finished harvesting cut out the spent canes at ground level. During the summer, top off the new canes and prune out all but the 6 to 8 strongest in late autumn.

If the bushes seem to be becoming an unsightly and inaccessible confusion, you may have to clear away some of the growth during the summer. Between mid-June and the beginning of August when the side shoots on each cane are between 8 to 20 inches long, cut them back to 2 leaves.

Currants and Gooseberries

Currants and gooseberries are members of the saxifrage family and are valued for their fruits' delicate taste in jellies, jams and desserts. Natives of northern Europe, both will produce well in northern zones of the U.S.

A general word about currants and gooseberries: because they can serve as an alternate host to white pine blister rust, their cultivation has been restricted or banned by law in certain states, mainly those along the Atlantic coast.

Weather, Soil and Nutrients

Both currants and gooseberries are extremely winter-hardy, and are, therefore, especially suitable for northern growing zones, although some gooseberry varieties do fairly well in southern zones.

Once the bushes are established, apply a little manure or compost late every spring, but work this in so it is shallow be-

cause the roots run out very close to the surface and you can damage them quite easily. At blossom time, and again after harvest, give them about 1/2 ounce of universal vegetable fertilizer per square yard.

Cultivation and Care

It's especially important to purchase disease-resistant currant and gooseberry bushes from a reputable nursery. Although you can plant in spring, it's best to do this in autumn. First, trim the thick roots to encourage root development. Set the bushes about 5 feet apart, and somewhat deeper than they were at the nursery. Water them well. The bushes will develop new canes every year.

Harvesting

Harvest the fruits as soon as they have developed their full color. Allow currants to hang until even the berries at the tips of the bunches are colored right through. The only berries that can be used green are gooseberries.

Special Cultivation Tips

Red Currants and Gooseberries

These two fruits have the best yield on 2 and 3-year-old wood, so pruning them can seem quite complicated. Cut out canes more than 4 years old at ground level; you can recognize them because their color is darker than younger canes and they have a very woody appearance. Old canes also bear very poorly. Cut younger canes back by about one-third in the autumn, to encourage good ramification, or branching out, and prune the bushes so that there are no more than 8 to 12 strong, well-branched canes per plant.

Black Currants

Black currants bear fruit on 2-year-old canes just like raspberries. Right after the harvest cut back the spent canes, either to ground level (when there are enough new canes available) or to the height of the first young cane.

Keep the soil around the bushes weed-free. Mulching is beneficial because deep digging and hoeing can damage the bushes' shallow roots. Water black currants in periods of drought or the berries will fall off.

Pests and Diseases

Mildew (blight), a disease that occurs during damp weather, can be very dangerous for gooseberries. The easiest remedy is to purchase plants that are resistant. The symptom to look for is a layer of white mold that covers the plant and renders the berries inedible. To avoid this disease, keep the bushes in full sunlight.

If the bushes are attacked, the only remedy is to cut out all infected canes and cut back the bush to the canes that are healthy.

Gardening Encyclopedia

A successful home gardener must know many important gardening terms, so we have provided simple explanations for some of them. Any **boldfaced** terms are defined elsewhere in this word list.

Alternating Crops

A rotation plan that provides for successive crops having unlike nutrient requirements. A **green manure crop** is usually included in a rotation plan. Alternating crops prevents **soil fatigue**. See also **crop rotation**.

Aphids

Tiny winged or wingless insects that damage plants in several ways. Usually appearing in large numbers, they cause the most obvious damage by sucking out the plant's sap and causing it to wither. However, as they feed, aphids also spread virus diseases from plant to plant.

Soil with good tilth

Bed Gardening

A traditional garden layout, in which the garden is divided into several beds, one for each type of plant. Paths then run between the beds.

Biannuals

Plants such as brassicas that store abundant nutrients during their first year, and use them to produce flowers in the second.

Blanch

1. Method for keeping vegetables light in color. Plants such as celery and leeks are often earthed up, or they are enclosed in cardboard tubes or black plastic. To blanch cauliflower, tie the leaves over the developing head. By cutting off the light, you prevent **chlorophyll** production, and the plant remains colorless. Blanching also can make the flavor somewhat milder.

2. Method of preparing vegetables for freezing by submerging them in boiling water for a short period of time, depending on the crop involved.

Bleeding

Heavy loss of plant fluid through injury. Since bleeding can lessen the value of root crops such as beets, always hoe and dig up these crops with care.

Bolt

Process by which some crops, such as lettuce and some brassicas form a flower stalk. This growth takes nutrients away from leaf production, and the flavor and texture are affected in such a way that the plant is no longer usable as a vegetable.

Breaking Down

The breakdown of the active poison in a pesticide. Because of chemical changes in the poison caused by the processes within the plant, the poison loses its potency. Breakdown speed varies considerably due to the different composition of various poisons, and the **waiting period** is determined by that speed. After the waiting period is over, no residues remain on or in the plant.

Broadcasting

A method for sowing seeds, in which you simply toss the seeds in all directions and let them more or less fend for themselves. This technique is effective if you are sowing a lawn or cover crop. Broadcasting the seeds results in a thick plant growth that is very advantageous for the **tilth** of the soil.

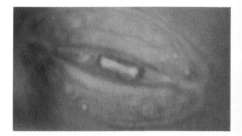

Typical leaf stomata

Canes

The new shoots that develop from the **crown** in berry bushes.

Clubroot

A disease characterized by swellings on the roots of brassicas, such as cabbage, large white radish, and mustard. This fungus disease is transmitted either through infected plant material or soil. There is no direct method of fighting it, apart from a relatively expensive soil sterilization process. Prevention relies on good **crop rotation** practices.

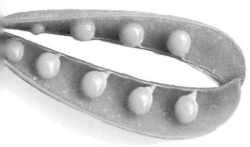

Peas in a pod

Compost

Compost is a mixture of rotted and decayed organic materials and soil. **Humus** is produced in the compost heap by the action of soil bacteria, moisture, and air. The heat that is produced by the decay process can reach 140 degrees F. (Some heaps containing fresh grass cuttings will actually smoke!) This heat can destroy weed seeds and some fungus disease viruses.

Composting

A method of continuing nature's natural decay cycle, thus

Hardening off in a cold frame

compensating for the disruptions caused by agricultural practices. Composting also speeds up the decay process.

Cover Crop

Crop sown to protect the soil and control weed growth in a fallow or unused field. Cover crops are often grown as mid-season or late crops. Also called **green fertilizer** or a **green manure crop**.

Crop Rotation

1. A regular alternation of plant varieties in the same bed, planned so that each crop has different nutrient requirements than the one before. A **green manure crop** should be included in crop rotation plans. 2. Because of the danger of transmitting diseases from one season to another, some crops must not be planted on the same soil two years in a row.

Cotyledons on bean seedlings

Crumb structures

The soil structure of loam soils and sandy loam soils. The soil particles have irregular shapes, and the soil itself has a better ratio of particles and air spaces. Soils having a crumb structure have the best **porosity**, and so hold water and air in a ratio that is the best for growing plants.

Cultivator

A versatile garden tool for aerating and loosening the soil. Some come with adjustable tines or prongs.

Curing

Method of setting out plants in a cool, well-ventilated place for a few days, long enough for them to dry, so they don't rot. Onions and garlic must be cured after harvesting, and cut seed potatoes must be cured before planting.

Decay

The breaking down of dead organisms in the soil into humus, with the help of bacteria and air.

Deep Cultivation Beds

Beds in which the soil is loosened and turned much more deeply than in the normal garden bed. As a result, plant roots can penetrate downward, rather than branching out sideways. You can plant seeds and seedlings quite closely together in a deep cultivation bed, and they still will be larger and stronger than those planted in a normal bed.

Earthing Up

This process may also be called *heaping* or *banking up*. To earth up, simply use a trowel to partially cover the lower parts of the plants. There are several reasons for earthing up a plant. In the case of dwarf beans, for instance, earthing up will give the plant better stability. In the case of fennel or leeks, you may want to blanch the stem or leaves. Then too, gardeners often earth up potatoes to form a loose layer of soil that facilitates well-formed tubers and easier harvesting.

F1 Hybrids

The letter F comes from the Latin *filia*, or daughter. Members of the first generation, F1 seeds are the result of cross-breeding two varieties of parent plants. Seeds developed from the F1 plants are called the F2 generation seeds (the second generation). F2 and F3 seeds lose some of the valuable F1 characteristics. As a result, to maintain a true F1 seed strain, horticulturists must continue the painstaking work of cross-pollination year after year to maintain the special characteristics they desire.

Cabbage suffering from cabbage flies

Flats

Seedbeds designed for starting seeds indoors.

Flea Beetle

A small, black or yellow striped beetle that eats minute holes in the leaves of brassicas, radishes, and large white radishes. When you approach plants that are infested, the beetles jump quickly away. Since they cannot stand dampness, you can hold them somewhat in check by providing the plants with plenty of water.

Friability

Ideal soil condition achieved by clumping soil particles together. See **Tilth.**

Frost Mellowness

Soil turned under in autumn, so that its structure allows the contracting and expanding of winter temperatures, and so that freezing and thawing water can split clumps of earth.

Fruit

The seed-containing structure of a plant. The names of the various fruit shapes depend on their botanical structure, or their relationship to the various plant families. For example: long pods (beans, peas), round pods (cabbages, large white radishes), soft fruits (tomatoes, sweet peppers, pumpkins, currants), drupes (cherries, plums), compound fruits (raspberries, strawberries), capsules (poppy).

Fungicides

Poisons designed to fight fungus diseases. Fungi produce no flowers, and after fertilization, they give off what are called spores, which then develop into new fungus plants. Fungicides function by inhibiting spore growth. More and more, chemical fungicides based on sulphur and copper are being replaced with organic fungicides, which are just as effective and less dangerous to humans and animals.

Green Fertilizer

See **Green Manure Crop.**

Green Manure Crop

An organic method of enriching the soil. The gardener broadcasts a seed mixture specifically designed for a green manure. Usually the mixture includes legumes for enriching the nitrogen content, and produces a large root mass and much foliage. After a set period ('at least 2 months), the plants are mown down and dug into the soil.

Hardening Off

The process of acclimating seedlings to the outdoors before placing them in a permanent bed. Seedlings can be hardened off under **hotcaps** or in a **cold frame.** Otherwise, they are set outdoors during the daytime, in a shaded area, for longer and longer periods, for about a week before they are transplanted into their permanent beds.

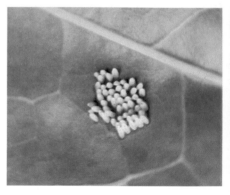

Cabbage moth eggs

Harrowing

Spring soil work. The surface crust is broken over in order to disrupt the soil **capillaries.** This retains valuable winter moisture and encourages microorganism development, which in turn releases new nutrients for new growth. Harrowing also allows better aeration and more thorough warming.

Herbicides

Poisons designed to combat weeds. Because of their potency and their long-lasting nature, herbicides are not recommended for use in the average garden.

A hill planting of squash

Hill Planting

Method for planting vine crops such as cucumbers, pumpkins, and zucchini. Several seeds are planted together in a single hole, called a drill. After germination, the number of plants is usually thinned, but more than one is left. Hill sowing makes it easier for germinating seedlings to push through the soil. It also increases the percentage of fertilization in cucurbits, and allows climbing plants to support each other.

Humus

A collective name for all organic substances in the soil, regardless of their state of decay. Humus is very important in all soil, because it encourages the growth of soil microorganisms, which are essential for plant growth and development.

Hybrids

From the Greek, meaning mixed origin. A hybrid is the result of cross-pollinating two parent plants whose individual strengths are desired in a single strain. The special qualities of the parent plants usually are products of long years of deliberate cultivation. Cross-pollination gives the plants of the first daughter generation (**F1 Hybrids**) complete uniformity of appearance, blossoms and fruit ripening. Most plant breeders are interested in improving yield, fruit quality, flavor, and/or disease resistance.

Incompatible Plants

Plants which, when grown near each other, adversely effect the growth of one or both. For a complete listing see the Gardening Guide. See also **companion planting**.

Inorganic (Non-Living)

Inorganic substances are those that have mineral origins—i.e. they do not come from the plant or animal worlds. Examples are such things as stones and salt.

Insecticides

Poisons designed to combat detrimental insects. If you must use pesticides, select those that are biodegradable, have a short **waiting period**, and will not harm helpful insects, such as honeybees.

Leaching

A process by which minerals are literally washed out of the soil. Leaching can occur if you overwater your crops, especially after applying **mineral fertilizers** (these products release all their strength at the same time). **Humus** and **organic fertilizers** release their nutrients over a longer period of time, so they are not as subject to leaching.

Legumes

Plants such as beans, peas, and various clovers, which have small root nodules containing microorganisms called **node bacteria**. These microorganisms take **nitrogen** from the air and transform it into a form plants can use. Legumes are often used as **green manure crops** because of their node bacteria, and because their extensive root systems loosen the soil.

Lime

A fertilizer valued for its ability to neutralize surplus soil acidity, expedite transplanting, and make available materials that are otherwise difficult for the plant to absorb.

Magnesium

The central building block of **chlorophyll** and thus extremely important in plant metabolism.

Main Plant Nutrients

The primary plant nutrients, which are nitrogen, phosphate, potassium, and, despite the fact

A well-developed root ball

that so little is needed, magnesium and calcium.

Manuring

Providing the soil with manure to increase the organic content of the soil. The best time to manure your soil is before sowing your seeds. You should dig composted or well-rotted manure into the soil. Later manurings, applied when the plants are already growing on the surface, are also known as "top dressing." The only time to dig in fresh manure is in the fall. It will then decompose over the winter and be ready for planting in the spring.

Maturity Dates

Quite accurate estimates of the number of days a certain variety must grow before it's ready to harvest.

Microorganisms

From the Greek *micro*, meaning small. The smallest living things, invisible to the naked eye, such as soil bacteria, which are important for the decay of plant remains.

Mildew

A fungus disease found on many plants. Mildew is usually a problem when there is high humidity and dense plant growth. A layer of whitish-gray mildew appears either on the underside or on the upperside of the leaf. Some newer vegetable varieties are resistant to mildew attacks.

Mineral Fertilizers

Plant nutrients supplied in inorganic form, at a much greater concentration than in **organic fertilizers**. The nutrients in mineral fertilizers also are released much more quickly than those in organic fertilizers.

Minerals

Minerals are inorganic nutrients required by plant, animal or human organisms for a multitude of functions. Minerals include, for example, calcium, potassium, phosphorus, magnesium, iron, and various trace elements.

Mixed Cultivation

Two or more types of plants grown together in the same bed for the mutual benefit of all. Mixed beds are likely to be more resistant to diseases and pests. To manage this technique successfully, you need to know whether plants are compatible or incompatible. For a complete listing see the Gardening Guide.

Mound Beds

A mound bed combines a traditional garden **bed** and a **compost** heap in a single unit. The raised surface of the bed enlarges its area. Growing and harvesting periods are lengthened because the decay taking place in the bed warms the soil. As a result, you can sow earlier in the spring and harvest longer in the autumn.

Mulching

Covering the soil with a layer of organic materials, such as grass, straw, or hay. Black plastic sheets are also used as a mulch to prevent weed growth. An organic mulch prevents evaporation and, to some extent, the germination of weeds. It also supplies humus to the soil as it decomposes. Mulches are especially useful under strawberries and various cucurbits, because they keep the fruit dry, which prevents rotting.

Natural Pest Control

Non-chemical methods of ridding your garden of pests. See **integrated plant protection**.

New Breeds / Varieties

Changes and improvements in the basic characteristics of plants are achieved through breeding and cultivation. The result is a new variety, which differs from other varieties in one or more characteristics. A new breed can be characterized by better and/or earlier yields, flavor improvement, and/or disease resistance. New varieties are patented by the companies that develop them, and often are only available through them.

Nitrogen

A basic element in **chlorophyll**, which is the basic building block in all plant proteins and the vehicle for **photosynthesis**. Nitrogen is indispensable in the life of every plant.

Nitrogen Deficiency

A nutrient deficiency that can shorten a plant's entire growth cycle. Nitrogen deficient plants grow poorly because they can't carry out photosynthesis efficiently. There are fewer fruits and seeds, and those that do form are small. Leaves remain a light green because they lack **chlorophyll**, and they turn yellow before they should because of the meager amount of protein material.

Nitrogen Excess

Too much nitrogen; which delays blossoming and rudimentary fruit formation. The leaves are dark green and abnormally large, due to their high chlorophyll content. Protein production is greatly accelerated, which causes the plant to consume carbohydrates at such a rate that it no longer has enough stocks to build up supporting tissues. As a result, the plant's rigidity and hardiness suffer. Nitrogen excess also makes the plant take in too much water, which increases its sensitivity to temperature fluctuations, making it more susceptible

to diseases and parasites. The increased formation of specific organic bonds such as asparagine and glutamine often impairs flavor in plants supplied with too much nitrogen.

Node Bacteria

Soil bacteria that invade the roots of legumes. The bacteria cause nodules of various sizes to form, and the bacteria then multiply within the nodules. Node bacteria are able to convert free gaseous nitrogen from the air into body protein. When the bacteria die, the nitrogen is released in a form that the plant can use. (Plants cannot utilize nitrogen in the form it has in the air.) After the death of the host plant, the

nodules decay, and the still-living bacteria return to the soil where they can penetrate another host plant. The nitrogen they have converted is then made available to any other plant growing on that soil. This is the basis of green manuring.

Nursery Bed

A garden bed prepared specifically for raising seedlings throughout the growing season, to ensure a steady supply of young plants. Crops started here include kale, late cabbage, and late kohlrabi. The seeds are sown thinly, and the young plants remain in the bed until transplanting time. A nursery bed can also be used to **harden off** seedlings started indoors or in a **cold frame**.

Nutrient Humus

Fresh organic material supplied to the soil, such as compost, dung, peat, mulch, or plant remains. When fully decayed, nutrient humus becomes **permanent humus**.

Onion Flies

The white maggots of the onion fly eat into the onion and cause the leaves to turn yellow. Ultimately you can pull the leaves right out of the bulbs. Plants that have been attacked should never be put on the compost pile. Instead they should be thrown in the garbage.

Open-Air Nursery Bed

See **Nursery Bed**.

Organic

Belonging to living nature. Organic materials, such as **humus** and **peat**, originate in the animal and plant kingdoms. The opposite of organic is inorganic. See **minerals**.

Organic Fertilizers

Fertilizers containing **nutrient humus**. Organic fertilizers, which can be either home-made or commercially produced, have a lower percentage of mineral nutrients than **mineral fertilizers**, release their nutrients more slowly, and improve the soil structure because of their high percentage of humus.

Peat

A soil conditioner made from a loose organic matter, predominately sphagnum moss dug from bogs and marshlands. As a soil conditioner, peat loosens clay soils and adds body to sandy soils. It is very porous and holds water well. However, due to the constant **leaching** in bog areas, peat has virtually no nutrient content. Leaching also makes it highly acidic, so it should always be applied with care.

Perennials

Plants which, once started, will continuing producing year after year. Rhubarb, raspberries, currants, and some herbs are just a few of the perennials you can grow in your garden.

pH Value

From the Latin, *potentia pydorgenii*. A measure of the acid or alkali condition of your soil. pH is measured on a scale from 0 to 14, with 0 being the most acidic and 14 being the most alkaline. Most crops grow best on a soil that has a pH of around 7, which is considered neutral.

Phosphorus

An essential part of specific proteins (nucleic acids) in every plant, thus essential for the production of new plant cells. Most importantly, phosphorus encourages the formation of the blossoms and fruit.

Photosynthesis

The conversion of carbon dioxide, in the presence of light, **chlorophyll** in the leaves, and nutrients and water from the soil, into sugars and starches. These materials are then used to build up roots, leaves, stems, flowers and fruits.

Pinching Off

Breaking off the **side shoots** in the leaf joints of plants, such as tomatoes, to eliminate diversions of food from the main, fruit-bearing stems. Otherwise the side shoots would take up some of this nourishment and possibly impair fruit formation.

Plant Breeding

The use of various plant husbandry practices to alter specific characteristics of a given plant. The aim is to develop valued

characteristics that will then be passed on to the next generation. In some cases, scientists develop entirely new breeds of a vegetable. The characteristics emphasized by plant breeders most often are increased yield, better flavor, earlier ripening, and disease resistance. Some varieties are bred specifically to meet problems only found in a given region.

Planting Strategies

Methods such as **crop rotation** and **mixed cultivation**, used as part of **integrated plant protection**, since **soil fatigue** results in weak plants that are susceptible to attack by both diseases and pests.

Porosity

A soil's ability to hold and release water. Clay and sand soils have poor porosity because they hold either too much or too little water. Crumb soils have the best water-retaining characteristics.

Potassium

Important in plant metabolism, because it regulates the plant's water balance. Good wa-

ter balance makes the plant more resistant to drought, temperature swings, and frost. Potassium also plays a role in the starch and sugar production, thus encouraging the root and **tuber** formation.

Potassium Deficiency

An inability to regulate water balance. The plant turns brown, withers, and, in the worst cases, literally dries up and dies.

Resistance

A plant's ability to resist a disease. Resistances are introduced into a variety through **plant breeding**. They then are passed on to the next generation of plants. Many new varieties are developed specifically because of their resistance to certain diseases.

Rhizome

A **root stock** that develops laterally, rather than in a concentrated root ball. A rhizome is planted just below the surface. Many berry bushes are propagated by using rhizomes.

Root Ball

The concentration of a plant's roots in the container in which it has grown. Seedlings having a concentrated root ball grow faster than those with a root system that is spread out and disorganized. To gradually increase the size of the root ball, repeatedly thin out the number of seedlings in a **flat,** or replant each seedling in a larger container as it grows.

Root Stock

Pieces of root taken from existing plants, and used to create new plants. Rhubarb, for instance, is propagated by using root stocks, as are several herbs. See also **rhizome.**

Runner

Runners are shoots that grow out sideways from a plant's stem or roots. They can then form a new plant by sending down roots at a distance from the mother plant. Strawberries form new plants by throwing out runners from the body of the mother plant. Some herbs, such as mint, form new plants by sending out root runners.

Seedling

A small, newly germinated plant, with or without a root ball, that is grown in a **seed starter** or in a small plant pot and later planted out in its final position in the garden.

Sets

Small bulbs used for growing onions.

Shade Mellowness

The crumb structure of the soil, which is maintained through shading the soil with a covering of plants, as in green manuring. The plant cover prevents drying out due to wind and sun, and prevents silting due to rain. See **cover crop.**

Shoot

The vertical plant shoot from which the side shoots, flowers and fruit-bearing stems branch off.

Side Shoots

Branching shoots that grow from the main shoot, and which can, in their turn, produce flowering shoots. Some plants, such as currants, will only form blossoms on side shoots such as these. However, if some plants form too many side shoots, the development of the main shoot will be weakened and the production of blossoms may be generally impaired. Therefore you should **pinch off** young side shoots growing from the leaf axels of, for example, tomatoes and eggplants.

Soil Mellowness

See **Tilth.**

Starting Soil

Soil mixture designed to meet all the needs of germinating seeds.

Stomata

Minute openings, or pores, in the surface of the leaf of higher plant forms. The pores lead to a cavity (breathing pit), and are surrounded by 2 cells capable of closing them. Stomata exist to regulate the release of water vapor (transpiration) and gas exchange. They often only take up 1 to 2% of the surface of the leaf, but, when fully open, they can release 50 to 70% of the amount of water that would evaporate from an open area of water of comparable size.

Systemic Pesticides

Poisons that are applied to the soil, and work through the plant's roots and circulatory system. Systemic pesticides are especially effective against sucking insects, such as aphids, but they do not harm insects that simply land on the leaves, such as honeybees, or insect predators such as praying mantises or ladybugs.

Thinning Out

The removal of a number of **seedlings** from a row of densely growing plants. Only the plants intended for further cultivation are left standing at the prescribed distances from each other. In the case of root vegetables such as carrots or onions, thinning out can take place over a period of time right in the permanent bed, since the small plants are especially tender.

Tilling

Spring work that follows **harrowing**. Tilling breaks soil to a fairly fine consistency. The loose layer of crumbs acts like a lid to hold winter moisture in the root area.

Tilth

The loose, crumb-like texture of the soil resulting from the action of microorganisms on the decomposition of organic substances, and through the mechanical working of the soil. Good tilth is characterized by a living, nutrient-rich soil that has a sweet, not putrid, smell.

Top Soil

The upper layer of soil that through careful cultivation is loosened and aerated, and that is penetrated by plant roots. Top soil contains more organic materials and more microorganisms than the soil layers below it.

Tuber

A storage organ formed in a plant's stem or root. Tubers also can be called bulbs or corms. Tubers are valuable sources of nourishment for both people and animals due to their starch and sugar storage.

Turning Under

Working the soil to break it into clumps that are easier for roots to penetrate. This method of turning over the soil is also used to work in fertilizers.

Universal Vegetable Fertilizer

A fertilizer that contains all the **main plant nutrients** (**nitrogen**, **phosphate**, and **potassium**), in relative proportions that will benefit all vegetables in your garden. (There are some mineral fertilizers especially designed for a given crop, and the nutrient rations will be adjusted accordingly.) Such ratios are given in percentages, based on the total weight, are indicated by letters and are always presented in the order N-P-K-Mg. The letters indicate: N = nitrogen, P = Phosphate, K = Potassium Oxide, Mg = Magnesium. A fertilizer with the label 10-10-15, therefore, contains 10% nitrogen, 10% phosphate and 15% potassium oxide.

Waiting Period

Period of time between the application of a pesticide and the time when the crop can be safely harvested. This time is required for the plant to **break down** the dangerous chemicals in the pesticide. It is especially important to respect the waiting period dictated by the product you use. This is especially important if you are using a **systemic pesticide**, which cannot be removed simply by washing the vegetable after harvesting it.

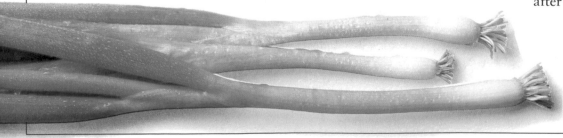

Introduction and Cooking Guide

Short Cooking Time for Young Vegetables

When you cook vegetables, be sure to add salt to the water—a good 1 to 2 teaspoons per pound—to prevent too many nutrients from leaching into the cooking water. Always have the water boiling before you add the vegetables. This too helps retain the nutrient content.

Instead of throwing away left-over cooking water, use it for sauces or gravies so you don't lose the minerals and vitamins extracted by boiling, especially water soluble ones, like C, B_1, B_6, and B_{12}.

If you sauté vegetables in fat, they cook in their own juices and are served with the very little liquid that they do lose. Steaming is another way to retain nutrients.

Always cover simmering saucepans—this holds in the steam and preserves nutrients. The cover also will keep the vegetables from boiling dry and holds in the delicate flavorings, so the vegetables are tastier.

How long should you cook vegetables before they'll lose their full value? Because of the variety among all kinds of vegetables, there can be no absolute cooking time. It will always depend on whether the vegetables are young or fully mature, coarse or tender, fresh or stored, whole or cut up.

Gardeners are lucky, because they are the ones who decide when to pick their crop. As a result they always know whether a vegetable is young or fully mature, fresh or stored. Just a trip into the garden and you can gather produce at the right time. Your biggest concern is storing vegetables when the yield is large. You'll find tips for this in both the garden and recipe sections.

Cooking time also is a matter of personal taste. Some people prefer vegetables that are stir-fried and still crunchy; others prefer them cooked until they are fork-tender.

In addition to controlling cooking time, you can try other ways to retain vegetable nutrients.

Always clean vegetables with a soft brush, and remove any bad parts. Unless absolutely necessary, don't trim away the very dark green leaves from savoys, celery, Chinese cabbage, leeks, and endives, because they contain the most vitamins and minerals. (As a general rule, remember that the greener the vegetable, the greater its nutritional value.)

Rinse vegetables *before* you peel or chop them, since many vitamins and flavoring agents are soluble in water, and are lost when vegetables are cut into small pieces before they're rinsed.

Prepare vegetables just before you are ready to cook them, and place them at once in boiling salt water or hot fat. Prepared too early, they lose juice, and the oxygen in the air will destroy some of their nutrients.

If you must prepare vegetables in advance, wrap them in aluminum foil or cellophane, or put them into plastic bags, and refrigerate them until you're ready for them. They'll be well protected and will remain fresh.

Herbs

Herbs are the crowning touch to many dishes.

To store herbs, don't stand them in a glass of water in the open. It is better to lightly sprinkle them with water and to put them in a plastic bag. Then blow it up and seal it. You can also wrap the herbs loosely in plastic wrap. They will keep fresh in the refrigerator for 3 to 4 days.

Basil
Finely cut basil leaves are especially good for flavoring tomato dishes and cold herbal sauces served with pasta, such as Pesto alla Genovese. Basil is also good with vegetables, soups such as minestrone, fresh salads, lamb, pork, or beef dishes, and with steamed and fried fish. Then, of course, there's always pizza.

Borage
Borage is the ideal flavoring for all cucumber dishes because it heightens their flavor. Add freshly chopped borage to leaf salads, mixed salads, and use it in cold savory sauces and herb sour cream mixtures. The delicate flowers make lovely garnishes.

Chervil

Chervil is an important ingredient in Frankfurt green sauce, and also in classical French cuisine, in combination with chives, parsley, and tarragon.

Egg dishes, sour cream, and cream cheese preparations can be flavored with chervil. It also goes into tomato dishes and fresh salads as well as into cream sauces for fish.

Chives

Chives—like parsley—are a universal herb for almost all salty dishes. Because of their onion-ey heritage, chives go with all dishes in which onions are used—stews, fancy salads and leaf salads, herb sour cream and herb butter, in soups and sauces, egg dishes, and toppings for bread. Chives are also popular with boiled fish and mayonnaise. Cut fine, they can be combined with all fresh herbs.

Dill

Dill is a versatile plant. Use the fresh leaves for flavoring dishes, and the dried dill blossoms for pickling cucumbers. Dill is a valuable addition to cucumber salad and it's an important seasoning for fish, lobster, and crab, as well as for their sauces. It's added to cooking water for fish and crustaceans, in cream marinades for butterhead lettuce and in all raw salads, in mayonnaise, light soups, and in herbal preparations. Dill can be combined with almost all herbs.

Lavender

Lavender is an important ingredient in provincial herbs (mixed herbs) and is used sparingly as a flavoring for provincial dishes. It also enhances the flavor of roast lamb, stews, fish soups, and is a valuable addition in herb butter, salads, and marinades for steaks and roasts, and in the cooking liquid for fish. It goes well with fennel and garlic.

Lemon Mint

Alone or combined with other herbs, lemon mint is suitable for leaf or mixed salads, for fancy salads, and for anything you might combine with lemon. This herb is used in herb sauces, herb sour cream, and herb butter, as well as in light sauces and soups, and is also suitable for fish and game. Added to sweet dishes, lemon mint gives fruit salads and dessert jellies that extra tang.

Lovage

Since lovage is highly aromatic, it doesn't lose its flavor when cooked. The dried, ground roots are a good seasoning standby for the winter. You can add lovage to spring soups and stews, pies, gravies, peas and beans, salads, herb sauces, potato soups and other potato dishes, or you can cook the herb right with the dishes. It also goes well with lettuce.

Marjoram

Marjoram is an indispensable ingredient for many kinds of cold sausage meats in everyday cuisine. It complements all vegetable or smoked meat dishes, and is used for preparing liver, fatty poultry, goose stuffings, for legume stews, liver pate, and dumplings.

Mint

Mint is primarily known for the tea made from its fresh leaves, but it is also indispensable for the mint sauce traditionally served with lamb. It is a valuable ingredient in game dishes, oriental dishes, and fresh leaf and mixed salads. Drinks and cocktails are also flavored with mint. It can be combined with basil and oregano.

Parsley

Parsley has numerous uses. Both the smooth and crinkly varieties are used in salads and cold sauces, peas, carrots, French beans, soups, boiled potatoes, and herbal dishes. It also goes with fish, seafoods, and poultry, and is indispensable as a garnish. Both leaf parsley and root parsley can be cooked with any dish.

Rosemary

Rosemary is excellent with roasts, grilled fish, and other grilled dishes; it makes tomato dishes even more savory, and is very suitable as a seasoning for meat and fish dishes baked in the oven. The Italians add rosemary to roast lamb. One version prepares roast leg of lamb with a mixture of garlic, fennel, rosemary, and basil. Rosemary also goes with chicken, eggplant, and zucchini.

Sage

Sage is almost indispensable for eel and other fish dishes having a high oil content. Used sparingly, sage is also good for all grilled dishes. Italian veal cutlets (saltimbocca) are not the real thing without sage. Sage is also a well-known accompaniment for liver, lamb, and roast pork.

Savory

This peppery, bean-flavored herb intensifies the flavor of all bean dishes, even those made from dried beans. Its flavoring is so strong that it can be cooked, complete with stems, in stews, with braised tomatoes, and in eggplant dishes. Savory even goes with bouillon, and is great with lamb dishes.

Tarragon

Tarragon is an indispensable ingredient in Sauce Bearnaise. It's also a typical seasoning for cold savory and mayonnaise sauces. Its sweet flavor adds much to stuffing in chicken, rabbit and veal roasts, as well as to sauerbraten (beef marinated in vinegar and roasted). Tarragon vinegar adds special character to any salad dressing.

Thyme

Thyme is a good seasoning for meat with dark sauces, such as game, pork, or roast lamb. It lends a slightly clove-like flavor to rabbit and poultry. It is suitable for all tomato dishes, zucchini and eggplant dishes, and also—in small amounts—for herb butter and fish dishes.

Wormwood

When used sparingly, wormwood gives hearty stews, roast pork, and roast goose an interesting flavor.

General Instructions for Canning

All canning instructions in the recipes here use the method called **water bath processing,** and follow the latest United States Department of Agriculture guidelines for preserving vegetables. If you wish to can your vegetables without a vinegar solution (green beans, for instance, or beets) you must use a pressure canner to be sure that the product will be safe from botulism growth and other bacteria problems. Instructions for these methods are available from your local County Agricultural Agent, as well as through the suppliers of various canning supplies.

Important Note:
Do *not* employ what is often

called the "open kettle" canning method, even with tomatoes. The acid content of some modern varieties is not high enough to ensure that the tomatoes will be safe.

Water Bath Processing

Equipment:
1. Water-bath Canner: A deep kettle that has a tight-fitting lid and a wooden or wire rack to hold the jars above the bottom of the kettle. You can purchase such a canner in most hardware stores.

2. Canning jars: You can use any glass jars with openings that will fit standard lid closures, as long as the jars are free from all cracks and nicks. Jars designed specifically for canning are required for pressure canning because they will not break under pressure and heat, but are not required for water-bath processing. They are the safest ones, however.

3. Self-sealing lids and rings. Lids and rings can be purchased in stores that handle canning materials. Although the rings can be used again and again, do *not* reuse old lids. They will not seal properly and the food will spoil.

4. A ready supply of soft towels and cloths for cleaning jars and rims during the canning procedures.

5. General equipment: rubber spatula, wide-mouth funnel, teakettle, jar-lifter.

Processing

1. Select only perfect, fresh vegetables, with no dark spots or damage.

2. Wash all fruits and vegetables carefully, and scrub with a soft vegetable brush. Remove the produce from the water each time, so the dirt doesn't settle back on it.

3. Wash the jars, lids, and rings in hot, soapy water, and rinse well. Prepare the lids according to the manufacturer's instructions.

4. Fill the canner at least $^2/_3$ full of hot water, and heat until steam is rising from the surface. Keep this water near boiling as you fill the jars. Have boiling water available in the teakettle.

5. Fill the jars firmly but do not pack so tightly that there's no room for the pickling solution. Always be sure to leave as much space at the top of the jar as the directions indicate—this is

called *headspace*, and is required in case the vegetables expand during processing. Add hot pickling liquid to cover.

6. Slide the spatula along the insides of the jars to remove any air bubbles. Otherwise these may prevent a good seal.

7. Clean the top rims and the shoulders with a clean, hot, damp cloth. Any juice or seeds along the rim will prevent a good seal.

8. Position the lids and bands according to the manufacturer's instructions. Follow these *to the letter*.

9. Place the jars in the canning rack, and lower them into the canner. If necessary, add enough water to the canner to bring the level between 1 and 2 inches above the tops of the jars. Do *not* pour boiling water directly on the jars.

10. Cover the canner, bring the water to a rolling boil, and process as long as indicated in the recipe.

11. Remove the jars from the canner as soon as the processing is complete. Set them on clean, dry towels, or on a cake rack or other device so that they can cool. The location should be draft-free. The jars should not touch each other, and they should not be covered.

12. Once the jars have cooled completely, test the seals by inverting the jars, or according to the manufacturer's directions.

If the seals are faulty, use the product at once, or reprocess it in clean jars with new lids.

13. Store in a cool, dark, dry location. Food processed in a water-bath canner will be good for at least a year.

General Instructions for Jellies

Jellies, jams, and preserves are prepared with a high enough sugar content that it isn't necessary to process them in a water bath, unless you live in a very warm, humid climate. Otherwise they can be prepared by the *open kettle* method. There are three general steps: sterilization of the jars, preparation of the jelly, and sealing the jars. The steps are as follows.

1. Select standard canning jars that are in perfect condition. Do not use nicked or cracked jars. Sterilize the jars in boiling water for 10 minutes. Leave them in the water until you are ready to use.

2. Use standard, two-piece canning lids. Prepare these accor-

ding to the manufacturer's directions. Remember that the rings can be reused, but the lids themselves must always be new.

3. Prepare the jelly according to the recipe. Keep in mind that a rolling boil is one that cannot be stirred down. Follow all instructions and measurements exactly.

4. Set the jars out on a dry folded kitchen towel, and fill them with the jelly up to $1/8$ to $1/4$ inch from the top of the jar. Wipe off the rims with a clean, damp cloth. Seal the jars immediately, and invert them on the towel for about 5 minutes. Turn them upright, and leave them in place for at least 12 hours, so they cool completely. Test the seals. Store any unsealed product in the refrigerator for immediate use.

Paraffin Seals
You can seal jelly jars with paraffin, but only when the jelly has a smooth surface. Do not use paraffin with jams, preserves, and conserves. Melt the paraffin carefully—it is flammable, and it can cause serious skin burns. Fill the sterilized jars to $1/2$ inch below the rim of each jar. Then add a $1/8$ to $1/4$-inch thick layer of paraffin over the surface. Be sure to seal the surface completely.

Water-Bath Processing
Fill the jars to within $1/4$ inch of the jar rim. Wipe the rims with a clean damp cloth. Process the jars according to the canning instructions above for 5 to 15 minutes, depending upon the kind of jelly you are preparing. As a general rule, jellies are processed for 5 minutes, jams for 10, and preserves and conserves for 15. The best source for exact information is your local County Extension Agent.

Gardener's Cookbook

The recipe section of this book contains a mine of information for all who want to enjoy their garden-fresh vegetables in delicious and fanciful meals. *The Creative Gardener's Cookbook* explores the bounty of your garden with recipes designed to maintain the nutrition you worked so hard for in your garden, without sacrificing fine taste. There are few recipes here that will use canned vegetables or packaged mixes. Instead, emphasis is on fresh fruits and vegetables, prepared from scratch. Preparation time may be a little longer, but you will find the efforts worthwhile. Whether you are fixing a simple breakfast or a complex menu for an elegant party, these selections will more than fill the bill.

Legumes

Tender and delicate as butter

African-Style Green Beans

(Illustrated above)

1 teaspoon salt
1 pound (500 g) green beans, rinsed and trimmed
2-3 sprigs savory, rinsed and patted dry
1 tablespoon butter *or* margarine
3 rounded tablespoons (50 g) butter *or* margarine
2 ¹/₂ ounces (75 g) grated coconut
  Dash ground turmeric
  Dash ground coriander
  Dash cayenne pepper

Fill a medium saucepan with water, add salt, and bring to a boil. Add beans and savory; return to a boil, and simmer for 20 minutes. Drain beans and remove the savory. In a small saucepan, melt butter, and pour it over beans; keep warm. In a small skillet, melt 3 rounded tablespoons of butter. Add coconut, and stir over medium heat until lightly browned. Add turmeric, coriander, and cayenne; pour over beans. Serve immediately. This dish is excellent with fried chicken.

Green Beans with Bacon

(Illustrated pp. 170-171)

1 teaspoon salt
1 pound (500 g) green beans, rinsed and trimmed
2-3 sprigs savory, rinsed and patted dry
8 strips lean bacon
3 tablespoons butter *or* margarine

Fill a medium saucepan with hot water, add salt, and bring to a boil. Add the beans and savory, return to a boil, and simmer gently for 20 minutes. Drain beans and remove the savory sprigs. Divide beans into 8 portions. Wrap each portion in a slice of bacon, and secure with a toothpick. Melt butter in a medium skillet; fry the bean portions on all sides for about 3 minutes. Serve with beef fillet or roast beef and potatoes.

Green Beans with Hollandaise Sauce

(Illustrated above)

1 ¹/₂ pounds (750 g) green beans, rinsed and
  trimmed
2-3 sprigs savory, rinsed and patted dry
1 teaspoon salt
  Hollandaise Sauce

Fill a medium saucepan half full with water, add
salt, and bring to a boil. Add the beans and savory,
return to a boil and simmer for 20 minutes. Drain
beans and remove savory. Place beans in a serving
dish. Prepare Hollandaise Sauce. Pour sauce over
beans, and serve immediately. Green Beans with
Hollandaise Sauce is excellent with smoked salmon
or beef fillet.

Hollandaise Sauce

5 tablespoons (70 g) butter *or* margarine
5 egg yolks
  Juice of 1 lemon
  Grated peel of 1 lemon
2 tablespoons water
  Salt and pepper to taste
  Dash of Tabasco sauce

In a small saucepan, melt butter; remove any foam
that appears until the butter is clear. In another
saucepan, combine egg yolks, lemon juice, peel,
and water. Season with salt, pepper and Tabasco
sauce to taste. Fill a medium bowl half full with
cold water, and place the saucepan in the water.
With an electric hand mixer, whip the egg yolk
mixture until it is foamy and light yellow in color.
Remove the pan from the water and, stirring
constantly, slowly add the melted butter to the egg
yolk mixture. Immediately pour over the beans.

Green Beans with Dill Cream

1 pound (500 g) green beans, trimmed, rinsed, and broken into 1-inch pieces
2-3 sprigs savory, rinsed and patted dry
1 teaspoon salt
1 medium onion, minced
2 tablespoons butter *or* margarine
8 ounces sour cream
2 tablespoons chopped fresh dill

Fill a medium saucepan half full with water, add salt, and bring to a boil. Add the beans and savory, and return to a boil; simmer for 20 minutes. In a medium skillet, melt the butter; add the onion and sauté until translucent. Add the drained beans, and toss. In a small saucepan, heat the sour cream until just warm. Add sour cream and the chopped dill to the beans. Stir gently. Serve immediately. Green Beans with Dill Cream is an excellent accompaniment to veal cutlets.

Green Beans and Broad Beans in Savory-Parsley Cream Sauce

1 teaspoon salt
1 1/2 pounds (750 g) green beans, rinsed and broken into 1-inch pieces
2-3 sprigs savory, rinsed and patted dry
2 tablespoons butter *or* margarine
1 onion, minced
1-2 cloves garlic, minced
1 pound (450 g) shelled broad beans, rinsed
1 cup (250 ml) cream
1-2 tablespoons chopped savory leaves
1-2 tablespoons chopped parsley

Fill a large saucepan half full with water, add salt, and bring to a boil. Add the beans and savory, return to a boil, and simmer for 20 minutes. Drain. Melt butter in a medium skillet, add onion and garlic, and sauté until onion is translucent. Add the broad beans to the onion mixture. Add enough water to cover, bring to a boil, and simmer for about 20 minutes; drain. Mix the two beans together. In a small saucepan, heat the cream until it has thickened slightly, add savory and parsley and stir into bean mixture. Serve immediately. Serve this dish with smoked pork chops.

Gourmet Bean Salad

(Illustrated opposite page)

1 teaspoon salt
1/2 pound (200 g) green beans, rinsed and trimmed
1/2 pound (200 g) fresh wax beans, rinsed
1 large carrot (about 200 g), cut into thin sticks
  Gourmet Dressing (see recipe below)
1/4 pound (125 g) small firm button mushrooms, rinsed, trimmed, and sliced
1 tablespoon lemon juice
4 thin ham slices
1 large tomato, peeled, cut into strips and seeded

Fill a medium saucepan half full with water, add salt and bring to a boil. Add beans, return to a boil, cover, and simmer until tender-crisp. Remove beans with a slotted spoon; drain. Add wax beans to the cooking water, bring to a boil, cover, and simmer until tender-crisp. Remove with a slotted spoon; drain. Add carrot sticks to the cooking water, bring to a boil, cover, and simmer for about 2 minutes. Drain. Prepare the Gourmet Dressing. Marinate beans and carrot sticks in the dressing for 1 to 2 hours. Sprinkle mushrooms with lemon juice. Place 1 ham slice each on 4 serving plates, arrange the mushrooms, tomato and other vegetables on top of the slices, and pour the Gourmet Dressing over. Serve immediately. Serve this salad with French bread and butter.

Gourmet Dressing

1 shallot, minced
3 tablespoons peanut oil
2-3 tablespoons white wine vinegar
  Salt, pepper and sugar to taste
2 tablespoons finely cut chives

Combine all ingredients in a small bowl; use as marinade and dressing.

Savory Green Beans

1 teaspoon salt
1 ½ pounds (750 g) green beans, rinsed and broken in half
2-3 sprigs savory, rinsed and patted dry
1 tablespoon chopped thyme leaves
1 tablespoon chopped rosemary leaves
½ cup (50 g) grated Parmesan cheese
3-5 tablespoons (50-75 g) butter *or* margarine

Fill a medium saucepan half full with water, add salt, and bring to a boil. Add beans and savory, return to a boil, cover, and simmer for 20 minutes. Place the beans in a pre-warmed serving bowl. Sprinkle beans with thyme and rosemary, and toss. Sprinkle with Parmesan cheese, and toss. In a small skillet, melt butter, and heat until it browns a little. Pour over beans, and serve.

Pickled Green, Wax, or Kidney Beans

(Illustrated below)

Earthenware crock
11 pounds beans, washed, trimmed, and cut into 1½-inch pieces
Pickling salt (¾ cup plus 4 teaspoons salt to 11 pounds beans)

A few hours before you are ready to begin, clean the crock thoroughly, and rinse with clear water. Invert on a cloth, and allow to drip dry. Place beans in a large dutch oven or cooking kettle, cover them with water, and bring to a boil. Remove from heat, and steep for 5 minutes. Drain; spread them out over a clean towel to cool. Alternately layer beans and salt in the crock. Shake beans down so that they settle together as closely as possible. Press them down as firmly as possible, cover with a linen cloth, and top with a board or lid. Weight down the board with a stone or any heavy implement. Leave the beans covered in a cool place. It will take them about 4 to 6 weeks to ferment.

Bean Goulash

3 tablespoons vegetable oil
1 pound ground pork
1 pound (500 g) onions, minced
  Salt and pepper to taste
1 cup (250 ml) meat stock
1 pound (500 g) green beans, rinsed and broken into
  pieces
1 cup sour cream
1 tablespoon cornstarch
1-2 tablespoons chopped savory leaves

In a medium saucepan, heat vegetable oil; add pork, and sauté slowly until well done. Add onions, and sauté until translucent. Season with salt and pepper. Add the meat stock, and bring to a boil; simmer for about 20 minutes. Add beans to meat mixture, and continue cooking for about 20 minutes. In a small mixing bowl, combine sour cream and cornstarch; stir into meat mixture. Simmer gently for 10 minutes, stirring constantly. Stir in the savory, season to taste, and serve immediately.

Green Bean Stew

1 tablespoon pork drippings *or* vegetable oil
1 ¹/₂ pounds ground pork
1 onion, diced
3 cups (750 ml) water
1 ¹/₂ pounds (750 g) green beans, rinsed and drained
1 ¹/₂ pounds (750 g) potatoes, peeled and quartered
  Salt to taste

In a large skillet, heat pork drippings, add pork, and sauté gently until lightly brown. Add onion, and sauté until translucent. Add 1 cup of water; simmer for about 20 minutes, stirring occasionally. Add beans and remaining water to the meat; season with salt. Bring mixture to a boil, cover, and simmer for about 25 minutes. Add the potato pieces, cover, and simmer for an additional 20 minutes. Serve immediately.

Bean Stew with Mutton

(Illustrated above)

2 1/4 pounds leg of mutton
2-3 tablespoons vegetable oil
  Salt and pepper to taste
2/3 pound (300 g) small onions, peeled and halved
2 cloves garlic, minced
1 1/2 pounds (750 g) green beans, rinsed and cut into
  1-inch pieces
1 pound (500 g) potatoes, peeled and cut into eighths
2 large green sweet peppers, cored, seeded, and cut
  into strips
2-3 sprigs of savory, rinsed and patted dry
4 cups (1 liter) water
1-2 tablespoons chopped parsley

Remove the meat from the mutton leg, and dice.
Heat oil in a large skillet, add meat, and sauté until
done on all sides. Season to taste. Add onions and
garlic to the meat; sauté until brown. Add beans,
potatoes, sweet peppers, savory sprigs, and water to
the meat mixture. Bring to a boil, cover, and simmer for about 1 hour, or until tender. Season to
taste; sprinkle with parsley and serve.

Butter Beans with Herb Cream

1 teaspoon salt
1 1/2 pounds (750 g) butter beans, rinsed
2-3 savory sprigs

1 teaspoon salt
  Herb Cream (see recipe below)
  Salt and pepper to taste

Fill a medium saucepan half full with water, add
salt, and bring to a boil. Add beans and savory,
return to a boil, cover, and simmer for about 20
minutes. Prepare the Herb Cream. Drain cooked
beans, stir in the Herb Cream carefully, and seaso
to taste with salt and pepper. Serve immediately.

Herb Cream

1 clove garlic, crushed
1 cup sour cream
1 tablespoon chopped herbs (tarragon, basil, dill,
  marjoram, parsley, chives, lemon mint)

Combine the ingredients, and mix with butter
beans.

Bean Salad with Feta Cheese and Basil

1 teaspoon salt
1 pound (500 g) green beans, rinsed and broken in
　　pieces
2-3 sprigs savory, rinsed and patted dry
4 ounces feta cheese
2-3 tablespoons chopped basil leaves
　　Bean Salad Dressing (see recipe below)

Fill a medium saucepan half full with water, add
salt, and bring to a boil. Add the beans and savory,
return to a boil, cover, and simmer for about 20
minutes. Save 2 tablespoons of the cooking water
for the dressing. Drain the beans; set aside to cool.
Prepare Bean Salad Dressing. Pour over the beans.
Crumble the cheese; add the cheese and the basil to
the beans. Marinate for 1 hour. Serve as an
appetizer or a side dish.

Bean Salad Dressing

2 tablespoons reserved cooking water
1 onion, minced
1 clove garlic, minced
5 tablespoons salad oil
3 tablespoons red wine vinegar
　　Salt and pepper to taste

Combine all the ingredients with reserved cooking
water. Pour over cooked beans.

Sliced Beans with Bacon

1 tablespoon butter or margarine
6 slices lean bacon, diced
1 1/2 pounds (750 g) green beans, washed, drained,
　　and sliced
2-3 savory sprigs, rinsed and patted dry
2 onions, minced
1 cup water
　　Salt and pepper to taste
2-3 tablespoons chopped parsley

Heat butter in a large skillet; sauté the bacon until
well browned. Add onions and sauté until
translucent. Add beans and savory; sauté on all
sides. Add water, cover, and simmer for about 20
minutes. Season to taste, stir in parsley, and serve
immediately. Serve sliced beans and bacon with
pork chops and baked potatoes.

Broad Beans with Carrots

(Illustrated above)

2 tablespoons butter *or* margarine
4 slices lean bacon, diced
1 pound (500 g) shelled broad beans (about 4 1/2
    pounds with the pods), *or* fresh limas, well rinsed
3/4 pounds (375 g) young carrots, rinsed and diced
3/4 pounds (375 g) potatoes, peeled and diced
1 onion, minced
12 sage leaves, rinsed, patted dry, and minced
    Salt, pepper and sugar to taste
1/2 cup (125 ml) water
4 tablespoons cream

Melt the butter in a large skillet, add bacon, and
sauté until brown. Add beans, carrots, potatoes,
onion and half the sage; sauté for 5 minutes. Season the mixture to taste. Add water, and simmer for
about 15 minutes, or until vegetables are fork-tender. Stir in cream, sprinkle on the remaining sage,
and serve. Serve with fried sausage, bratwurst or
chops.

Broad Beans with Sour Cream and Marjoram

1 teaspoon salt
1 pound (500 g) shelled broad beans (about 4 ¹/₂ pounds with the pods) *or* fresh limas, rinsed
2 tablespoons butter *or* margarine
2-3 onions, minced
1 cup sour cream
  Salt and pepper to taste
1 tablespoon chopped marjoram leaves
1 tablespoon chopped savory leaves
1 cup vanilla yogurt

Fill a medium saucepan half full with water, add salt, and bring to a boil. Add beans, return to a boil, cover, and simmer for 15 minutes, or until tender. Drain and set aside. Melt butter in a large skillet; add onions, and sauté until translucent. Add cooked beans, and braise for about 10 minutes. Stir in sour cream, and heat through. Season to taste. Add marjoram, savory, and yogurt. Stir gently and serve. Serve with lamb or pork chops.

Broad Bean Ragout with Meatballs

(Illustrated this page)

1 teaspoon salt
1 ¹/₄ pounds (600 g) shelled broad beans (about 5 pounds with pods), *or* fresh limas, rinsed
1 bread roll, torn into small pieces
¹/₂ pound (250 g) ground sausage
¹/₄ pound ground beef
¹/₄ pound ground pork
1 egg
1 onion, minced
  Salt, pepper, and sweet paprika to taste
2 cups (500 ml) water
1 tablespoon vegetable oil
1 pound (500 g) lean bacon, minced
1 onion, diced
³/₄ pound fresh tomatoes, cut into chunks
¹/₄ cup (40 g) flour
2 tablespoons tomato puree
4 ounces cream cheese
¹/₂ pound fresh tomatoes, peeled, seeded, and diced
2 tablespoons chopped parsley

Fill a medium saucepan half full with water, add

salt, and bring to a boil. Add beans, return to a boil, cover, and simmer for 20 minutes. Drain, reserving the cooking liquid. Set both aside. Soak the bread pieces in water and then squeeze. In a medium mixing bowl, combine bread with meats, egg, and onion. Season to taste with salt, pepper, and paprika. Shape into 1-inch meatballs. Place the reserved cooking water in a large saucepan, bring to a boil, and add the meatballs. Return to a boil, and simmer the meatballs about 5 to 7 minutes. Remove meatballs with a slotted spoon. Add 2 more cups of water to liquid; set aside. In a large skillet, heat the oil, add bacon and onion; sauté until onion is translucent. Add tomato chunks, and simmer for 2 minutes. Sprinkle flour over the bacon mixture, stir and simmer for about 5 minutes. Add reserved cooking water, stir well, bring to a boil, and simmer for about 5 minutes. Press the entire mixture through a sieve; return to a large saucepan. Season with salt, pepper, and paprika. Add the tomato puree and the cream cheese. Heat slowly, stirring constantly, until the cream cheese is completely melted. Add beans and meatballs; simmer until they are heated through. Add the diced tomatoes, and heat through. Sprinkle parsley over the mixture, and serve. Serve with baked potatoes.

Sugar Pea Pods with Lemon Mint Sauce

(Illustrated below)

1 teaspoon salt
1 ¹/₄ pounds (600 g) sugar pea pods, trimmed and rinsed
2 tablespoons vegetable oil
  Lemon Mint Sauce (see recipe below)

Fill a medium saucepan half full with water, add the salt, and bring to a boil. Add pea pods and oil, return to a boil, cover, and simmer for 5 to 7 minutes. Prepare Lemon Mint Sauce. Drain the peas; place in a warmed serving dish. Serve the sauce as a side dish. Serve with steak fillets or pork chops.

Lemon Mint Sauce

1 cup sour cream
2 tablespoons yogurt
  Grated peel from 1 lemon
  Salt, pepper, and sugar to taste
1-2 tablespoons chopped lemon mint leaves

Combine the sour cream, yogurt, and lemon peel; add salt, pepper, and sugar to taste. Stir in lemon mint. Serve with the peas.

Sugar Pea Pods with Almond Butter

1 teaspoon salt
1 ¹/₄ pounds (600 g) sugar pea pods, rinsed and trimmed
¹/₄ pound (50 g) butter *or* margarine
¹/₄ cup (40 g) chopped almonds
  Salt and pepper to taste

Fill a medium saucepan half full with water, add salt, and bring to a boil. Add pea pods, return to a boil, cover, and simmer for about 5 minutes. Drain, and set aside. In a medium skillet, melt and lightly brown the butter. Add almonds; sauté until lightly browned. Add pea pods; toss well. Season to taste, and serve immediately. You may substitute fresh shelled peas for the pea pods. Serve with steak, pork chops, or other meat entrees.

Sweet and Sour Sugar Pea Pods with Pork Tenderloin

1/4 cup red wine vinegar
1/4 cup tomato catsup
1/4 cup sugar
1/4 cup vegetable oil
1 pound (500 g) pork tenderloin, thinly sliced
   Salt to taste
2 slices fresh ginger root, minced
1 clove garlic, minced
1 pound (500 g) sugar pea pods, rinsed and trimmed

In a small mixing bowl, combine the vinegar, catsup and sugar; set aside. In a large skillet, heat the vegetable oil, and quick-fry the tenderloin slices, turning often, for about 1 minute. Add salt to taste. Add garlic and ginger, and sauté for about 1 minute longer. Add pea pods; sauté for about 1 minute. Add the vinegar mixture, and bring to a boil. Simmer for 2 or 3 minutes, and serve immediately.

Piquant Sugar Pea Pod Stew

5 tablespoons vegetable oil, divided
3/4 to 1 pound boneless chuck roast, thinly sliced
   Salt and pepper
2 tablespoons vegetable oil
3-4 onions, diced
3/4 pounds sugar pea pods, rinsed and trimmed
2 sprigs basil, rinsed and patted dry
1/2 cup (125 ml) water
2 fresh tomatoes (about 3/4 pound), peeled and diced
3 tablespoons soy sauce

In a large skillet, heat 3 tablespoons vegetable oil. Add meat, and sauté for about 3 minutes, turning constantly. Season to taste, remove from the skillet with a slotted spoon, and set aside. Add the remaining oil to the juices in the skillet. Add onions, and sauté until translucent. Add pea pods, basil and water. Season with salt and pepper to taste; cover, and simmer for about 3 minutes. Add tomatoes, cover, and simmer for about 3 minutes. Add the soy sauce, stir well; cover, and simmer for 2 to 3 minutes more. Season to taste, and serve immediately. This dish is best served with rice.

Rice Salad with Chicken and Peas

(Illustrated above)

8 cups (2 liters) water
1 teaspoon salt
3/4 cup (200 g) long grain rice
1 teaspoon salt
1/2 pound (300 g) shelled peas, rinsed
1 teaspoon salt
1 small Chinese cabbage (about 1/2 pound), cleaned and halved
2 cups (500 g) cooked chicken meat, skinned and sliced
    Rice Salad Dressing (see recipe below)

In a medium saucepan, bring the water and salt to a boil. Add the rice, bring back to a boil, and boil gently for about 20 minutes. Drain the cooked rice in a colander, and rinse well with cold water. Fill a medium saucepan half full with water, add the salt, and bring to a·boil. Add the peas, bring back to a

boil, cover, and simmer for about 10 minutes. Drain and set aside. Remove the cabbage core, wash the leaves, and slice them in very thin strips. Drain well. In a large mixing bowl, combine the rice, peas and cabbage. Toss well. Arrange on individual serving dishes, and place chicken on top. Top with Rice Salad Dressing, and allow to marinate for 1/2 hour before serving.

Rice Salad Dressing

1/3 cup plus 1 tablespoon (100 ml) white wine vinegar
1 tablespoon hot mustard
    Salt and pepper to taste
1/2 cup (125 ml) salad oil
    Lemon juice to taste

Combine vinegar, mustard, salt and pepper; mix thoroughly. Gradually beat in salad oil. Beat until liquid has a thick consistency. Add lemon juice to taste. Pour over the salad servings.

Melt the butter in a large skillet. Add onion and garlic, and sauté both until the onion is translucent. Add peas and cream; cook until cream is thickened. Add the cheese, stirring well, and season to taste. Cook for about 10 minutes, stirring occasionally. Serve immediately. Serve this dish with ham and baked potatoes.

Omelets Stuffed with Peas, French Style

(Illustrated this page)

3-4 tablespoons butter *or* margarine
1 bunch spring onions, cleaned, trimmed, and sliced
1 head lettuce, cleaned, drained, and broken
1 pound shelled peas (about 2 1/4 pounds with pods), rinsed
  Salt, white pepper, and sugar to taste
  All-Purpose Omelets (see recipe below)

In a large skillet, melt butter. Add onions, and sauté until translucent. Add the lettuce, and cook until wilted. Add the peas and season to taste; cover, and simmer for about 20 minutes. Set aside while you prepare All-Purpose Omelets.

All-Purpose Omelets

8 eggs
2 tablespoons milk
  Salt to taste
1 tablespoon butter *or* margarine

Using a wire whisk, combine the eggs with milk and salt in a small mixing bowl. Melt butter in a heavy-bottomed frying pan or an omelet pan, and add 1/4 of the egg mixture. With very low heat, cover the pan, and allow egg mixture to slowly set (about 10 minutes). Check occasionally by lifting the edge of the omelet. The top must remain soft, but the bottom surface should be brown. When the omelet is done, remove it from the pan, and keep it warm while you prepare the other three. When all four are finished, divide the filling between them, fold them over and serve immediately.

Peas in Parmesan Cream

1 tablespoon butter *or* margarine
1 onion, minced
1 clove garlic, minced
1 pound (500 g) shelled young peas
1 cup (250 ml) cream
1 cup (100 g) grated Parmesan cheese
  Salt and pepper to taste

Pea Soufflé

(Illustrated opposite page)

3 1/3 tablespoons (50 g) butter *or* margarine
1/4 cup (40 g) flour
2 cups (500 ml) milk
   Salt, pepper and grated nutmeg to taste
2 egg yolks, beaten
1 pound shelled peas (about 2 1/4 pounds with pods),
   rinsed and drained
2 egg whites
   Cornstarch *or* flour

Preheat the oven to 350° F. In a medium skillet, melt the butter. Add flour, and cook gently until the flour becomes light yellow in color. Remove from heat. Add milk, and mix with a wire whisk, taking care that there are no lumps. Return to the stove, and bring to a boil; cover, and simmer for about 5 minutes. Season to taste. Add the egg yolks, and mix in. Remove from heat, and allow sauce to cool for 10 minutes before adding the peas. Whip the egg whites until stiff, and fold into the sauce. Grease a soufflé dish, and dust it with cornstarch; fill with the soufflé mix. Bake for about 20 minutes; serve immediately.

Mashed Potato Nests with Peas and Ham Filling

(Illustrated opposite page)

Mashed Potato Nests

1 1/2 pounds (750 g) unpeeled potatoes, rinsed
2 eggs, lightly beaten
1-2 tablespoons butter *or* margarine
   Salt, pepper and ground nutmeg to taste
1 egg yolk thinned with a little cold water
   Peas and Ham Filling

Preheat the oven to 350° F. Place potatoes in a medium saucepan, cover with water, and bring to a boil. Boil gently for 20 to 25 minutes, or until they are fork-tender. Drain, allow the steam to evaporate, and peel while they are still hot. Mash them until smooth. Stir in eggs and butter; beat well. Season to taste with salt, pepper and nutmeg. Fit an icing bag with a large rosette nozzle. Fill the bag with the mashed potatoes, and squeeze out 4 to

6 nests onto a well-greased baking tray. Use a pastry brush to brush each nest with a coating of egg yolk. Place the tray in the center of the oven, and bake for 10 to 15 minutes, or until the nests are just beginning to brown. As they bake, prepare Peas and Ham Filling. When the nests are done, fill them with the filling. Serve immediately. Serve with pork fillets or chops.

Peas and Ham Filling

2 tablespoons butter *or* margarine
2 slices (2 ounces) boiled ham, julienned
1/2 pound shelled peas, washed
1/2 cup (125 ml) water
   Salt and pepper to taste
1 tablespoon white wine
1 teaspoon cornstarch

Melt butter in a medium skillet; add ham and peas, and sauté for about 3 minutes. Add the water, bring the mixture to a boil, cover, and simmer for about 8 to 10 minutes. Season to taste. In a small mixing bowl, combine the wine and cornstarch. Add to the pea mixture; cook for 2 minutes. Fill the nests.

Peas and Shrimp on Toast

(Illustrated opposite page)

1 stick softened butter *or* margarine
1/4 pound (100 g) shelled peas, rinsed
   Salt and pepper to taste
   Garlic salt to taste
1/4 pound (100 g) shrimp, cooked
8 ounces (200 g) Boursin *or* cream cheese, softened
4 slices toasted bread
2 tablespoons finely chopped dill

Melt 2 tablespoons butter in a medium skillet. Add the peas, and sauté gently for about 8 minutes, or until tender. Season to taste, and remove from heat. Allow to cool; then add 4 tablespoons butter, garlic salt, and shrimp. In a small mixing bowl, combine the cream cheese with salt and pepper to taste. Spread each of the toasted bread slices with remaining butter, then with cream cheese mixture, and top with the pea mixture. Sprinkle each slice with 1/2 tablespoon of chopped dill, and serve. Serve as an appetizer.

Pea Soup with Prawns

(Illustrated opposite page)

2 1/4 pounds beef soup bones, rinsed
8 cups (2 liters) cold water
1 cup chopped celery with leaves
1 bunch parsley, rinsed
2 bay leaves
1 teaspoon white peppercorns
  Salt to taste
1 pound shelled peas (about 2 1/4 pounds with pods)
2 egg yolks
4 tablespoons cream
2-3 tablespoons chopped chervil leaves
1-2 tablespoons butter or margarine
4 shelled prawns

In a dutch oven, place the bones, and cover them with cold water. Bring to a boil, and skim off the foam. Add celery, parsley, bay leaves, and the peppercorns. Return the mixture to a boil, simmer for about an hour, or until there is about 1 quart of stock remaining. Salt to taste. Strain the mixture through a sieve or fine colander. Return to the dutch oven. Add the peas, bring to a boil, cover, and simmer for about 15 minutes. (This mixture may need to be pureed somewhat. Force it through a sieve or run it through a blender.) In a small mixing bowl, combine egg yolks and cream, and add slowly to the soup mixture, stirring constantly. Heat the mixture, but *do not boil*. When the mixture is thickened slightly, add chervil and salt to taste. Melt the butter in a small skillet, and sauté prawns about 2 to 3 minutes on all sides, until bright pink in color. Place one prawn each in warm soup bowls, and pour the pea soup over. Serve immediately with French bread slices and butter.

Pureed Pea Soup

(Illustrated opposite page)

1 tablespoon butter or margarine
2 slices lean bacon
1 onion, minced
3/4 pound shelled peas, rinsed
2-3 tablespoons chopped parsley
1 cup (250 ml) boiling water
  Salt and white pepper to taste
1 tablespoon butter or margarine
4 all-meat wieners
1 tablespoon butter or margarine

1 slice toasted bread, cubed

Melt the butter in a dutch oven, and add the bacon. Sauté until browned. Add onion, peas, parsley, and boiling water to the bacon. Stew for about 15 minutes. Remove the bacon and puree the peas. Measure the puree, and add enough water to have 3 cups. Return this to the dutch oven, and bring to a boil. Add the butter and the wieners. Heat the mixture thoroughly. Melt the butter in a small skillet, and sauté the bread cubes in butter until a golden yellow. Serve in soupbowls; garnish with the bread cubes.

Pea Soup with Light Dumplings

(Illustrated opposite page)

2 tablespoons margarine
1/2 pound (250 g) shelled peas (about 1 pound with pods), rinsed
4 cups (1 liter) chicken stock
  Light Dumplings (see recipe below)
  Chopped parsley

Melt the butter in a medium saucepan, add the peas, and braise. Add the stock, and bring to a boil. Simmer for about 7 minutes. Prepare the Light Dumplings. Drop by spoonfuls onto the surface of the soup. Bring the mixture to a boil; cover, and simmer for about 10 minutes, stirring occasionally. Sprinkle the soup with parsley, and serve immediately.

Light Dumplings

1/2 cup flour
1 teaspoon baking powder
1 tablespoon minced parsley
  Dash of salt
  Dash of nutmeg
1/3 cup milk
1 egg, beaten
2 tablespoons oil

In a medium bowl combine flour, baking powder, parsley, salt and nutmeg. In a small bowl combine milk, egg, and oil. Pour milk mixture over dry ingredients; stir until just moistened. Add to soup.

Fruit-bearing Vegetables, Fennel and Rhubarb

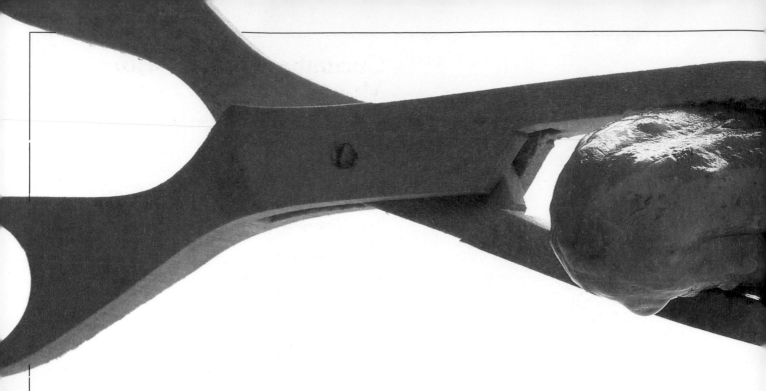

Pickled Gherkins

(Illustrated on pp. 190-191)

9 pounds small gherkins *or* cucumbers, rinsed
   Salt water (4 cups water to $1/4$ cup plus
   1 tablespoon *or* 75 g salt)
6-8 onions (about 375 g), peeled and sliced
2 $1/2$ ounces (75 g) horseradish root, cleaned and
   diced
3-4 fresh sweet red peppers, rinsed and patted dry
   Dill sprigs, rinsed and patted dry
3-4 sprigs tarragon, rinsed and patted dry
1-2 tablespoons mustard seeds
1 tablespoon peppercorns
5-6 bay leaves
   Vinegar-Sugar Bath (see recipe below)

Place the gherkins in a large kettle, and cover with
salt water. Cover the kettle, and set in a cool place
for 12 to 24 hours. Remove the gherkins, and drain.
Discard the salt water. Scrub the gherkins with a
soft vegetable brush, and pat dry. Cut away any bad
spots. Prepare the Vinegar-Sugar Bath; keep hot.
Prepare the jars and lids for canning as directed in
the Introduction. Combine all the ingredients except the Vinegar-Sugar Bath. Fill the jars firmly but
not so tightly that there is no room for the Vinegar-
Sugar Bath. Add enough bath to fill the jars, leaving 1 inch of headspace. Wipe rims clean with a
damp cloth. Place the lids on the jars, then screw
on the metal bands tightly. (Always follow the instructions that come with the lids and bands.) Process the jars in a boiling water bath for 5 minutes.
(See instructions for the water bath process in the
Introduction.) Remove the jars from the canner, and
set them out on a dry towel to cool. Do not cover
the jars; keep them in a draft-free area for 12 to 24
hours while they are cooling. Check the seals for
tightness; if any are not tight, use the product immediately, or reprocess the contents in a clean jar.
Store sealed jars in a cool, dark, dry place.

Vinegar-Sugar Bath

6 cups (1 $1/2$ liters) wine vinegar
6 cups (1 $1/2$ liters) water
1 $1/4$-1 $1/2$ cups (300-375 g) sugar

In a large saucepan, combine the vinegar, water and
sugar; bring to a boil. Remove from heat; keep hot
until ready to use.

Cucumbers in Curried Cream

(Illustrated opposite page)

2-3 cucumbers (about 4 pounds), rinsed, peeled, and
   halved
2 tablespoons butter *or* margarine
1 onion, minced
2 tablespoons lemon juice
1 teaspoon sugar
$1/2$ teaspoon grated lemon peel
   Salt and white pepper to taste
8 tablespoons cream
   Curry powder and lemon juice *or* white wine
   Lemon peel

Lemon mint leaves, rinsed and patted dry

Remove seeds from the cucumbers with a spoon, and cut the flesh into strips about ¹/₄ inch wide. In a large skillet, melt the margarine, and sauté onion until translucent. Add cucumber slices, lemon juice, and sugar; season to taste. Cover, and simmer for about 7 minutes. Stir in cream, and heat through. Season to taste with curry powder and lemon juice. Garnish with lemon peel and lemon mint leaves.

Cucumbers Pickled with Mustard

11 pounds large mature cucumbers, rinsed, peeled, and halved
³/₄ cup plus 4 teaspoons (200 g) salt
¹/₂ pound (250 g) pearl onions, peeled
¹/₂ piece small horseradish root, cleaned, peeled, and diced
10 pickling spice seeds
3 bay leaves
15-20 white and black peppercorns
3 ¹/₄ ounces (100 g) yellow mustard seeds
Vinegar-Sugar Solution (see recipe below)

Scoop out seeds from cucumber halves with a spoon, and cut the halves into finger-length strips. In a washed, dry earthenware or china crock, layer the cucumbers and the salt. Cover the crock, and place it in a cool place for 12 to 24 hours. Drain the slices, and dry them carefully. Prepare the Vinegar-Sugar Solution; keep hot until ready to use. Prepare the canning jars as instructed in the Introduction. Layer the slices with the onions, horseradish, and the seasonings in the jars. Pack the jars firmly. Pour Vinegar-Sugar Solution over the vegetables. Seal according to the instructions provided by the lid manufacturer. Process the jars in a boiling water bath for 5 minutes. Remove the jars, and set them on a dry towel in a draft-free area for 12 to 24 hours. Check for faulty seals; use unsealed products immediately, or reprocess in clean jars. Store in a cool, dark, dry place.

Vinegar-Sugar Solution

6 cups (1 ¹/₂ liters) white wine vinegar
4 cups (1 liter) water
2 ¹/₂ cups (600 g) sugar

In a large saucepan, combine the vinegar, water, and sugar. Bring to a boil, and remove from the heat. Keep hot until ready to use.

Cold Cucumber and Tomato Soup

(Illustrated above)

1 cucumber (about ³/₄ pound), rinsed, peeled, and halved
4 cups heavy cream
1 clove garlic, crushed
1 tablespoon chopped parsley
  Salt and pepper to taste
³/₄ pound fresh tomatoes, rinsed, halved, seeded, and diced

Scoop out seeds from cucumber halves with a spoon; dice the halves. Sprinkle with salt, and set aside for 5 minutes. Combine the cream, garlic, and parsley; season to taste. (If the mixture seems thick,

add a little milk.) Add the cucumber and tomatoes; cover and refrigerate for ¹/₂ hour before serving.

Stuffed Cucumber

1 cucumber (about 1 pound), rinsed, dried, and quartered
4 walnut halves
4 small sprigs dill, rinsed and patted dry
  Lettuce leaves, rinsed
4 small tomatoes, rinsed and cut in wedges
  Herb-Cream Filling (see recipe below)

Cut the ends off the cucumber quarters; scoop out the seeds with a spoon so that you have a shell that is about ¹/₄ inch thick. Discard seeds. Prepare the

192

Herb-Cream Filling. Attach a large star nozzle to a frosting bag, and fill with the herb mixture. Pipe mixture into the cucumber shells, finishing off each with a rosette. Garnish each with a walnut half and a small dill sprig, and place on lettuce leaves on individual serving dishes. Arrange tomato wedges around each, and serve with whole-wheat bread.

Herb-Cream Filling

6 ounces (150g) Boursin *or* cream cheese
1 heaping tablespoon sour cream
1 tablespoon chopped dill
1 tablespoon chopped tarragon leaves
1 tablespoon chopped lemon mint leaves
 Salt and pepper to taste

In a medium mixing bowl, combine the Boursin and sour cream until smooth. Stir in the dill, tarragon and lemon mint leaves. Season to taste, and fill cucumber shells.

Cold Cucumber Soup with Shrimp

1 cucumber (about 300g), rinsed, peeled, and halved
 lengthwise
3 6-ounce cartons (each 150 g) plain yogurt
1 6-ounce carton (150 g) sour cream
1/2 cup (125 ml) milk
6 1/2 ounces (200 g) shrimp, thawed, peeled
1 tablespoon chopped mint leaves *or* chopped
 tarragon leaves
1 teaspoon chopped dill
1 teaspoon chopped parsley
1-2 cloves garlic, diced
 Salt and pepper to taste
 Lettuce leaves, rinsed
1 hard-boiled egg, chopped
 Mint *or* dill sprigs, rinsed and patted dry

Scoop out the cucumber seeds with a spoon, and cut the halves into fine strips. Combine the yogurt, sour cream, and milk, mixing thoroughly. Add cucumber, shrimp, and herbs. Mix gently. Add garlic, and season to taste. Refrigerate for at least 4 hours. Line a glass bowl with lettuce leaves; fill with the soup. Garnish with egg and mint or dill

sprigs. Serve with whole-wheat bread and butter, or sliced white bread fried in butter.

Cucumber Cocktail
(Illustrated below)

2-3 cucumbers, rinsed and halved lengthwise
 Lemon juice to taste
 Salt, pepper, sugar, and celery salt to taste

Scoop out the cucumber seeds with a spoon, and dice the halves. Run diced pulp through a juicer, or liquify in a blender. Season the juice with lemon juice, salt, pepper, sugar, and celery salt. Chill until ready to serve. Serve sprinkled with pepper.

Zucchini with Meatballs

(Illustrated above)

   Mild Meatballs (see recipe below)
1-2 tablespoons butter *or* margarine
5-6 onions (about ¹/₂ pound), minced
1 ¹/₂ pounds (750 g) small zucchini, rinsed, dried, and cut into thin slices
   Salt and pepper to taste
5 sage leaves, rinsed, patted dry, and chopped coarsely
6 tablespoons white wine

Prepare the Mild Meatballs. In a large skillet melt the butter, and sauté the onions until translucent. Add the zucchini slices, and season to taste. Add the sage and wine. Cover and simmer for about 7 minutes, or until the zucchini slices are tender. Place the mixture on a serving platter, and arrange the meatballs on top. Serve immediately.

Mild Meatballs

3 slices white bread, crusts removed, and torn into small pieces
¹/₂ cup (125 ml) lukewarm water
1 onion, minced
¹/₂ pound ground beef
1 pound ground pork
1 egg
1 teaspoon mustard
   Salt and pepper to taste
1 tablespoon butter *or* margarine

Soak bread pieces in water and then squeeze. Combine the bread, onion, ground beef, ground pork, egg, and mustard; mix thoroughly. Season to taste. Form the mixture into meatballs about ¹/₂ inch in diameter. In a large skillet, melt the butter, and sauté the meatballs until they are golden brown. Set aside, and keep warm.

Roman Zucchini

(Illustrated above)

1 tablespoon vegetable oil
2 slices lean bacon, diced
1 onion, diced
1 clove garlic, diced
1 pound fresh tomatoes, peeled and diced
1 tablespoon chopped oregano leaves
   Salt and pepper to taste
1 pound (500 g) zucchinis, washed and halved
   lengthwise
   Salt to taste
   Zucchini Herb Topping

Preheat the oven to 375° F. In a large skillet, heat the vegetable oil, and sauté the bacon until brown. Add onion and garlic; sauté until the onion is translucent. Add tomatoes and oregano to the skillet, and season to taste. Cook until the sauce becomes fairly thick. Pour the sauce into a medium casserole. Prepare Zucchini Herb Topping. Arrange zucchini on top of tomato sauce, then spread topping over zucchini. Bake for 20 to 25 minutes.

Zucchini Herb Topping

2 tablespoons fine bread crumbs
2 tablespoons chopped parsley
1 tablespoon finely cut chives
1 tablespoon finely chopped dill
1/2 cup (40 g) grated Parmesan cheese
6 tablespoons cream

Combine all the ingredients, and mix to a spreading consistency.

Fennel and Fish Soup

(Illustrated below)

3-4 pounds fresh salmon, turbot *or* other large fish,
  cleaned and bones reserved
2 teaspoons salt
8 cups (2 liters) water
  Juice of 1 lemon
4 tablespoons olive oil
4-5 fennel tubers, trimmed, rinsed, and cut into
  eighths (reserve the greens, which should be rinsed
  and patted dry)
4 onions (about 200 g), diced
1/2 cup chopped parsley
1 clove garlic, minced or crushed
1/2 cup (100 g) uncooked long grain rice
1 teaspoon sweet pickle relish
2 bay leaves
1/2 pound (250 g) tomatoes, peeled, seeded, and
  diced
2 tablespoons chopped parsley

Rinse the fish, and fillet it carefully. Set aside. In a large saucepan, place the water, salt and fish bones; bring to a boil, and simmer for 10 to 15 minutes. Rinse the fillets, and pat dry. Cut them into 1 to 2-inch pieces. Sprinkle lemon juice over fish, and let the pieces stand while the bones are cooking. Strain the cooking liquid through a fine sieve, collecting the broth. Discard the bones. Heat the olive oil in a large skillet, and add fennel, onions, parsley, garlic, and rice. Sauté until onions are translucent, stirring constantly. Transfer the mixture to saucepan. Add the fish stock, pickle relish, and bay leaves. Cover and simmer for about 20 minutes. Skim off the foam. Add fish pieces and tomatoes to soup. Heat, uncovered, for 8 to 10 minutes, but *do not* allow the soup to boil. Chop the fennel greens, and add them and the chopped parsley to the soup. Serve immediately.

Stuffed Fennel

1 teaspoon salt
4 large fennel tubers (about 3 1/3 pounds), trimmed, rinsed, and halved lengthwise (reserve the greens)
6 ounces (150 g) sour cream
1 6-ounce carton (150 g) plain yogurt
Fennel greens, rinsed, patted dry, and minced

Salt, pepper, and sweet paprika to taste
Stuffed Fennel Topping (see recipe below)
8 strips lean bacon (about 160 g), halved

Preheat the oven to 325° F. Fill a large saucepan half full with water, add the salt, and bring it to a boil. Add the fennel halves, return to a boil, cover, and simmer for about 7 minutes. Drain, and set aside. Combine the sour cream and yogurt, stirring until smooth. Add the fennel greens, and season to taste. Place the mixture in a medium casserole. Prepare the Stuffed Fennel Topping. Spread it over the cut face of the fennel halves. Set the halves on top of the sour cream mixture. Lay 2 pieces of bacon on top of each fennel half in a cross pattern. Bake about 45 minutes, or until the fennel is fork-tender. Serve Stuffed Fennel with rice.

Stuffed Fennel Topping

4 ounces (125 g) Swiss Emmanthaler cheese, diced
12 ounces (375 g) ground sausage
1 egg
Salt and pepper to taste

Combine the cheese, sausage, and egg. Season to taste.

Fennel Puree

3 tablespoons (40 g) butter *or* margarine
2 large or 4 small fennel tubers, trimmed, rinsed, and minced
Salt and pepper to taste
6 ounces (150 g) sour cream
Fennel greens, rinsed, patted dry, and minced

Melt the butter in a large skillet, and sauté the minced fennel for 1 or 2 minutes. Season it to taste, cover, and simmer for about 5 minutes, stirring occasionally. Stir in the sour cream and heat, uncovered, until just warmed. Season to taste. Add the fennel greens, and serve immediately. Serve with lamb cutlets or with rump steak.

Marinated Eggplant Slices

(Illustrated below)

1 teaspoon salt
4 small eggplants (about 1 pound), trimmed and
  rinsed
2-3 cloves garlic, crushed
  Salt
  Coarse cayenne pepper
  Juice of 1 lemon
  Lemon juice
3 tablespoons olive oil
1 6-ounce carton (150 g) plain yogurt
  Small tomato slices, optional
  Basil leaves, optional

Fill a medium saucepan half full with water, add
salt, and bring to a boil. Add the eggplants return
to a boil, and simmer for about 10 minutes. Drain,
and slice lengthwise. Spread the garlic over eggplant
slices, and sprinkle with salt, cayenne, lemon juice,
and olive oil. Marinate for at least 2 hours. If necessary, sprinkle a second time with lemon juice. Stir
the yogurt, and serve with eggplant slices. If desired, garnish with tomato slices and basil leaves.

Delicate Stuffed Eggplant

4-5 medium-sized eggplants, trimmed and rinsed and
  patted dry
  Salt and pepper to taste
  Seafood Filling
4 tablespoons grated Parmesan cheese
1-2 tablespoons butter _or_ margarine
  Tangy Tomato Sauce

Preheat the oven to 350° F. Dry the eggplants, and
halve them lengthwise. Sprinkle the cut surfaces
with salt and pepper. Lay them on a baking tray,
cut side up, and bake for about 15 minutes, or until
fork-tender. Remove the pulp leaving the shells
intact, about 1/4-inch thick. Prepare the Seafood
Filling using the baked pulp, and fill the eggplant
shells. Sprinkle each with grated cheese, and dot
with butter. Bake for about 10 minutes, or until
cheese is slightly browned. Prepare the Tangy
Tomato Sauce. Serve eggplant with the sauce as a
side dish. Serve Delicate Stuffed Eggplant with
French bread, garlic butter, and a fresh green salad.

Seafood Filling

1 tablespoon butter *or* margarine
2 lean slices bacon, diced
1 onion, diced
8 fish fillets, washed and cut into strips
1/2 pound shrimp, peeled
  Eggplant pulp
8 medium tomatoes, peeled and diced
1 clove garlic, crushed
2 tablespoons chopped parsley
1 tablespoon chopped thyme
  Salt and pepper to taste

In a large skillet, melt butter, and sauté bacon for about 2 minutes. Add the onion, and sauté until translucent. Add the fish and shrimp; sauté over a high heat, stirring constantly. Add eggplant, tomatoes, garlic, parsley, and thyme; season to taste. Heat through, but do not cook, stirring constantly. Fill the eggplant shells.

Tangy Tomato Sauce

1 cup (250 ml) all-vegetable juice
1-2 tablespoons tomato catsup
  Salt, pepper, sweet paprika, and sugar to taste
1 tablespoon flour
4 tablespoons cream
1-2 tablespoons brandy
1 tablespoon chopped thyme leaves

In a small saucepan, heat the vegetable juice. Add catsup, and season to taste. In a small mixing bowl, combine flour and cream; carefully blend with catsup mixture, stirring constantly. Stir in brandy, and heat through. Serve sprinkled with thyme leaves.

Grilled Pumpkin

(Illustrated opposite page)

6 1/2 tablespoons (100 g) soft butter *or* margarine
1 teaspoon mixed herbs
   Salt and pepper to taste
2 1/4 pounds fresh pumpkin, peeled, cleaned, and cut into slivers
   Lemon juice

Preheat the oven to 350° F. Combine the butter and herbs; season to taste. Arrange the pumpkin slivers on a baking tray, spread with a little herb butter, and bake for about 30 minutes, or until fork-tender. Baste the slivers with the butter as needed during baking. Before serving, season to taste, and sprinkle with lemon juice. Serve with fish fillets.

Pumpkin Vegetable Dish

(Illustrated opposite page)

3 tablespoons butter *or* margarine
2 1/4 pounds fresh pumpkin, peeled, cleaned, and cut into sticks
1/2 cup (125 ml) meat stock
   Salt, pepper, sugar, and vinegar to taste
2 tablespoons finely chopped dill
2 tablespoons finely chopped parsley

In a large skillet, melt the butter, and braise the pumpkin sticks. Add the meat stock, bring to a boil, and simmer for about 8 minutes, or until fork-tender. Season to taste. Stir in dill and parsley. Serve immediately. Serve with pan-fried liver and rice.

Pumpkin Stew

(Illustrated opposite page)

5 cups (1 1/4 liters) water
1 teaspoon salt
1 pound (500 g) stewing beef
1/2 cup chopped celery
3 tablespoons vegetable oil
3 onions, sliced
2 1/4 pounds fresh pumpkin, cubed
1 pound (500 g) fresh tomatoes, peeled, halved, and seeded
2 tablespoons chopped basil leaves
   Salt and pepper to taste
   Vinegar to taste

Combine the water and salt in a medium saucepan, bring to a boil, and add the beef and celery. Return to a boil, cover, and simmer for about 1 hour, skimming away any foam as needed. Remove meat with a slotted spoon; dice. Strain the liquid, saving 1 quart, and discarding the celery. In a dutch oven, heat the oil, add onions, and sauté until translucent. Add the pumpkin; braise for about 5 minutes. Add the tomatoes, the measured stock, the beef, and the basil to the soup. Simmer for about 5 minutes. Season to taste. Add vinegar as desired. Serve immediately.

Pumpkin Soup

(Illustrated opposite page)

3 tablespoons butter *or* margarine
2 1/4 pounds fresh pumpkin, peeled, cleaned, and diced
1 cup (250 ml) meat stock
   Salt, pepper, sugar, and vinegar to taste
1 pound Polish sausage, sliced
1 tablespoon minced chives
1 tablespoon chopped parsley

In a large saucepan, melt the butter, and braise the pumpkin for about 5 minutes. Add the stock, and bring to a boil. Cover, and simmer for about 10 minutes, or until fork-tender. Remove half of the mixture, puree in a blender, and return to the saucepan. Season to taste. Add the sausage, and heat through. Ladle into individual serving bowls, and sprinkle with chives and parsley before serving.

Stuffed Sweet Peppers

(Illustrated this page)

7 large sweet peppers (about 3 1/2 pounds), rinsed,
    hollowed out, tops reserved
    Salt and pepper to taste
    Meaty Tomato Filling (see recipe below)
    Butter *or* margarine
    Tomato Sauce (see recipe below)

Preheat the oven to 350° F. Season peppers inside
with salt and pepper. Set aside. Prepare the Meaty
Tomato Filling. Stuff the peppers, and dot the mixture with butter. Replace the tops. Set them aside.
Prepare the Tomato Sauce and place in baking dish;
set peppers in sauce. Cover the casserole and bake
for 55 minutes or until fork-tender.

Meaty Tomato Filling

2-3 slices boiled ham, diced
1 1/2 pounds (750 g) boneless chicken breast, minced
    or ground, *or* 3/4 pound ground beef and 3/4
    pound ground pork
3 large fresh tomatoes, peeled, seeded, and diced,
    reserving seeds and juices
2 eggs
4 tablespoons chopped parsley
    Salt, pepper, cayenne pepper, and Worcestershire
    sauce to taste

In a large mixing bowl, combine all the ingredients
well. Fill the peppers with the mixture.

Tomato Sauce

1 pound (500 g) fresh tomatoes, peeled, seeded, and
    diced
2 tablespoons tomato paste
1 cup (250 ml) cream
    Salt, pepper, sweet paprika, and lemon juice to
    taste

Combine the reserved seeds and juices from the
Meaty Tomato Filling with the tomatoes. Puree in a
blender. Combine with tomato paste and cream.
Season to taste.

Sweet Pepper and Cream Soup

2-3 tablespoons vegetable oil
4 onions (about 200 g), minced
3-4 sweet peppers, rinsed, seeded, and cut into strips
6 1/2 ounces (200 g) sauerkraut
4 cups (1 liter), heated meat stock
    Salt to taste
3-4 tablespoons white wine
1/2 cup (125 ml) cream

In a large skillet, heat the oil, add onions, and sauté until translucent. Add the sweet peppers and sauerkraut, and heat through. Add the meat stock, bring to a boil, and simmer for about 20 minutes. Season to taste. Add wine; stir in cream. Heat through, and serve immediately.

Sweet Pepper Salad

3-4 sweet peppers, rinsed, seeded, and cut into strips
1-2 onions, sliced
   Tarragon Dressing

Prepare the vegetables and the Tarragon Dressing. Toss, then marinate for about $1/2$ hour. If necessary, season with additional salt and pepper.

Tarragon Dressing

3 tablespoons salad oil
2-3 tablespoons herb vinegar
   Salt, pepper, and sugar to taste
1 tablespoon chopped tarragon leaves

In a small mixing bowl, combine the ingredients.

Colorful Vegetable Salad

(Illustrated below)

2 teaspoons salt, divided
3 large ears of sweet corn (about 2 1/4 pounds),
   cleaned and rinsed
6 1/2 ounces (200 g) shelled peas, rinsed
Herb and Onion Dressing
1 red sweet pepper, rinsed, seeded, and diced
2 tablespoons salad oil

Fill a medium saucepan half full with water, add 1 teaspoon salt, and bring to a boil. Add the ears of corn, return to a boil, and simmer for about 10 minutes. With a sharp paring knife, remove the kernels from the ears, and set them aside to cool. Fill a medium saucepan half full with water, add 1 teaspoon salt, and bring to a boil. Add the peas, return to a boil, cover, and simmer for about 10 minutes. Drain, and set aside to cool. Prepare the Herb and Onion Dressing. Once the vegetables are cooled, combine them with red sweet pepper and Herb and Onion Dressing. Stir in the salad oil. Refrigerate, and marinate for at least 1 hour before serving.

Herb and Onion Dressing

1 onion, diced
1 cup (250 ml) water
7 tablespoons vinegar
2 teaspoons salt

3 tablespoons sugar
   Pepper and onion powder to taste
3 tablespoons chopped herbs (parsley, chives, dill)

Combine all the ingredients well. Mix with the cooled vegetables.

Delicate Corn Soup

(Illustrated opposite page)

1 teaspoon salt
3 large ears of sweet corn (about 2 1/4 pounds),
   cleaned and rinsed
3 cups (750 ml) chicken stock
1 tablespoon cornstarch dissolved in 2 tablespoons
   cold water
   Salt, pepper, and onion salt to taste
2 egg yolks
1/2 cup (125 ml) cream
1 tablespoon minced chives

Fill a medium saucepan half full with water, add salt, and bring to a boil. Add the ears of corn, return to a boil, and simmer for about 10 minutes. Drain the ears, and remove the kernels with a sharp paring knife. Set aside 2 tablespoons of kernels, and puree the rest by rubbing through a sieve or running through a blender. Return the puree to the saucepan, add stock, and bring to a boil. Slowly add cornstarch mixture, stirring constantly. Add the remaining corn kernels, and heat through. Season to taste. In a small mixing bowl, combine egg yolks and cream; add slowly to the soup, stirring constantly. Serve in individual soup bowls, garnished with chives.

Sweet Corn and Tomato Souffle

1 teaspoon salt
3 large ears of sweet corn (about 2 1/4 pounds),
   cleaned and rinsed
2 beefsteak tomatoes (about 1 pound), peeled and
   sliced
   Salt and pepper to taste
   Minced marjoram leaves
   Minced basil leaves
6 eggs
1/2 cup (125 ml) milk
   Sweet paprika
1/4 pound (125 g) pepperoni slices

Preheat the oven to 350° F. Fill a medium saucepan half full with water, add salt, and bring to a boil. Add the ears of corn, return to a boil, and simmer for 10 minutes. Drain, and remove the kernels with a sharp knife. Set aside 1 cup of kernels. Grease a medium casserole, and line the bottom with the tomato slices. Season to taste. Sprinkle with marjoram and basil, and cover with the corn kernels. In a large mixing bowl, combine the eggs, milk and paprika. Season to taste. Pour the egg mixture into the casserole, and top with the pepperoni slices. Bake for about 45 minutes, or until a knife inserted near the center comes out clean. Serve immediately.

Canned Rhubarb

(Illustrated this page)

5 pounds of rhubarb, rinsed, trimmed, and cut into
    1-1 $1/2$ inch pieces
    Sugar

Place rhubarb in a large kettle, and add sugar. Mix together thoroughly, and let sit for at least $1/2$ hour to draw out juice. Prepare the jars for processing as instructed in the Introduction. Heat rhubarb mixture, and bring to a boil. Pack the jars so that there is $1/2$ inch of headspace. Wipe the rims clean with a damp cloth. Apply the lids according to the manufacturer's instructions. Process the jars in a boiling water bath (see instructions in the Introduction) for 10 minutes. Remove the jars from the processor, and set out on a dry towel in a draft-free location. Cool for 12 to 24 hours. Check the seals; use any unsealed product immediately, or reprocess in clean jars. Store in a cool, dark, dry place. Makes 4 quarts.

Rhubarb Juice

(Illustrated this page)

11 pounds (5 kg) rhubarb, rinsed, and cut into small
    pieces
4 cups (1 liter) water
9 cups (2 kg) sugar
1 packet citric acid preservative, optional

Prepare the jars for processing as instructed in the Introduction. Combine rhubarb with the water in a dutch oven, and bring to a boil. Cover and simmer for about 5 minutes. Drain the puree through a jelly bag or several layers of cheesecloth. Once the puree is cool, squeeze the bag to remove all the juice you can. Weigh or measure the juice. For 2 $1/4$ pounds or 1 quart juice, use 1 $3/4$ to 2 $1/4$ cups sugar; bring to a boil. Skim off the foam. Return the juice to the dutch oven, add the preservative to the juice, if desired. Pour the juice into the jars, leaving $1/2$ inch headspace. Wipe the rims clean with a damp cloth. Apply the lids according to the manufacturer's instructions. Process the jars in a boiling water bath (see instructions in the Introduction) for 10 minutes. Remove the jars from the processor, and set out on a dry towel in a draft-free location. Cool for 12 to 24 hours. Check the seals; use any unsealed product immediately, or reprocess in clean dry jars. Store in a cool, dark, dry place.

Rhubarb Jelly

(Illustrated this page)

2 $1/2$ pounds (1250 g) rhubarb (weighed after preparing), rinsed, trimmed and cut into very small piece
1 $1/2$ cups (375 ml) water
3 $1/3$ cups rhubarb juice
1 packet pectin
4 $1/8$ cups (1000 g) sugar

actly 30 seconds, stirring constantly. Remove from the heat. For filling the jars and storing the jelly see the Introduction.

Rhubarb Soufflé

1 pound (500 g) rhubarb, trimmed, rinsed, and cut into 1-inch pieces
$^1/_2$ cup (125 g) sugar
2 tablespoons raspberry syrup
4 ounces (125 g) Holland rusks (about 10 pieces)
3 egg yolks
$^1/_2$ cup (125 ml) cream
1 teaspoon vanilla
$^1/_4$ cup (50 g) finely chopped hazelnuts
3 egg whites
$^1/_4$ cup less 2 teaspoons (50 g) sugar

Preheat the oven to 325° F. If necessary, halve any especially thick pieces of rhubarb. In a large mixing bowl, combine rhubarb with the sugar and raspberry syrup and set aside for about 20 minutes, to draw out the juice. Place the rhubarb mixture into a large dutch oven, and bring to a boil. Simmer until soft, but not falling apart. Set aside. Line a greased soufflé dish with the rusks. Combine thoroughly egg yolks, cream, hazelnuts, vanilla and rhubarb; pour over the rusks. Whip the egg whites and sugar until they form stiff peaks. Spread over the rhubarb mixture, sculpting the top in peaks and swirls. Bake for about 25 minutes, or until a knife inserted in the center comes out clean.

Combine rhubarb with the water in a large kettle, and heat, while stirring, until almost boiling. Cover, and simmer for about 5 minutes, to free the juice. Strain the puree through a juice bag or several layers of cheesecloth. When the puree has cooled, squeeze the bag to remove all the juice. Measure the juice, and put 3 $^1/_3$ cups into a dutch oven or a kettle. (If necessary, add water to equal 3 $^1/_3$ cups.) Sprinkle the pectin over the surface. With the heat set on high, bring the juice to a boil quickly, stirring constantly to dissolve the pectin. (Should any lumps form, crush them against the side of the kettle with your spoon.) As soon as the juice boils, without lowering the heat, add all of the sugar. (Do not use any less than the amount called for.) Bring the mixture back to a rolling boil, and boil for *ex-*

Tomatoes
Slices of summer sun

Tomato and Tuna Fish Salad

1 pound (500 g) tomatoes, rinsed, dried, and sliced
2 large red onions, sliced and separated into rings
1 6 ¹/₂-ounce can oil-packed tuna, drained and
   flaked
   Wine Vinegar Dressing (see recipe below)
2 tablespoons chopped parsley

Gently toss the salad ingredients. Prepare the Wine
Vinegar Dressing. Combine the dressing and salad
mixture; refrigerate for 20 minutes. Sprinkle with
parsley, and serve.

Wine Vinegar Dressing

2 tablespoons salad oil
1 tablespoon red wine vinegar *or* herb vinegar
   Salt, pepper, and sugar to taste

Combine all the ingredients. Fold into the salad.

Tomato Salad

   Chive Dressing (see recipe below)
1 ¹/₂ pounds (750 g) tomatoes, rinsed, dried, and
   sliced
2 tablespoons basil leaves

Prepare the Chive Dressing. Pour the dressing over
the tomato slices, sprinkle with basil, and serve.

Chive Dressing

1-2 onions, minced
4-5 tablespoons vegetable oil
1 teaspoon white vinegar
4 teaspoons water
   Salt, pepper, and sugar to taste
2 tablespoons finely chopped chives

Mix the onions, oil, vinegar, water, and seasonings.
Stir in the chives. Pour over the tomato slices.

Geronese Tomato Bowl

(Illustrated above)

1 pound (500 g) tomatoes, rinsed and sliced
2 large onions, sliced
  Geronese Salad Dressing
4 slices lean bacon, diced
2-3 tablespoons chopped basil leaves
  Chopped egg white, reserved

Arrange the tomato and onion slices in a shallow serving bowl. Prepare the Geronese Salad Dressing, and pour it over the tomato mixture. In a small skillet, sauté the bacon until crisp and brown. Garnish the salad with bacon, basil and reserved chopped egg white.

Geronese Salad Dressing

1 hard-boiled egg
3 tablespoons vegetable oil
2 tablespoons vinegar
$1/2$ teaspoon mustard
Salt, pepper, and sugar to taste
2 cloves garlic, minced

Separate the egg white and yolk. Chop the white, and reserve. Rub the yolk through a sieve, and set aside. Combine the oil, vinegar, mustard, and seasonings. Add the yolk and the garlic. Mix thoroughly.

Tomatoes and Braised Beef

Herb-Wine Marinade
3 1/4 pounds chuck roast or bottom round, rinsed
    and patted dry
3 cloves garlic, crushed
    Salt and pepper to taste
1 teaspoon thyme leaves
3 tablespoons olive oil
1 stalk celery (about 150 g), diced
1/2 pound (250 g) carrots, peeled and diced
8 small onions, peeled
1-1 1/2 pound (500-750 g) tomatoes, peeled and
    diced
    Salt, pepper, and sugar to taste

Prepare Herb-Wine Marinade. Place the beef in a
large mixing bowl, and pour the marinade over it.
Cover and refrigerate for 12 to 24 hours. Preheat
the oven to 350° F. Remove meat from the
marinade, and pat dry. Remove the herbs from the
marinade, and discard. Set aside marinade,
including its vegetables. Rub the meat with the
garlic; add seasonings and thyme. Heat the olive oil
in a dutch oven, and braise the meat on all sides,
stirring constantly. Add celery, carrots, and onions
to the meat, and braise them. Add the marinated
vegetables, and half of the marinade. Cover the
dutch oven, and roast for 1 1/2 hours. Add the
remaining marinade; roast for another 45 minutes,

uncovered. Put the dutch oven back on top of the
stove, add tomatoes, cover, and simmer for another
10 to 15 minutes. Place meat on a warm platter, and
slice. Season vegetable sauce to taste with salt,
pepper and sugar. Serve separately.

Herb-Wine Marinade

4 tablespoons olive oil
2 onions, diced
2 cloves garlic, diced
1 piece celery, peeled and diced
1 carrot, peeled and diced
1 sprig thyme
1 sprig rosemary
1 sprig marjoram
1 sprig parsley
1 1/2 cups (375 ml) red wine

In a medium skillet, heat the oil, and sauté the
onions, garlic, celery, and carrot. Add the herbs and
wine. Bring to a boil, cover, and simmer for about
5 minutes; then cool. Pour over the meat.

Chili Tomatoes

Chili Salad Dressing (see recipe below)
1 pound (500 g) fresh tomatoes, peeled, seeded and sliced
Salt to taste
2 onions, minced
1 bunch spring onions, rinsed, trimmed to 6 inches of green, and cut into rings

Prepare the Chili Salad Dressing at least 12 hours in advance. Season the tomato slices to taste. Toss the tomatoes and all the onions in a medium salad bowl; pour the dressing over the mixture. Refrigerate for at least ¹/₂ hour before serving.

Chili Salad Dressing

4 tablespoons vegetable oil
1 tablespoon wine vinegar
8 chili peppers, rinsed, seeded, and chopped

Combine all the ingredients in a blender, and mix on high for 1 minute. Cover, and refrigerate at least 12 hours before using.

Tomato-Pasta Souffle

(Illustrated above)

6 cups (1 ¹/₂ liters) water
1 teaspoon salt
6 ¹/₂ ounces (200 g) noodles
1 ¹/₂ pound (750 g) tomatoes, peeled and sliced
5 ounces (150 g) ham, diced
3 eggs
¹/₂ cup (125 ml) milk
2 tablespoons chopped parsley
2 tablespoons finely cut chives
Salt and pepper to taste
2 tablespoons grated Parmesan cheese
2 tablespoons fine bread crumbs

Preheat the oven to 325° F. Fill a medium saucepan with the water, add salt, and bring to a boil. Add the noodles, return to a boil, cover, and simmer for about 8 minutes. Rinse with cold water, and allow to drain. Grease a soufflé dish, and layer in the tomatoes, noodles and ham. Combine the eggs and the milk. Add the parsley and chives, and season to taste. Pour the egg mixture over the noodles. Combine the Parmesan and the bread crumbs; sprinkle over the noodles. Bake for about 35 minutes, or until just lightly browned. If necessary, cover the soufflé with aluminum foil towards the end of the baking time.

Classic Tomato Sauce
(Illustrated this page)

1 tablespoon vegetable oil
4 slices lean bacon, diced
1 onion, diced
2 ¼ pounds (1 kg) plum tomatoes, rinsed and cubed
  Salt and pepper to taste
3 sprigs marjoram, rinsed and patted dry
2 sprigs basil, rinsed and patted dry
2 ¼ ounces (70 g) tomato paste
  Salt, pepper, and sugar

In a dutch oven, heat oil. Add the bacon and onion; sauté until the onion is translucent. Add the tomatoes and herbs, and season to taste. Cover, and simmer for about 15 minutes. Rub the mixture through a sieve. Add the tomato paste; season to taste and serve.

Meaty Tomato Sauce

(Illustrated this page)

2 tablespoons vegetable oil
1/2 pound ground beef
1/4 pound ground pork
2-3 medium onions, diced
    Salt, pepper, and sweet paprika
1 tablespoon tomato paste
1 3/4 to 2 1/4 pounds fresh tomatoes, peeled and
    diced
1 sprig thyme, rinsed and patted dry
1 sprig basil, rinsed and patted dry
1 sprig marjoram, rinsed and patted dry
4-6 tablespoons red wine
2 tablespoons flour mixed with 1 tablespoon water,
    optional

In a large skillet, heat the oil. Add ground beef and
pork, and sauté until the meat loses its redness.
Add onions, and sauté until translucent. Season to
taste. Add the tomato paste, tomatoes, herbs, and
wine. Cover and simmer for 15 minutes. Remove
the herbs. Season to taste once more. If desired, stir
in the flour mixture to thicken the sauce. Cover,
and simmer for about 5 minutes. Serve immediately.
Serve with noodles, macaroni, or spaghetti, along
with Parmesan cheese and a fresh green salad.

Tomato and Onion Sauce

(Illustrated this page)

3 tablespoons vegetable oil
4-5 onions, peeled and sliced
2 garlic cloves, peeled and sliced
1 pound (500 g) tomatoes, peeled and diced
4 tablespoons red wine
2 1/4 ounces (70 g) tomato paste
1 tablespoon chopped marjoram leaves
1 tablespoon finely cut chives
    Salt and pepper

In a large skillet, heat the oil. Add the onions and
garlic, and sauté until the onions are translucent.
Add the tomatoes, wine, tomato paste, and herbs.
Season to taste. Stir well, and simmer for about 10-
15 minutes. Serve with steamed fish and rice.

Tomato Pizza

    Basic pizza crust mix for one crust
1 tablespoon chopped marjoram leaves
1 tablespoon chopped basil leaves
1 tablespoon olive oil
1 pound (500 g) tomatoes, rinsed and sliced
    Pepper
2 1/2 ounces (75 g) pepperoni slices
1/4-1/2 pound (150-200 g) Gouda cheese, grated
    coarsely

Preheat the oven to 375° F. Prepare the pizza crust
as the package directs. Spread half of the herbs on
the pastry, and lay the tomato slices on top of
herbs. Top tomatoes with the pepperoni slices.
Sprinkle the cheese, remaining herbs, and the oil
over the top. Bake for about 20 minutes, or until
the cheese is lightly browned.

T-Bone Steaks in a Tomato and Red Wine Marinade

(Illustrated this page)

Tomato and Red Wine Marinade (see recipe below)
8 T-bone steaks, each weighing about ³/₄ pound

Prepare the Tomato and Red Wine Marinade. In a dutch oven or other large kettle, place the steaks, pour the marinade over them, and marinate for 24 hours, turning occasionally. Drain the steaks, reserving the marinade. Pat the steaks dry, and grill for 10 to 15 minutes, or until they reach the desired state of doneness. Baste the steaks with the marinade occasionally as they cook.

Tomato and Red Wine Marinade

¹/₂ pound (250 g) tomatoes, peeled, seeded, and chopped
6 tablespoons olive oil
6 tablespoons red wine vinegar
¹/₂ cup (125 ml) red wine
2 tablespoons sweet pickle relish
3 onions (about 125 g), peeled and diced
2-3 cloves garlic, minced
2-3 bay leaves

In a blender or food processor, combine tomatoes, oil, vinegar, wine, and relish. Puree the mixture. Add onions, garlic, and bay leaves. Pour over steaks.

Pickled Tomatoes

4 ¹/₂ pounds small, ripe, firm tomatoes, rinsed and patted dry
Pickling Solution

Prepare the jars for processing as instructed in the Introduction. Prepare the Pickling Solution. Prick each tomato 15 to 20 times with a toothpick, and place in carefully washed canning jars. Add the simmering Pickling Solution; leave a 1-inch headspace. Wipe the rims clean with a damp cloth. Apply the lids according to the manfacturer's instructions. Process the jars in a boiling water bath. Remove the jars from the processor, and set out on a dry towel in a draft-free location for 12 to

24 hours. Check the seals; use any unsealed product immediately, or reprocess in clean dry jars. Store in a cool, dark, dry place.

Pickling Solution

4 cups (1 liter) wine vinegar
1 cup (250 ml) water
1 tablespoon plus 1 teaspoon (20 g) salt
1 tablespoon plus 1 teaspoon (20 g) sugar
2 cloves
3 tablespoons (20 g) peppercorns
3 tablespoons (20 g) mustard seeds
4 shallots *or* small onions, peeled and diced
In a medium saucepan, combine all ingredients.
    Bring to a boil, and remove from heat; keep hot
    until ready to use.

Green Tomato Preserve

1 ³/₄ pound (900 g) prepared green tomatoes, rinsed,
    dried, and either minced or ground coarsely
1 packet pectin
1 teaspoon vanilla extract
    Grated rind of 1 lemon
    Pinch of ground ginger *or* cinnamon
4 ¹/₂ cups plus 3 tablespoons (1125 g) sugar
2-3 tablespoons lemon juice

In a kettle, combine the tomatoes, pectin, vanilla, lemon rind, and the ginger. Turn the heat to high, and bring to a rolling boil, stirring constantly. Add the sugar (measure *exactly*), and return to a boil, stirring constantly. As soon as the boil is rolling, continue boiling 1 minute. Remove the mixture from the heat; stir in the lemon juice. Prepare the jars for processing as instructed in the Introduction. Pack the jars so that there is a 1-inch headspace. Wipe the rims clean with a damp cloth. Apply the lids according to the manufacturer's instructions. Process the jars for 10 minutes in a boiling water bath (see instructions in the Introduction). Remove the jars from the processor, and set out on a dry towel in a draft-free location for 12 to 24 hours. Check the seals; use any unsealed product immediately, or reprocess in clean, dry jars. Store in a cool, dark, dry place.

Baked Tomatoes Stuffed with Cheese

(Illustrated this page)

8 large tomatoes, hollowed out, tops reserved
1/2 cup (125 ml) milk
3 1/2 ounces (100 g) bleu cheese, crumbled
2 teaspoons cornstarch, dissolved in 1 teaspoon water
2 egg yolks, beaten until light yellow
2 egg whites, whipped into stiff peaks
  Salt and pepper to taste
1 tablespoon chopped tarragon leaves

Preheat the oven to 375° F. Set the tomatoes upside down on paper towels to drain. In a medium saucepan, heat the milk over a low heat. Stir in the bleu cheese, and continue stirring until the cheese melts. Add the cornstarch mixture, stirring constantly, and continue cooking until the mixture thickens. Remove the pan from the heat, and allow to cool for 5 minutes. Slowly stir some of the milk mixture into the egg yolks, then add the egg yolk mixture to the milk mixture. Season to taste. Add the tarragon leaves. Fill the tomatoes, cover with whipped egg whites and set the tops in place. Place the tomatoes in a greased casserole, and bake for about 15 minutes.

Baked Tomatoes with Mushroom-Ham Filling

(Illustrated this page)

4 medium tomatoes, hollowed out
  Mushroom-Ham Filling (see recipe below)
  Salt and pepper to taste
  Butter or margarine
  Chopped chives

Preheat the broiler. Prepare the Mushroom-Ham Filling. Sprinkle the tomato cavities with salt and pepper; then add the filling. Dot the tomato openings with butter; broil for about 15 minutes. Garnish with chives, and serve immediately.

Mushroom-Ham Filling

3/8 pound (150 g) fresh mushrooms, cleaned, and diced
  Juice of 1 lemon
2 tablespoons white wine

1 teaspoon butter *or* margarine
3 tablespoons cream
2 slices boiled ham, diced

Sprinkle the mushrooms with lemon juice. In a small skillet, heat the wine, add the mushrooms, and braise over a low heat, 5 to 8 minutes, or until tender. Allow them to cool for 5 minutes. Add butter and rewarm mushrooms over a low heat. Stir in the cream, and continue to heat until the cream thickens. Add the ham, and season to taste. Remove from heat, and fill the tomatoes with the mushroom mixture.

Baked Tomatoes with Spiced Bratwurst Filling

4 tomatoes, rinsed, dried, and halved horizontally
   Salt and pepper to taste
3 tablespoons vegetable oil
4 tablespoons fine bread crumbs
   Spiced Bratwurst Filling (see recipe below)
4 tablespoons fine bread crumbs

Preheat the oven to 375° F. Sprinkle the cut surfaces of the tomato halves with salt and pepper. Heat 3 tablespoons oil in a small skillet; place tomatoes cut side down. Saute for 5 minutes over low to medium heat. Prepare Spiced Bratwurst filling. In an ovenproof dish, divide the mixture between the 8 tomato halves, cut side up, and baste with some of the oil. Sprinkle the tops with the bread crumbs, and baste with remaining oil. Bake the dish for about 15 minutes.

Spiced Bratwurst Filling

1/4 pound Bratwurst, casing removed
1 small onion, diced
1 clove garlic, diced
2 hard-boiled eggs, diced
2 tablespoons chopped parsley
   Salt and pepper to taste

In a medium mixing bowl, combine the bratwurst meat, onion, garlic, eggs, and parsley. Season to taste.

Tomato Soup

(Illustrated this page)

1 tablespoon vegetable oil
6 slices lean bacon, diced
1 onion, diced
1 clove garlic, diced
2 1/4 pounds (1 kg) ripe tomatoes, rinsed, dried, and
   diced
   Salt and pepper to taste
1 tablespoon chopped marjoram leaves
1 tablespoon chopped basil leaves
2 cups (500 ml) water
1 egg yolk, mixed with 1 heaping teaspoon cornstarch
   and 1 tablespoon water
1 tablespoon chopped basil leaves
   Salt, pepper, and sugar
4 teaspoons sour cream

In a dutch oven, heat the oil; add bacon, and sauté until brown. Add onion and garlic, sauté until onion is translucent. Add the tomatoes, and sauté for 1 or 2 minutes. Season to taste, and add the marjoram, basil, and water. Bring the mixture to a boil, cover, and simmer for about 10 minutes. Force the mixture through a sieve, return to the dutch oven, and warm over a low heat. Add the egg yolk mixture, stirring constantly, and heat until thickened. Stir in the basil leaves, and season to taste with salt, pepper, and sugar. Ladle the soup into 4 individual serving bowls, and top each with a teaspoon of sour cream. Serve immediately.

Gazpacho

2 1/4 pounds (1 kg) tomatoes, peeled, seeded, and
   diced
1 sweet pepper, rinsed. cored, seeded, and diced
1/2 cucumber, peeled and cut into pieces
2 onions, chopped coarsely
2 cloves garlic, chopped coarsely
1 mild pickled pepper, cut in half lengthwise and
   seeded
1/3 cup (40 g) peeled almonds
2-3 slices white bread, with crust removed and cubed
2 tablespoons red wine vinegar
4 tablespoons olive oil
   Salt to taste

Run the tomatoes, sweet pepper, cucumber, onions, garlic, pickled pepper, and almonds through a food

processor or a blender to make a puree. Soak the bread cubes in the vinegar and oil, then mix together well, and stir into the vegetable puree. Season to taste. Cover and refrigerate for at least 2 hours. Serve well chilled. Serve gazpacho with diced tomatoes, sweet pepper rings, cucumber slices, chopped spring onions, black olives, and toasted cubes of white bread.

Tomato Soup with Strips of Leek

(Illustrated this page)

4 cups (1 liter) water
1 teaspoon salt
1/2 cup (4 ounces) long grain rice
3 tablespoons and 1 teaspoon (50 g) butter *or* margarine
2 medium onions, diced
6 to 8 slices lean bacon, diced
2-3 leeks (about 375 g), trimmed to about 4 inches of green, cleaned, and cut into fine lengthwise strips
1 1/2 pounds (750 g) tomatoes, peeled and sliced
6 cups (1 1/2 liters) meat stock, heated
3 rounded tablespoons cornstarch, dissolved in 4 tablespoons cold milk
  Salt to taste
1 tablespoon tomato paste
2 tablespoons port wine
2 egg yolks
5 tablespoons cream

Fill a medium saucepan with the water, add salt, and bring to a boil. Add the rice, return to a boil, cover, and simmer for 12 to 15 minutes, or until the rice is tender. Strain the rice through a colander, rinse with cold water, and drain. In a dutch oven, melt the butter; and sauté bacon and onions until the onions are translucent. Add leeks and tomatoes, cover, and simmer for about 10 minutes. Add meat stock; bring to a boil, cover, and simmer for about 25 minutes. Slowly stir in the cornstarch mixture, and heat until the soup is thickened. Season to taste. Stir in the tomato paste and wine. In a small bowl, combine the egg yolks and cream. Add this to the soup slowly, stirring constantly, and continue simmering until the soup is thick. Add rice, and heat through.

Fish and Tomato Kebabs with Dill-Herb Marinade

(Illustrated this page)

Dill-Herb Marinade (see recipe below)
$2/3$ pound (300 g), eel, cleaned and cut into 1-inch pieces
$3/8$ pound (200 g) fillet of cod, cleaned and cut into 1-inch pieces
6 $1/2$ ounces (200 g) large scampi, shelled
12 cherry tomatoes, rinsed and dried
$1/4$ cucumber, sliced into $1/2$ inch slices
7 tablespoons butter *or* margarine
Salt and pepper to taste
Lemon wedges

Prepare the Dill-Herb Marinade. Place the eel, cod, and scampi in a large mixing bowl, and pour the marinade over them. Marinate for at least 30 minutes, turning occasionally. Remove and drain. Skewer the seafood and the vegetables alternately onto 6 kebab spikes. In a large skillet, melt the butter, and lay the skewers in. Saute them on all sides for about 10 minutes. Season to taste. Serve immediately.

Dill-Herb Marinade

3 tablespoons vegetable oil
Juice from 1 lemon
1 teaspoon mustard *or* Tabasco *or* Worcestershire sauce
Salt, white pepper, and sweet paprika to taste
1-2 teaspoons finely chopped dill

In a small mixing bowl, combine the oil, lemon juice, mustard, and seasonings. Stir in the dill.

Tomato and Bean Casserole

1 teaspoon salt
$3/4$ pound (375 g) green beans, rinsed and broken in pieces
4-5 stalks of savory, rinsed and patted dry
6 slices lean bacon, diced
2 small onions, diced
1 $1/2$ pounds (750 g) tomatoes, peeled and diced
Salt, pepper, and sugar to taste

Fill a medium saucepan half full with water, add salt, and bring to a boil. Add the beans and savory, return to a boil, cover, and simmer for about 10 minutes, or until fork-tender. In a medium skillet, sauté the bacon until it is brown. Add the onions and beans; sauté for about 5 minutes. Add the tomatoes; cover, and simmer for an additional 5 minutes. Season to taste. Serve immediately.

Midnight Soup
(Illustrated this page)

3 tablespoons vegetable oil
12 slices lean bacon, divided
5-6 large onions, diced
1 sweet pepper, diced
5 ounces (150 g) sauerkraut, diced
3 cups (750 ml) meat stock
4-5 cloves garlic, crushed or minced
2 ¹/₂ pounds (1 kg) tomatoes, peeled and diced
1 bay leaf
3 ¹/₄ ounces (100 g) tomato paste
¹/₂ cup (125 ml) white wine
¹/₂ teaspoon paprika

1 teaspoon sugar
  Salt and Tabasco to taste
6 slices lean bacon, sliced
¹/₄ cup Tequila
6 ounces (150 g) sour cream

In a dutch oven, heat the oil, and brown 6 slices of diced bacon. Add the onions, and sauté until translucent. Add pepper and sauerkraut; cover, and simmer for about 2 minutes. Add the meat stock, bring to a boil; cover, and simmer for about 5 minutes. Add garlic, tomatoes, and bay leaf to the mixture; cover, and simmer for about 5 minutes. Stir in the tomato paste and wine, return to a boil; cover, and simmer for about 5 more minutes. Remove the bay leaf. Season the soup with paprika, sugar, salt, and Tabasco. In a medium skillet, sauté the remaining bacon until crisp; crumble and add to the soup. In a small saucepan, heat the Tequila. Pour it over the soup, and light it. Serve sour cream separately.

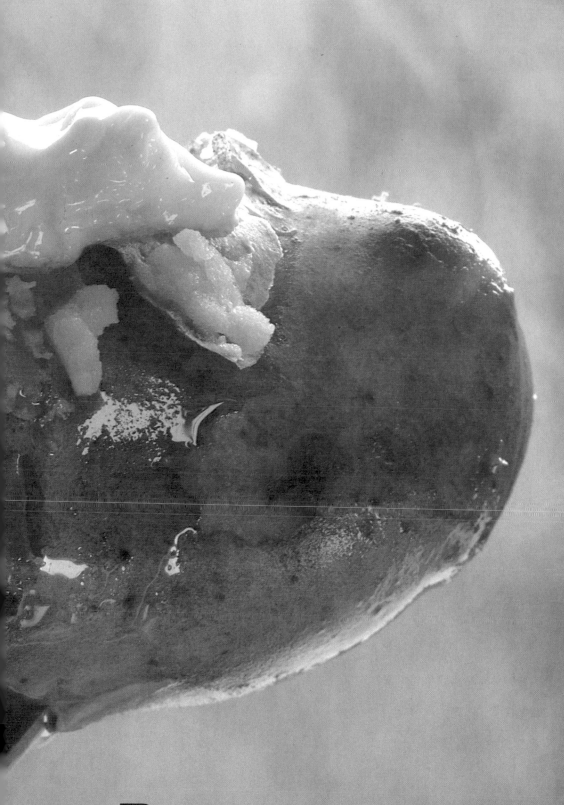

Potatoes
Bounty from beneath the soil

Baked Potatoes
(Illustrated on previous page)

8 medium-sized potatoes, washed and dried

Preheat the oven to 350° F. Place the potatoes on a baking sheet; bake for 40 to 60 minutes, or until fork-tender. Cut a cross into the cooked potatoes, press the cuts open, and hollow out the opening somewhat. Serve immediately.

Potato Soup with Sweet Peppers and Sausages
(Illustrated this page)

6 cups (1 ¹/₂ liters) cold water
1 teaspoon salt
1 pound (500 g) beef spareribs
2-3 soup bones
¹/₄ cup chopped parsley
¹/₃ pound lean bacon, diced
4 onions, diced
2 ¹/₄ pounds (1 kg) potatoes, peeled and diced
2-3 green sweet peppers, rinsed and cut into strips
** Salt and pepper to taste**
4 smoked sausages, sliced

In a dutch oven, place the water, salt, spareribs, and soup bones. Over high heat, bring the water to a boil, and skim off any foam that forms. Add parsley, return to a boil, cover, and simmer for about 1 ¹/₂ to 2 hours. Strain the stock, remove the meat from the bones, and discard them. Dice the meat, and set it aside. In a medium saucepan, sauté the bacon until browned. Add the onions, and sauté until translucent. Combine the stock, bacon, onions, and potatoes in the dutch oven. Bring the soup to a boil, cover, and simmer for about 5 minutes. Add the sweet pepper, return to a boil, cover, and simmer for about 10 minutes. Season to taste. Add the sausages and rib meat to the soup, heat through, and serve immediately.

Potato Soup with Egg Royale

** Egg Royale (see recipe below)**
1 tablespoon butter *or* margarine
4 slices of lean bacon, diced
¹/₂ cup chopped parsley

4 cups (1 liter) meat stock
1 pound (500 g) potatoes, peeled and diced
1 egg yolk
¹/₂ cup (125 ml) cream
** Salt and pepper to taste**
3 tablespoons cress leaves

Prepare the Egg Royale and set aside. In a dutch oven, melt the butter, and sauté bacon until it is brown. Add parsley and braise for 2 minutes. Add the meat stock, and bring mixture to a boil. Add the potatoes, return to a boil, cover, and simmer for about 12 to 15 minutes. Puree the mixture in a

blender or food processor. Return the puree to the dutch oven. In a small mixing bowl, combine the egg yolk and cream. Stir it into the soup, and heat until the mixture thickens. Season to taste. Add the Egg Royale to the soup, and heat through. Sprinkle cress leaves over the soup. Serve immediately.

Egg Royale

2 eggs
¹/₂ cup (125 ml) cold milk
    Salt and grated nutmeg to taste
2 tablespoons butter *or* margarine

In a small mixing bowl, combine the eggs, milk, salt, and nutmeg. Turn this into a small ovenproof bowl, greased with butter. Cover the bowl with aluminum foil. Fill a medium saucepan half full with water, and bring to a boil. Set the bowl into the water, return to a boil, cover the saucepan, and turn off the heat. Let the mixture set for 30 minutes. Then remove the bowl from the pan, and turn the egg mixture out onto a cutting board. Cut the mixture into cubes, and set aside until the soup is ready.

Potato Dumplings

(Illustrated this page)

1 ¹/₂ pounds (750 g) potatoes, rinsed
¹/₄ cup flour
1 egg
  Salt to taste
  Grated nutmeg to taste, optional
1 tablespoon butter *or* margarine
1 slice white bread, cubed
1 teaspoon salt

Place the potatoes in a large saucepan, cover with water, and bring to a boil. Cover, and simmer for 20 to 25 minutes, or until fork-tender. Pour off the water, allow the steam to evaporate, and peel and mash them while still warm. Knead in the flour, egg, salt, and nutmeg, if desired. In a small skillet, melt the butter. Add the cubed bread, and sauté until golden yellow. Flour your hands, and shape the potato dough into dumplings. Force a bread cube into the center of each one; seal. Fill a medium saucepan half full with water, add salt, and bring to a boil. Add the dumplings, return to a boil, cover, and simmer for about 15 minutes. Serve immediately. Serve these with sauerbraten or roast.

Potato Soup with Tomatoes

(Illustrated on pp. 226-227)

2 tablespoons butter *or* margarine
2 onions, diced
¹/₂ cup chopped parsley
4 cups (1 liter) meat stock
1-1 ¹/₄ pounds (500-600 g) potatoes,
  peeled and cubed
6 ounces (150 g) sour cream
1 tablespoon chopped basil leaves
2 tablespoons finely chopped chives
³/₄ pound fresh tomatoes, peeled, seeded, and diced
  Salt and pepper to taste

In a dutch oven, melt the butter, and sauté onions and parsley until the onions are translucent. Add the stock, and bring it to a boil. Add the potatoes, return to a boil, cover, and simmer for about 12 to 15 minutes. Puree mixture in a food processor or blender. Return it to the dutch oven. Stir in the sour cream; add basil leaves, chives, and tomatoes. Heat the soup through, but do not boil. Season to taste, and serve immediately.

Potato Soup with Garlic Sausage

(Illustrated on pp. 226-227)

1 pound (500 g) beef spareribs
2 pimientos, sliced
2 bay leaves
6 cups (1 ¹/₂ liters) cold water
1 teaspoon salt
1 cup chopped celery with leaves
2 ¹/₄ pounds (1 kg) potatoes, peeled and diced
1 tablespoon chopped marjoram leaves
1-2 tablespoons butter *or* margarine
³/₄ pound garlic summer sausage, skinned and sliced
  Salt and pepper to taste
  Chopped parsley

Put the spareribs, pimientos and bay leaves into a dutch oven, cover with cold water, and add salt. Bring to a boil, and skim off any foam that develops. Add celery, return to a boil, cover, and simmer for about 1 ¹/₂ to 2 hours. Drain the mixture

through a colander, saving the broth. Separate the ribs from the celery, cut away beef from the ribs, and dice the meat. Discard the bones. Reserve the greens and diced meat. Return the broth to the dutch oven, and bring it to a boil. Add the potatoes and marjoram, cover, and simmer for about 12 to 15 minutes. Use a slotted spoon to remove about ¹/₃ of the cooked potatoes. Set these aside. Add reserved celery to the broth, and puree the mixture in a food processor or blender. Return puree to the dutch oven. Add meat and reserved potatoes to the soup, and heat through. In a medium skillet, melt the butter, and brown the sausage slices on both sides; add slices to the soup. Season to taste. Sprinkle with parsley, and serve immediately.

Potato Soup with Chicken and Leek

(Illustrated on pp. 226-227)

2 ¹/₄ pounds (1 kg) chicken pieces

1 teaspoon salt
1 pound (500 g) chicken breasts
6 cups (1 ¹/₂ liters) cold water
2 onions, quartered
1 cup chopped celery with leaves
2 ¹/₄ pounds (1 kg) potatoes, peeled and cubed
2-3 carrots (about 200 g), trimmed, peeled, and cut into strips
2 leeks (about 400 g), trimmed leaving 3 inches of green, rinsed and sliced
  Salt and pepper to taste
3 tablespoons chopped parsley

Place the chicken pieces into a dutch oven, and cover with the water. Add the salt, and heat to boiling; skim off any foam that forms. Add the onions and celery to the dutch oven, return to a boil, cover, and simmer for about 1 ¹/₄ hours. Strain the soup through a colander (reserve the broth). Remove the chicken meat from the bones, and dice; discard the bones. Return the stock to the dutch oven. Add the potatoes, bring the stock to a boil, cover, and simmer for about 5 minutes. Add the carrots, return to a boil, cover, and simmer for about 7 minutes. Add the leeks, return to a boil, cover, and simmer for an additional 3 to 5 minutes. Add the chicken meat, and season to taste. Heat the soup through, sprinkle with parsley and serve immediately.

Boiled Potatoes in Cream Sauce

(Illustrated this page)

1 ¹/₂ pound (750 g) potatoes, washed
   Cream Sauce
6 ounces (200 g) boiled ham, diced
   Salt and pepper to taste
   Grated nutmeg to taste, optional
2 tablespoons chopped dill

Place the potatoes in a large saucepan, and cover with cold water. Bring the water to a boil, cover, and simmer for 20 to 25 minutes, or until fork-tender. Pour off the water, allow the steam to evaporate, and skin the potatoes while they are still hot. Cut them into large cubes. Prepare Cream Sauce. Add the potato cubes and the ham to the sauce, and heat through. Season to taste, and carefully stir in the dill. Serve with a mixed green salad.

Cream Sauce

2 ²/₃ tablespoons (40 g) butter *or* margarine
¹/₄ cup flour
1 ¹/₂ cups (375 ml) milk
1 cup (250 ml) cream

In a medium saucepan, melt the butter. Reduce heat to low, slowly add the flour, stirring constantly. Heat until the mixture turns a light yellow. Add the milk, and bring the mixture to a boil while beating

it with a wire whisk, to prevent any lumps from forming. As soon as the mixture boils, turn it down to low, cover, and continue simmering for 5 minutes; add the cream.

Potatoes au Gratin

(Illustrated this page)

2 1/4 pounds (1 kg) potatoes, peeled and rinsed
1 clove garlic
7 1/4 ounces (200 g) Gruyere cheese, grated
   Salt and pepper to taste
1 cup (250 ml) milk
1 cup (250 ml) cream
3 eggs
   Salt, pepper, and grated nutmeg to taste
3-4 tablespoons chopped herbs (dill, parsley, chives, tarragon, lemon mint, marjoram)
Butter *or* **margarine**

Preheat the oven to 325° F. Slice the potatoes in very thin strips, 1/4 to 1/8 inches thick, rinse again, and drain. Rub the garlic over the inside surface of a medium casserole. Grease the casserole. Place a layer of potatoes over the bottom of the casserole, then cover this with a layer of grated cheese. Continue layering until all potatoes and cheese are used. Sprinkle with salt and pepper. In a medium mixing bowl, combine milk, cream, and eggs. Season to taste. Stir in the chopped herbs, and pour the mixture over the potatoes. Dot the top of the casserole with butter. Bake for 60 to 70 minutes, or until the potatoes are fork-tender. If necessary to prevent burning the top, cover the dish with aluminum foil during the last 20 minutes of baking time.

Fried Potatoes with Grilled Sausages

(Illustrated on p. 233)

2 1/4 pounds (1 kg) potatoes, rinsed
1 teaspoon caraway seeds
1 teaspoon salt
2 tablespoons butter
6 slices lean bacon, diced
   Salt and pepper to taste
2 tablespoons vegetable oil
1 onion, diced
1 red sweet pepper, cut into strips
2 small zucchini, rinsed and sliced
1/2 pound (250 g) tomatoes, peeled, seeded, and
   quartered
2 tablespoons vegetable oil
8 to 16 smoked link-type sausages
2-3 tablespoons chopped parsley

Put potatoes and caraway seeds into a large saucepan, cover with cold water, and add the salt. Bring
to a boil, cover, and simmer for 20 to 25 minutes.
Pour off the water, allow the steam to evaporate,
and peel and slice the potatoes while they are hot.
In a dutch oven, melt the butter, and sauté bacon
until brown. Add potato slices, and season to taste.
Sauté the mixture for 10 to 15 minutes, or until the
potato slices are brown and crisp. Keep warm. In a
large skillet, heat the oil, and sauté the onion until
translucent. Add the pepper and zucchini, and sauté
for about 5 minutes. Add the onion mixture and
the tomatoes to the potato mixture. Heat through;
season to taste. Place in a warm serving dish; keep
warm. Heat the oil in a medium skillet. Sauté the
sausages until browned on all sides. Arrange the
sausages over the potatoes; sprinkle with parsley.
Serve immediately.

Herbed Potato Pancakes with Creamed Mushrooms

(Illustrated this page)

3 1/4 pounds (1 1/2 kg) large potatoes, peeled and
grated

   Creamed Mushrooms
1/2 cup (125 ml) milk
4 eggs
   Salt and pepper to taste
1 onion, grated
1 tablespoon chopped dill
2-3 tablespoons finely cut chives
2-3 tablespoons chopped parsley
1 tablespoon chopped lemon mint leaves
6 2/3 tablespoons (3 1/4 ounces) margarine

Set a colander over a large mixing bowl, line the
colander with a cotton towel, and place the grated
potatoes inside to drain for about 10 minutes. Reserve the liquid. Prepare the Creamed Mushrooms.
The liquid from the grated potatoes will be quite
clear for the most part. Pour off the clear portion
carefully, and you will find a starchy, thick layer at

In a large skillet, melt the butter, and sauté the onion until translucent. Add the mushrooms and season to taste. Cover the skillet, and cook for 8 to 10 minutes. Add the sour cream, and heat, stirring gently, until just warmed. Stir in the parsley. Keep warm until the pancakes are prepared. Serve as a side dish.

Potato Souffle with Apples and Sausage

(Illustrated on pp. 234-235)

1 ¹/₂ pounds (750 g) potatoes, peeled and diced
1 teaspoon salt
¹/₂ cup (125 ml) milk
   Salt, pepper, and grated nutmeg to taste
2 tablespoons vegetable oil
2 onions, peeled and sliced
1 pound (500 g) ground smoked sausage
   Salt and pepper to taste
1-2 tablespoons chopped marjoram leaves
2 medium-sized cooking apples, sliced very thin
3 tablespoons chopped parsley

Preheat the oven to 350° F. Place the potatoes and the salt in a medium saucepan, cover with cold water, and bring to a boil. Cover the pan, and boil slowly for 12 to 15 minutes, or until fork-tender. Pour off the water, and allow the steam to evaporate. Combine the milk and the potatoes, and puree in a food processor or blender. Season to taste. In a large skillet, heat the oil, and sauté the onion until translucent. Add the sausage, and cook for about 5 minutes. Season to taste, and add the marjoram leaves. Drain the fat from the pan into a small mixing bowl, and set aside. Spoon half of the potato puree into a large, well-greased casserole. Sprinkle the surface lightly with some of the parsley. On top of the puree, layer half of the sausage mixture, and all of the apple slices. Then finish with the remaining sausage, topped with the last half of the puree. Sprinkle the top with remaining parsley. Pour 2 tablespoons of reserved fat over the top of the casserole, and bake for about 30 minutes, or until the top is golden brown.

the bottom of the bowl. Add the grated potatoes to the bowl and mix them with the starchy liquid. Add the milk, eggs, and seasonings; mix well. Add the onion and herbs; mix well. Over medium heat, melt some of the butter in a small skillet. Ladle enough of the potato mixture into the pan to thinly cover the bottom. Fry the pancake until it is crispy brown on both sides. Repeat this process until all of the batter is used. Keep the pancakes warm until ready to serve.

Creamed Mushrooms

2 tablespoons butter *or* margarine
1 onion, diced
1 pound (500 g) small button mushrooms, cleaned
   Salt and pepper to taste
6 ounces (150 g) sour cream
2 tablespoons chopped parsley

Potato Soufflé with Cod

(Illustrated this page)

1 1/2 pounds (750 g) potatoes, peeled and diced
1 teaspoon salt
1 tablespoon butter *or* margarine
1/2 cup (125 ml) milk
1/2 cup (125 ml) sour cream
   Salt, pepper, and grated nutmeg to taste
1 pound 3 ounces (600 g) fillet of cod, rinsed, patted
   dry, and cut into chunks
   Lemon juice
3 tablespoons vegetable oil
1-2 carrots (about 150 g), peeled and diced
2 onions, sliced
1 pound (500 g) fresh tomatoes, peeled, seeded and
   diced
2 tablespoons chopped mixed herbs (parsley, chives,
   dill, chervil)
   Salt and pepper to taste
   Souffle Sauce (see recipe below)

Preheat the oven to 350° F. Put the potatoes and salt into a medium saucepan, and add enough cold water to cover. Bring to a boil, cover, and simmer for 12 to 15 minutes, or until fork-tender. Pour off the water, and allow the steam to evaporate. Combine the potatoes with butter, milk, and sour cream, and puree in a food processor or a blender. Season to taste, and set aside. In a medium mixing bowl, sprinkle the fish chunks with lemon juice; set aside for 15 minutes. Pat the fish dry, sprinkle with salt, and set aside. In a large skillet, heat the oil, and add the onions and carrots. Saute for about 5 minutes. Add the tomatoes and mixed herbs. Cover, and cook for 7 more minutes; season to taste. Prepare the Souffle Sauce. Fasten a serrated nozzle to a frosting bag, and fill the bag with potato puree. Using all of the puree, pipe around the edge of a well-greased casserole to create a border. Combine fish and vegetables, and arrange them inside the border. Pour the sauce over the vegetable mixture. Bake for about 30 minutes, or until the fish is flake-tender and the border is lightly browned.

Soufflé Sauce

1 tablespoon butter *or* margarine
1 tablespoon flour
1/2 cup (125 ml) milk
1/2 cup (125 ml) cream
   Salt and pepper to taste
   Worcestershire sauce, to taste

In a small saucepan, melt the butter. Stirring constantly, add the flour and continue heating until the flour is light yellow in color. Slowly add the milk and cream, and heat while whipping with a wire whisk to prevent lump formation. Season with salt, pepper, and Worcestershire.

Meaty Potato and Leek Souffle

(Illustrated this page)

1 1/2 pounds (750 g) potatoes, rinsed
   Salt
4 leeks (about 1 pound), trimmed to about 3 inches
   of green, sliced, and rinsed thoroughly
2 tablespoons vegetable oil

2 onions, minced
2 cloves garlic, minced
¹/₂ pound ground beef
¹/₂ pound ground pork
 Salt, pepper, and cayenne pepper to taste
2 cups (250 g) sour cream
2 tablespoons chopped parsley
¹/₂ cup (50 g) grated Swiss Emmental cheese
 Butter *or* margarine

Preheat the oven to 350° F. Place the potatoes in a medium saucepan, and fill with enough water to cover. Add 1 teaspoon salt, and bring to a boil. Simmer for 20 to 25 minutes; then drain and allow the steam to evaporate. Peel the potatoes while they are still hot, and slice them. Set aside. Fill a me-dium saucepan half full with water, add 1 teaspoon salt, and bring to a boil. Add the leeks, return to a boil, cover, and simmer for 2 to 3 minutes. Drain, and set aside. In a large skillet, heat the oil, and sauté the onions and garlic until translucent. Add the ground meats, and sauté until browned, stirring occasionally. Season to taste. In a medium mixing bowl, combine the sour cream and parsley. Season to taste. Place half of the potatoes into a large, well-greased casserole, then add half of the leeks. Sprin-kle with salt. Pour on half of the sour cream; add the browned meats, the remaining leeks, and the remaining potatoes. Pour the remaining sour cream over the ingredients. Sprinkle cheese evenly over the top, and dot with butter. Bake for about 30 min-utes.

Delicate Colorful Salad

(Illustrated this page)

1 1/2 pounds (750 g) small potatoes, rinsed
3 hard-boiled eggs, diced
2 medium-sized onions, minced
3/4 pound (300 g) garlic summer sausage, ground or
  minced
1 large cooking apple, minced
3-4 sweet pickles, minced
  Delicate Dressing
2 tablespoons chopped parsley

Place the potatoes in a medium saucepan, add enough water to cover, and bring to a boil. Simmer 20 to 25 minutes, or until fork-tender. Drain, and allow the steam to evaporate; quarter and slice. In a large serving bowl, combine all the salad ingredients, and toss carefully. Prepare the Delicate Dressing. Pour it over the vegetables, and toss gently.

Sprinkle the parsley over the top, cover, and refrigerate for at least 2 hours before serving.

Delicate Dressing

4-5 tablespoons salad oil
2 tablespoons herb vinegar
1 teaspoon hot mustard
  Salt, pepper, and sugar to taste

Combine all the ingredients, and pour over the salad vegetables.

Pomeranian Style Potato Salad

(Illustrated this page)

2 1/4 pounds (1 kg) salad potatoes, rinsed
2 onions, sliced in very thin slices

2 sweet pickles, sliced in very thin slices
  Pomeranian Dressing (see recipe below)
3 tablespoons vegetable oil
8 slices lean bacon, diced
5 tablespoons water

Place the potatoes in a large saucepan, add enough water to cover, and bring to a boil. Cover, and simmer for 20 to 25 minutes, or until fork-tender. Drain, and allow the steam to evaporate. Peel them while they are still hot, and slice in thin slices. Place potato slices, onions and pickles into a large serving bowl, and toss gently. Prepare the Pomeranian Dressing. Pour it over the salad vegetables, cover, and refrigerate for at least an hour. In a medium skillet, heat the oil, and sauté the bacon until it is browned. Add the water, and bring to a boil, stirring to loosen any browned bits. Pour the bacon and water over the potato salad. Serve immediately.

Pomeranian Dressing

4 tablespoons salad oil
5 tablespoons herb vinegar
  Salt, pepper, and sugar to taste

Mix the oil and vinegar, season to taste, and pour over the vegetables.

Harz Mountain-Style Warm Potato Salad

(Illustrated opposite page)

2 ¼ pounds (1 kg) small potatoes, rinsed
  Harz Mountain Dressing
  Salt, pepper, and vinegar to taste
1 tablespoon minced chives

Preheat the oven to 325° F. Place the potatoes in a medium saucepan, add enough water to cover, and bring to a boil. Simmer for 20 to 25 minutes, or until fork-tender. Drain, and allow the steam to evaporate. Peel, and slice. Prepare the Harz Mountain Dressing. Place the potato slices in an oven-proof serving bowl. Pour the dressing over the potatoes, toss gently, and place the dish in the oven. Turn off the heat, and leave the bowl in the oven for 30 to 45 minutes, occasionally tossing gently. Season to taste with salt, pepper, and vinegar. Stir in the chives, and serve immediately.

Harz Mountain Dressing

6 slices fatty bacon, diced
1 onion, diced
½ cup (125 ml) hot water
4-5 tablespoons vinegar
  Salt, pepper, and sugar to taste

In a medium skillet, sauté the bacon until it is limp and translucent. Remove with a slotted spoon, and set aside. Add the onion, and sauté for about 5 minutes. Add water, vinegar, and seasonings, and heat through. Add the bacon. Pour dressing over the potato slices.

Potato Salad with Tomato

(Illustrated opposite page)

2 ¼ pounds (1 kg) small potatoes, rinsed
2 small onions, sliced
½ pound (250 g) canned mushrooms, sliced
1-2 sweet pickles, sliced
½ cup (125 ml) meat stock
3-4 tablespoons herb vinegar
  Salt, pepper, and sugar to taste
4 tablespoons sour cream
1 cup (250 g) cream
1 tablespoon mustard
1 teaspoon sugar
5 fresh tomatoes, rinsed and cut into wedges
4 hard-boiled eggs, sliced
  Sweet pickle slices

Place the potatoes in a large saucepan, add enough water to cover, and bring to a boil. Cover, and simmer for 20 to 25 minutes, or until fork-tender. Drain, and allow the steam to evaporate. Peel them while they are still hot, and slice into a large serving bowl. Add onions, mushrooms, and pickles, and toss. In a medium mixing bowl, combine the stock, vinegar, and seasonings. Pour the mixture over the vegetables, and refrigerate for at least 1 hour. In a small mixing bowl, combine the sour cream, cream, mustard, and sugar. Combine this with marinated vegetables. Reserve the slices from one of the tomatoes and one of the eggs. Add the remaining tomato and egg slices to the salad ingredients, and toss gently. Garnish with reserved tomato and egg and sliced pickles. Serve immediately.

Brassicas

Multi-colored strength and vitality

Classic Cauliflower

(Illustrated above)

1 teaspoon salt
2 small cauliflower heads (each about 1 pound),
   trimmed, separated, and rinsed
3 $^1/_3$ tablespoons (50 g) butter *or* margarine
4 tablespoons fine bread crumbs

Fill a medium saucepan half full with water, add
salt, and bring to a boil. Add the cauliflower, return
to a boil, cover, and simmer for about 15 minutes,
or until fork-tender. Remove the cauliflower from
the water with a slotted spoon, place in a large
serving bowl, and keep warm. In a small skillet,
melt butter, and add the breadcrumbs. Saute at a
medium temperature until the crumbs are lightly
browned. Pour over the cauliflower, and serve immediately. Serve Classic Cauliflower with peas, carrots and saddle of veal.

Cauliflower Soufflé with Cheese Topping

1 teaspoon salt
1 medium-sized cauliflower (about 3 pounds),
   trimmed, separated, and rinsed
6 $^1/_2$ ounces (200 g) boiled ham, chopped coarsely
   and pureed
$^3/_4$ cup plus 4 teaspoons (200 ml) cream
1 egg
1 teaspoon sweet pickle relish
4 ounces (125 g) ham, minced
3 $^1/_3$ tablespoons (50 g) butter *or* margarine
$^1/_8$ cup (20 g) flour
$^1/_2$ cup (125 ml) milk
3 egg yolks
$^1/_2$ cup (50 g) grated Parmesan cheese
3 egg whites
   Canned or homemade tomato sauce

Preheat the oven to 325° F. Fill a medium saucepan
half full with water, add salt, and bring to a boil.
Add the cauliflower, return to a boil, cover, and
simmer for about 10 to 12 minutes. Drain the
cauliflower, and break the heads into florets. In a

medium mixing bowl, combine the pureed ham, cream, egg, pickle relish, and minced ham. Place half of the ham mixture into a well-greased 1-quart casserole, and press half of the cauliflower florets into the mixture; repeat. In a small saucepan, melt the butter over a low heat. Add the flour, stirring constantly to be sure that no lumps form. Cook mixture over low heat until the flour turns light yellow. Add in the milk very slowly, stirring constantly. Bring mixture to a boil, cover, and simmer for about 5 minutes. Remove from the heat. In a medium mixing bowl, combine egg yolks and Parmesan cheese. Add this slowly to the milk mixture. Whip the egg whites until they form stiff peaks; fold into the milk mixture. Spread the milk mixture over the casserole; bake for about 35 minutes, or until a knife inserted near the center comes out clean. Serve with a side dish of tomato sauce.

Oriental Style Cauliflower

1 teaspoon salt
1 large cauliflower (about 2 kg), trimmed, separated, and rinsed
3/4 cup (200 g) butter *or* margarine
1 tablespoon turmeric
1 tablespoon ground coriander
1 tablespoon Chinese 5-spice powder
  Salt to taste
1/3 cup (50 g) unsalted cashew nuts, coarsely chopped

Fill a medium saucepan half full with water, add salt, and bring to a boil. Add cauliflower; return to a boil, cover, and simmer for about 15 minutes, or until fork-tender. Drain and loosen the florets from the stalk. In a large skillet, melt the butter. In a small mixing bowl, combine the turmeric, coriander, Chinese spice, and salt. Add herbs to the butter, stirring constantly, and heat. Add the florets, stirring until they are covered with the butter mixture. Turn the cauliflower into a warm serving bowl. In a small ungreased skillet, sauté cashews until they are a golden brown; sprinkle over the cauliflower. Serve immediately.

Broccoli with Almond Butter

(Illustrated this page)

1 ¾ pounds (800 g) broccoli, trimmed and rinsed
1 teaspoon salt
3 ⅓-5 tablespoons (50-75 g) butter *or* margarine
¼ cup (50 g) peeled chopped almonds

If necessary, peel the stems of the broccoli, and cut a crosshatch into the bases to speed cooking. Fill a medium saucepan half full with water, add salt, and bring to a boil. Add the broccoli, return to a boil, cover, and simmer for about 8 to 10 minutes, or until fork-tender. Drain, and place in a warm serving bowl. In a small skillet melt the butter. Add the almonds, and sauté until lightly browned. Sprinkle the almonds over the broccoli and serve immediately. Serve with steaks and baked potatoes.

Broccoli with Sauce Vinaigrette

(Illustrated this page)

1 ¾ pounds (800 g) broccoli, trimmed and rinsed
1 teaspoon salt
  Sauce Vinaigrette (see recipe below)

If necessary, peel the broccoli stalks, and cut a crosshatch in the base to speed cooking. Fill a medium saucepan half full with water, add salt, and bring to a boil. Add the broccoli, return to a boil, cover, and simmer for about 8 to 10 minutes, or until fork-tender. Prepare the Sauce Vinaigrette. Arrange the broccoli on a large serving platter, pour Sauce Vinaigrette over, and refrigerate for at least 3 hours before serving.

Sauce Vinaigrette

4 tablespoons salad oil
3 tablespoons vinegar
1 teaspoon mustard
  Salt, pepper, and sugar to taste
1 tablespoon finely chopped chives
1 tablespoon chopped parsley
1 tablespoon chopped lemon mint leaves
1 tablespoon chopped borage leaves
1 tablespoon chopped tarragon leaves
1 tablespoon chopped basil leaves

Combine the oil, vinegar, mustard, salt, pepper, and sugar. Stir in the herbs. Pour over the cooked broccoli.

Broccoli with Herb Hollandaise

(Illustrated this page)

8 cups (2 liters) cold water
1 teaspoon salt
1 1/2 pounds (750 g) broccoli, trimmed
  and rinsed
1 tablespoon butter *or* margarine
1 clove garlic, crushed
1 teaspoon sugar

Fill a large saucepan half full with water, add salt, and bring to a boil. Add the broccoli, garlic, butter, and sugar. Return to a boil, cover, and simmer for about 8 to 10 minutes, or until fork-tender. Drain, and arrange on a warm platter. Keep warm. Prepare Herb Hollandaise, and serve separately.

Herb Hollandaise

3/4 cup (200 g) butter *or* margarine
4 egg yolks
1-2 teaspoons lemon juice
3 tablespoons white wine
  Salt, pepper, sugar, and Worcestershire sauce to taste
2-3 tablespoons chopped smooth parsley
2-3 tablespoons finely chopped chives
2-3 tablespoons chopped dill
1 tablespoon chopped thyme leaves
2-3 tablespoons chopped basil leaves
  Salt and pepper to taste, optional

In a small saucepan, heat the butter over a low flame. Remove any foam that forms, until the butter is clear. Turn the heat very low. (Check often; do not scorch!) In a small mixing bowl, combine the egg yolks, lemon juice, and white wine, and season to taste. Fill a medium bowl about 1/4 full with cold water, set the smaller bowl in the water bath, and mix with an electric hand mixer for about 5 minutes, or until the mixture is foamy and light yellow in color. With the mixer still running, slowly stir in the hot butter in a steady stream, and continue beating until the sauce has a creamy consistency. With a wooden spoon, stir in the herbs. If necessary, season to taste.

Kohlrabi and Potatoes au Gratin

(Illustrated this page)

3-4 small kohlrabi (about 1 pound), trimmed, peeled, rinsed, and thinly sliced
1 pound (500 g) potatoes, peeled and thinly sliced
3-4 onions, thinly sliced
1/2 pound salami slices, cut into strips
2 cups (200 g) grated Swiss Emmental cheese
  Salt and pepper to taste
1 cup (250 ml) milk
1/2 cup (125 ml) cream
2 eggs
  Salt and sweet paprika to taste

2-3 tablespoons fine bread crumbs
1-2 tablespoons butter or margarine

Preheat the oven to 325° F. Beginning and ending with a layer of potatoes, alternate the vegetables and salami in a well-greased soufflé dish. As you alternate, sprinkle each layer of kohlrabi and potato with a little of the cheese. Season to taste. In a medium mixing bowl, beat together the milk, cream, and eggs. Season with salt and paprika, and pour over the soufflé. Combine remaining cheese with the breadcrumbs, and sprinkle over the top. Melt butter and spoon this evenly over the top. Bake for about 45 minutes. About half-way through the baking period, cover the souffle dish with aluminum foil so that the top does not become too dark.

In a large skillet, melt butter, and sauté the onion until translucent. Add the rutabaga, and sauté for about 2 minutes. Add the meat stock and bring to a boil; cover, and simmer for 5 minutes. Add the kohlrabi, carrots, bay leaves, juniper berries, and peppercorns. Bring the soup to a boil, turn down to a simmer, cover, and prepare the Hearty Meatballs. After 15 minutes, add meatballs. Return to a boil, cover, and simmer for an additional 7 to 10 minutes, or until the meatballs are done. Season to taste. Rinse and drain the reserved kohlrabi leaves, and add them to the soup. Serve immediately.

Hearty Meatballs

$^1/_2$ bread roll, torn into pieces
1 small onion, minced
$^3/_8$ pound ground beef
$^3/_8$ pound ground pork
1 egg
  Salt and pepper to taste

Soak in cold water and then squeeze. Place it in a medium mixing bowl. Add the onion, ground meats, and egg, and season to taste. Shape the mixture into 1-inch meatballs, and add them to the soup.

Kohlrabi Stew

3 cups (750 ml) water
4 smoked uncooked bratwurst
1 pound (500 g) potatoes, peeled and sliced into
  strips $^1/_4$-inch wide
6-7 kohlrabi (about 3 $^1/_2$ pounds), trimmed, peeled,
  rinsed, and cut into strips $^1/_4$ inch wide
  Salt and pepper to taste
1 tablespoon flour
$^1/_2$ cup (125 ml) cream
  Salt, pepper, and grated nutmeg to taste
1-2 tablespoons chopped dill

Put the water into a large saucepan, add the bratwurst, and bring to a boil. Cover, and simmer for about 5 minutes. Add the potatoes, return to a boil, cover, and simmer for about 5 minutes. Add the kohlrabi, season to taste, return to a boil, cover, and simmer for about 10 minutes. In a small mixing bowl, combine the flour and cream; add to the stew, stirring constantly. Bring the mixture to a boil, cover, and simmer for an additional 2 to 3 minutes. Season to taste. Sprinkle dill over the top, and serve.

Kohlrabi Soup with Hearty Meatballs

(Illustrated this page)

2-3 tablespoons butter *or* margarine
1 onion, diced
1 rutabaga (about 1 pound), peeled and diced
4 cups (1 liter) meat stock
3-4 kohlrabi (about 2 $^1/_4$ pounds), trimmed, peeled,
  rinsed, and diced (reserve the leaves)
2-3 carrots (about 1 pound), peeled and sliced
1-2 bay leaves
2 juniper berries
10 black peppercorns
  Hearty Meatballs (see recipe below)
  Salt to taste

Corned Beef with Red Cabbage

(Illustrated this page)

2 tablespoons pork drippings
1 medium-sized onion, minced
1/4 pound (600 g) corned beef, cut into slices
1/2 cup (125 ml) meat stock
2 cloves
1 piece of orange peel
  Pepper and sugar to taste
1 red cabbage head (about 1 1/2 pounds), trimmed, rinsed, and cut into eighths
3/4 pound (400 g) small cooking pears, peeled
3-4 tablespoons Madeira
  Salt, pepper, and sugar to taste

In a 5-quart pressure cooker, heat the pork drippings, and sauté the onion until translucent. Add the beef slices, stock, cloves, and orange peel, and season to taste. Close the pressure cooker, and cook for about 20 minutes. Add the cabbage, pears, and Madeira. Stir together, close the cooker, and cook for an additional 10 minutes. If necessary, season to taste before serving.

Stewed Red Cabbage

6 slices bacon, diced
2 onions, diced
1 head of red cabbage, rinsed, quartered, and stalk removed
3 tablespoons herb vinegar
5 juniper berries
3 cloves
1 bay leaf
  Salt, pepper, and sugar to taste
1 cup (250 ml) red wine
1 pound (500 g) cooking apples, peeled, cored, and sliced

In a large skillet, sauté the bacon and onions together for about 3 minutes. Add cabbage, and sauté for 5 minutes more. Add the vinegar and herbs, and season to taste. Stir well. Pour in the wine, and add the apples. Mix well. Cover, and simmer the mixture for about 30 minutes, stirring occasionally to prevent sticking. Season to taste. Serve immediately. Serve with game, poultry, or grilled bratwurst.

Red Cabbage with Prunes and Apple Rings

1 ¹/₂ ounces (50 g) pork drippings
1 head of red cabbage (about 800 g), trimmed,
  rinsed, and grated
¹/₂ pound (250 g) pitted prunes, rinsed
3-4 tablespoons vinegar
¹/₂-1 cup (125-250 ml) water
  Salt, sugar, and vinegar to taste
1 cup (250 ml) water
1 heaping tablespoon sugar
2 tablespoons lemon juice
3 apples (about 350 g), peeled, cored, and cut into
  ¹/₄-inch thick slices

In a large dutch oven, melt the pork drippings, add
the cabbage, and heat over a low heat, stirring
constantly. Add the prunes, vinegar, water, and
seasonings. Bring the mixture to a boil, cover, and
simmer for 30 minutes, stirring occasionally. In a
medium saucepan, combine the water, sugar, and
lemon juice, and bring to a boil. Add the apple
slices, and stew them for about 3 minutes. Arrange
the cabbage in the center of a warm serving platter,
and lay the apple slices in a ring around it.

Piquant White Cabbage with Mackerel

(Illustrated above)

1 ¹/₂ ounces (50 g) pork drippings
8-10 medium-sized onions (about ¹/₂ pound), quartered
1 small white cabbage (about 1 ¹/₂ pounds), trimmed, rinsed, cut into strips, and the core removed
5 juniper berries
1 bay leaf
¹/₂ cup (125 ml) water
2 cooking apples
    Salt and pepper to taste
    Vinegar
2 oven-ready mackerel (about 2 ³/₄ pounds), rinsed and patted dry
    Lemon juice

In a large skillet, melt the drippings, and sauté the onions until they are a light yellow. Add the cabbage, and sauté the two together for 3 to 5 minutes. Season to taste. Add the juniper berries, bay leaf, and water. Cover, and simmer for about 5 minutes. Add the apples, cover, and simmer for another 10 minutes. Season to taste with salt, pepper, and vine-

gar. Turn the mixture out in the center of a large serving platter; keep warm. Preheat the broiler. Sprinkle the mackerel with lemon juice, and let stand for 15 minutes. Sprinkle the inside and outside with salt and pepper. Score the backs of both fish in several places, then place on a baking sheet and broil for about 7 minutes on each side. Lay fish across the cabbage; serve immediately. Serve with potatoes boiled in bouillon water.

Cabbage Rolls

1 head of white cabbage or savory (about 4 ¹/₂ pounds), trimmed and rinsed
1 teaspoon salt
    Meat Filling
5 tablespoons (75 g) butter or margarine
1-2 tablespoons flour, combined with 3 tablespoons cold water
    Salt and pepper to taste

Fill a medium saucepan half full with water, add salt, and bring to a boil. Place the cabbage head in a wire basket, and immerse the head in the boiling water until the outer leaves break away from the head. Remove the loosened leaves and place in a

Soak the bread pieces in water; squeeze them well. Combine bread with the onion, eggs, and ground meats. Season to taste.

Sauerkraut

Firm, fresh white cabbage heads, trimmed, rinsed, stalks removed, and grated
Salt (3 ¹/₄ ounces *or* 100 g salt to 2 pounds cabbage)

Thoroughly wash and dry an earthenware crock. Place a layer of cabbage inside, then a layer of salt. Use a wooden mallet or other device to pack down cabbage, in order to remove as much air space as possible. Then, as the pickling juice forms, the cabbage will always lie beneath it. Continue layering and packing until crock is full. Cover cabbage with a linen cloth, place a board over that, and weight down the board with a stone or other heavy device. Store in a cool place, such as a cellar. The sauerkraut will be ready in about 4 to 6 weeks.

colander to drain, and repeat the process until all the leaves are free. Drain, and cut any thick ribs so that the leaves lay flat; set them aside. Prepare the Meat Filling. Lay 2 or 3 large cabbage leaves over each other, spread the filling over them, and roll up the leaves. To keep them together, wind them with thread or string. Repeat until you have used all the filling. In a large skillet, melt the butter, and heat over a medium heat. Lay the rolls carefully in the butter, and sauté them on all sides. Add water to a depth of ¹/₂-inch in the skillet, cover, and simmer for 35 to 45 minutes, turning occasionally. As necessary, add more water. Remove the rolls from the pan with tongs, and arrange on a warm serving platter. Remove string gently. Keep warm. Stirring constantly, add the flour mixture to the cooking liquid. Cook slowly until the liquid has thickened. Season to taste. Pour the gravy over the rolls, and serve immediately.

Cabbage Salad

1 teaspoon salt
1 small head white cabbage (about 1 ¹/₂ pounds), trimmed, rinsed, cored, and cut into fine strips
Herb Vinegar Sauce (see recipe below)
6-8 slices lean bacon
Vinegar to taste

Fill a medium saucepan half full with water, add salt, and bring to a boil. Add the cabbage, return to a boil, cover, and simmer for about 1 minute. Drain. Prepare the Herb Vinegar Sauce. In a small skillet, sauté the bacon until browned. Drain, crumble and fold into the cabbage. Season to taste. Serve warm.

Meat Filling

1 bread roll, torn into pieces
1 medium-sized onion, diced
1 egg
³/₈ pound ground beef
³/₈ pound ground pork
Salt and pepper to taste

Herb Vinegar Sauce

4 tablespoons vinegar
¹/₈ teaspoon caraway seed
Salt, pepper, and sugar to taste

In a small mixing bowl, combine all the ingredients. Pour over the cabbage.

Savoy with Bacon

(Illustrated this page)

6 to 8 slices lean bacon
2-3 medium onions (about ¹/₄ pound), sliced
1 pound (500 g) beef chuck, quartered
1 head savoy (about 2 ¹/₄ pounds), trimmed, rinsed, cored, and chopped
  Salt and pepper to taste
¹/₂ cup (125 ml) water

Preheat the oven to 325° F. Line a medium-size, ovenproof top-of-range baking dish with the bacon slices, and lay onion slices on top of them. Cook the two over medium heat for about 10 minutes. Place the beef and savoy on top of the onions. Season to taste, and add the water. Cover the dish snugly, and bake for about 1 ¹/₂ hours, or until meat is fork-tender.

Savoy Soup

(Illustrated this page)

¹/₄ pound (100 g) dried navy beans, rinsed
2 cups (500 ml) water
1 pound chunk of salt pork *or* jowl bacon
4 cups (1 liter) water
1 ham bone (about 1 pound), rinsed and patted dry
4 cups (1 liter) water
1 head savoy (about 3 ¹/₂ pounds), trimmed, rinsed, cored, and chopped
3 onions, sliced
4 cloves garlic, crushed
2 carrots (about ¹/₄ pound), peeled and sliced
2 parsley roots, peeled and sliced
2 leeks (about ¹/₂ pound), trimmed to about 5 inches of green, sliced and washed thoroughly
2 sprigs thyme, trimmed and rinsed
2 sprigs marjoram, trimmed and rinsed
2-3 sprigs parsley, trimmed and rinsed
2-3 celery leaves, trimmed and rinsed
2-3 bay leaves
1 pound (500 g) firm potatoes, peeled and diced

1 pound (500 g) garlic summer sausage
  Salt and pepper to taste

Put the beans into a large mixing bowl, pour in the water, and let them soak for 12 to 24 hours. In a large kettle, combine the salt pork and water, bring to a boil, cover, and simmer for 1 hour. Add the ham bone, beans, and the water they have soaked in. Add 4 cups of water and the prepared vegetables. Bring to a boil, cover, and simmer for 45 minutes. Add the herbs, potatoes and sausage. Return to a boil, cover, and simmer for an additional 15 to 20 minutes. Remove the ham bone, salt pork, and sausage chunks. Trim and dice any meat from the ham bone. Trim the rind from the bacon, and dice. Slice the sausage into thin slices. Return the meats to the kettle, and heat through. Season to taste, and serve immediately.

Lamb Stew with Savoy

(Illustrated opposite page)

2-3 slices lean bacon, diced
1 1/2 pounds (750 g) lamb, trimmed from soup bones and diced
  Salt and pepper to taste
2 onions, diced
1 small head savoy, trimmed, rinsed, cored, and cut into strips
1 leek (about 150 g), trimmed to about 5 inches of green, washed and thinly sliced
2 large carrots (about 150 g), peeled and thinly sliced
  Salt, pepper, and sweet paprika to taste
1-2 tablespoons chopped thyme leaves
1 to 1 1/2 pounds (500-750 g) firm potatoes, peeled and thinly sliced
2 cups (500 ml) meat stock
6 strips lean bacon (about 75 g)
2-3 tablespoons chopped parsley

In a 5-quart pressure cooker, sauté the bacon until it is limp and translucent. Add the lamb, and season to taste. Saute over a medium heat, until all sides are browned. Add the onions, and sauté for 5 more minutes. Add the savoy, leek, and carrots, stir carefully, and season to taste with salt, pepper, and sweet paprika. Stir in the thyme. Layer the potato slices over the mixture, and pour in enough meat stock to cover some but not all of the potatoes. Salt and pepper the potatoes, and lay the uncooked bacon slices on top of them. Close the pressure cooker, and cook for about 8 minutes. Pour the stew into a large serving tureen, and sprinkle with parsley before serving.

Kale, Bremen Style

(Illustrated below)

1 teaspoon salt

3 1/4 pounds (1 1/2 kg) kale, cleaned, rinsed, and ribs removed

1/4 cup (100 g) pork drippings

2 medium onions, diced

2 tablespoons oatmeal

1-1 1/2 pounds (500-750 g) smoked pork spareribs, meat trimmed, bones reserved

1/2 pound (250 g) lean bacon, cut in thick slices

1 1/2 cups (375 ml) water
   Salt to taste

4 smoked sausages
   Salt, pepper, grated nutmeg, and sugar to taste

Fill a medium saucepan half full with water, add salt, and bring to a boil. Add the kale, return to a boil, cover, and simmer for about 1 to 2 minutes. Drain, reserving cooking water, and chop the kale coarsely. In a large skillet, heat the drippings, add

onions, and sauté until translucent. Add the kale, and stir in oatmeal. Heat through. Add reserved water, rib meat, rib bones and bacon. Season to taste with salt, return to a boil, cover, and simmer for about 30 minutes. Add the smoked sausages, return to a boil, cover, and simmer for about 20 minutes. Season to taste. Remove rib bones, and discard. Remove the sparerib meat, sausages and bacon, slice and arrange on a large serving platter with drained kale. Serve with baked potatoes.

Kale Stew

1 teaspoon salt
3 ¹/₄ pounds (1 ¹/₂ kg) kale, cleaned, rinsed, and ribs removed
2-3 tablespoons vegetable oil
6 slices lean bacon, diced
1 pound (500 g) stewing beef, cubed
2 onions, diced
    Salt and pepper to taste
2 cups (500 ml) water, or more as needed
¹/₂ pound (250 g) carrots, peeled and diced

Fill a medium saucepan half full with water, add salt, and bring to a boil. Add the kale, return to a boil, cover, and simmer for about 1 to 2 minutes. Drain, chop coarsely, and set aside. In a large skillet, heat the oil, and sauté bacon until it is well browned. Add beef cubes, and sauté until well browned. Add the onions, and sauté until translucent. Season to taste. Add water, bring to a boil, cover, and simmer for about 20 minutes. Add kale, cover, and simmer for about 45 minutes. Add carrots, cover, and simmer for an additional 10 to 15 minutes. Season to taste. Serve immediately. Serve with potato dumplings.

Stewed Kale

1 teaspoon salt
3 ¹/₄ pounds (1 ¹/₂ kg) kale, cleaned, rinsed, and ribs removed
6-8 slices fatty bacon, diced
2 onions, diced
2 teaspoons medium-hot mustard
    Salt and pepper to taste
2 cups (500 ml) meat stock

Fill a medium saucepan half full with water, add salt, and bring to a boil. Add kale, return to a boil, cover, and simmer for about 1 to 2 minutes. Drain, chop coarsely, and set aside. In a dutch oven, sauté the bacon until it is well browned. Add the onions, and sauté until translucent. Add the kale, mustard, and season to taste. Add the meat stock, cover, and continue simmering for another 15 to 20 minutes. If necessary, add more stock, so the kale doesn't scorch. Season to taste. Serve immediately. Serve stewed kale with bratwurst, smoked pork and baked potatoes, or fried liver.

Cold Stuffed Beef Slices

(Illustrated below)

1 Chinese cabbage (about 9 1/2 ounces), cleaned, rinsed, halved, and core removed
1 tablespoon vegetable oil
1/2 cup (50 g) grated Parmesan cheese
1/2 cup (50 g) fine bread crumbs
2 eggs
2 tablespoons chopped parsley
2-3 tablespoons milk
8 very thin slices of beef
  Salt and pepper to taste
  Vegetable oil
  Garlic Marinade (see recipe below)

Preheat the oven to 350° F. Rinse and drain the Chinese cabbage leaves, and chop very fine. In a large skillet, heat the oil, and gently braise the leaves. Remove from the heat. Add Parmesan, bread-crumbs, eggs and parsley. If the mixture tends to crumble, add milk to help it hold together. Sprinkle beef slices with salt and pepper, spread with cabbage mixture, and roll up. Lightly grease 8 pieces of aluminum foil, and wrap the beef rolls. Seal the foil loosely, but well. Lay them 1 inch apart on a baking tray, and bake for 45 minutes. Let the rolls cool in the foil. Prepare Garlic Marinade. Remove the foil, and slice rolls into thin slices. Arrange them on a large serving platter, and ladle marinade over the slices. Serve with French bread or fried potatoes.

Garlic Marinade

2 cloves garlic, minced
3 tablespoons vegetable oil
  Juice of 1 lemon
  Salt and pepper to taste
2 tablespoons chopped parsley

Combine the ingredients well; pour over the beef roll slices.

Sauteed Stuffed Chinese Cabbage Rolls

2 Chinese cabbages (about 1 pound), cleaned and rinsed
1 cup (250 ml) vegetable oil
  Chicken Filling
  Sherry Sauce

Break cabbage leaves away from the stalks of the plants, and split the ribs, so the leaves will lay somewhat flat. Fill a large mixing bowl with very cold water. Fill a medium saucepan half full with water, and bring to a boil. Add cabbage leaves, return to a boil, cover, and simmer for about 30 seconds. Remove them, and immediately put them into the very cold water. Remove them from the mixing bowl, and drain. Prepare the Chicken Filling. Lay one cabbage leaf over another, spread filling over them, and roll them up, tying them firmly with thread or string. Repeat this until all the

filling is used. In a dutch oven, or deep frying cooker, heat the oil to 450° F., and deep-fry the cabbage rolls until they are golden yellow. Drain on paper towels. Keep warm. Prepare the Sherry Sauce. Pour the sauce over the rolls, and serve immediately. Serve with buttered rice and a fresh green salad.

Chicken Filling

1 tablespoon vegetable oil
2 green onions, trimmed to about 6 inches of green, rinsed, and sliced
1 large carrot, peeled and diced
$^1/_4$ cup bean sprouts
1 $^1/_2$ ounces (50 g) fresh mushrooms, minced
6 $^1/_2$ ounces (200 g) cooked chicken *or* turkey breast, minced *or* ground
Salt, pepper, and soy sauce to taste

In a large skillet, heat the oil, and sauté onions, carrot, sprouts, and mushrooms about 5 minutes. Remove from heat. Add chicken, season to taste, and fill the cabbage slices.

Sherry Sauce

4 tablespoons dry sherry
1 tablespoon lemon juice
1 teaspoon honey
Soy sauce to taste

Combine the ingredients, and pour over the cabbage rolls.

255

Stewed Brussels Sprouts

(Illustrated above)

2 tablespoons butter *or* margarine
1 onion, diced
2 1/4 pounds (1 kg) Brussels sprouts, cleaned, rinsed,
    and a cross-hatch cut into each base
    Salt and grated nutmeg to taste
1/2 cup (125 ml) water
2 tablespoons sour cream
2 tablespoons chopped parsley
    Salt and grated nutmeg to taste

In a large skillet, melt the butter, add the onion,
and sauté until translucent. Add the Brussels
sprouts, and season to taste. Add the water, bring
to a boil, cover, and simmer for 15 to 20 minutes,
or until fork-tender. Stir in the sour cream and
parsley, and season to taste. Serve immediately.
Serve with game, roast pork, or roast beef.

Brussels Sprouts Salad

3/8 pound (200 g) small firm button mushrooms,
    rinsed
3/8 pound (200 g) carrots, peeled and sliced
1 pound (500 g) Brussels sprouts, cleaned, rinsed,
    and cross-hatched at base
1 leek trimmed to about 4 inches of green,
    halved lengthwise, and thoroughly cleaned
    Creamy Tomato Sauce
    Tomato wedges
    Parsley

Fill a large saucepan half full with water, and bring
to a boil. Add carrots, return to a boil, cover, and
simmer for about 5 minutes. Remove with a slotted
spoon, and drain. Add mushrooms to the vegetable
water, return to a boil, cover, and simmer for about
3 minutes. Remove with a slotted spoon, and drain.
Add Brussels sprouts to the vegetable water, return
to a boil, cover, and simmer for about 10 minutes.
Remove with a slotted spoon, and drain. In a large
mixing bowl, combine all the above, and allow
them to cool. Cut the leek into fine slices, and add

to the vegetables. Prepare the Creamy Tomato
Sauce. Mix the sauce well with the vegetables and
refrigerate for at least 2 hours before serving. If
necessary, season with salt and pepper. Garnish
with tomato wedges and parsley. Serve with
whole-wheat bread and butter.

Creamy Tomato Sauce

6 ounces (150 g) sour cream
3 tablespoons tomato catsup
  Salt, pepper, and cayenne pepper to taste
3 tablespoons chopped herbs (lemon mint, tarragon,
  parsley)

Combine the sour cream and catsup, and season to
taste. Stir in the herbs. Mix with the Brussels
Sprouts Salad.

Cream of Brussels Sprouts Soup

1 cup (250 ml) water
1 teaspoon salt
1 pound (500 g) Brussels sprouts, cleaned, rinsed,
  and crosshatched at base
2 cups (500 ml) hot water
1 teaspoon meat extract
1 teaspoon cornstarch mixed with 1 tablespoon cold
  water
1 egg yolk
2 tablespoons sour cream
1 tablespoon soft butter or margarine
  Salt, cayenne pepper, and sugar to taste
  Chopped parsley

Put the water and the salt into a medium saucepan,
and bring to a boil. Add the Brussels sprouts,
return to a boil, cover, and simmer for about 10
minutes. Shortly before the end of the cooking
time, remove about 10 sprouts, quarter them, and
reserve. Puree remaining sprouts and cooking liquid
in a blender or a food processor. Return puree to
the saucepan, add water and meat extract, and
bring to a boil. In a small mixing bowl, combine
cornstarch mixture, egg yolk and sour cream. Add
this to the soup, stirring constantly. Heat through,
but do not boil. Add butter, and season to taste.
Add reserved sprouts, and heat through. Ladle the
soup into individual bowls, sprinkle with parsley,
and serve immediately.

Leek Varieties
Long and delicious

Greek Leeks

(Illustrated pp. 258-259)

2 1/4 pounds (1 kg) leeks (about 10 thin leeks),
  rinsed, and trimmed to about 4 inches of green
1/2 cup (125 ml) water
1/2 cup (125 ml) dry white wine
5-6 tablespoons lemon juice
5 tablespoons olive oil
10 sprigs parsley, rinsed, patted dry, and thick stalk
  cut away
1 tablespoon coriander seeds
6 bay leaves
  Salt and pepper to taste

Make several lengthwise cuts in the leeks, but do
not separate them. Using kitchen thread, tie them
into small bunches. In a medium saucepan, combine the water, wine, lemon juice, and olive oil.
Add parsley, coriander, and bay; season to taste.
Bring to a boil, cover, and simmer for about 10
minutes. Add the bunches of leeks, return to a boil,
cover, and simmer for another 30 minutes, or until
fork-tender. Allow the leeks to cool in the liquid;
remove with a slotted spoon. Remove the thread,
and arrange the leeks on a medium serving platter.
Pour a little of the cooled liquid over them, and
serve. Serve Greek Leeks as an appetizer.

Leek Stew

(Illustrated this page)

1 tablespoon vegetable oil
2 1/2 ounces (75 g) lean bacon, diced
2 carrots, peeled and sliced
1 stalk celery (about 150 g), diced
1 onion, peeled and diced
1 1/2 pounds (750 g) potatoes, peeled and diced
4 cups (1 liter) meat stock
4 smoked sausages
2 1/4 pounds (1 kg) leeks (about 10 leeks), trimmed,
  rinsed, cut to about 4 inches of green, halved, and
  cut into 1/2-inch chunks
  Salt and pepper to taste
  Additional meat stock, as needed
1-2 tablespoons chopped parsley

In a large skillet, heat the oil, and sauté the bacon
until crisp. Add the carrots, onion, and celery;
sauté gently for about 5 minutes. Add the potatoes,
stock, and sausages. Bring to a boil, cover, and simmer for about 10 minutes. Add the leeks, and sea-

son with salt and pepper. If necessary, add a little
more meat stock. Bring to a boil, cover, and cook
for 5 to 7 minutes. Remove the sausages, slice, and
return them to the skillet. Season to taste. Sprinkle
with chopped parsley. Serve immediately.

Leek Salad with Smoked Turkey Breast

1 teaspoon salt
1 1/2 pounds (750 g) leeks (about 8 leeks), rinsed,
  trimmed to about 4 inches of green, and cut
  diagonally into thin slices
  Lemon-Ginger Dressing
1 1/2 ounces (50 g) smoked turkey breast, cut into
  strips
  Sugar and salt to taste

Fill a medium saucepan half full with water, add
salt, and bring to a boil. Add the leeks, return to a
boil and cook until fork-tender. Drain the leeks in a
colander, and rinse with cold water. Set aside; cool.
Prepare the Lemon-Ginger Dressing. In a medium
serving bowl, combine the leeks and turkey strips.
Pour dressing over leek mixture; toss gently. Cover,
and refrigerate for 1/2 hour. Season with sugar and
salt. Serve immediately.

Lemon-Ginger Dressing

6 tablespoons salad oil
4 tablespoons lemon juice
4 teaspoons (10 g) peeled and grated fresh ginger root

In a small mixing bowl, combine the oil, juice, and ginger. Pour over the salad. Serve this salad with rye bread rolls and butter.

Curried Pork with Leek

4 tablespoons vegetable oil
1 pound (500 g) fillet of pork, cut into strips
2-3 onions (about 4 ounces), peeled, halved, and sliced

1 heaping tablespoon curry powder
Salt to taste
7 tablespoons orange juice
2 cloves garlic, diced
2 slices fresh ginger root, diced
1 yellow sweet pepper, rinsed, cored, and cut into strips
2 ¼ pounds (1 kg) leeks (about 10 leeks), rinsed, trimmed to about 4 inches of green, and sliced

In a large skillet, heat the oil, and sauté meat and onions until onions are translucent. Stir often. Add the curry powder, and simmer for a short time (do not allow the curry powder to become too dark). Season with salt, and add orange juice. Add garlic and ginger to the curry, cover, and simmer for about 5 minutes. Add sweet pepper and leeks, cover, and cook for about 5 minutes. Season to taste. Serve with rice.

Creamed Onions

(Illustrated below)

1-2 tablespoons butter
1 pound (500 g) onions, sliced and separated into
  rings
  Salt and pepper to taste
  Thyme to taste
1 cup (250 ml) cream
  Salt to taste
1/4 cup (150 g) medium-ripe Gouda cheese, grated
4 slices toasted bread, crusts trimmed away and cut
  into small croutons
2 tablespoons butter

Preheat the oven to 325° F. In a large skillet, melt
the butter, add onions, and sauté until translucent.
Season with salt and pepper, and add a few thyme
leaves. Divide the onions between 4 small baking
dishes. Season the cream with salt to taste, and
pour enough over the onion rings to just cover
them. Sprinkle cheese and croutons evenly over the
cream. Dot the top with butter. Bake for 20 to 30
minutes. Serve immediately.

Port Wine Onions

(Illustrated below)

2 1/4 pounds (1 kg) medium onions, peeled
1 cup (250 ml) red wine vinegar
1/2 pound (250 g) sugar
2 teaspoons salt
8 sage leaves, rinsed and patted dry
4 bay leaves
1 tablespoon plus 2 teaspoons (20 g) fresh, peeled,
  sliced ginger root
5 cloves
10 black peppercorns
1 piece cinnamon stick
  Rind from 1 lemon
1 cup (250 ml) red port wine

Prepare the jars for canning as instructed in the
Introduction. Fill the water-bath canner 2/3 full,
and begin heating the water. Fill a large saucepan
half full with water, and bring to a boil. Add the
onions, return to a boil, cover, and simmer for
about 10 minutes. Remove the onions from the water with a slotted spoon, and place them in cold
water for about 10 minutes. Remove them, and allow them to drain. In a medium mixing bowl, combine the vinegar with 1/2 of the sugar and salt. Set
aside. In a medium saucepan, caramelize the remaining sugar, stirring continuously. Add the vinegar mixture; stir well until all of the caramel has
dissolved. In a dutch oven, combine the onions,
vinegar mixture, sage, bay leaves, ginger, cloves,
black peppercorns, cinnamon stick, and lemon rind.
Bring the mixture to a boil, cover, and simmer for
about 5 minutes. Remove from the heat, and add
the wine. Marinate for 30 minutes. Remove the
onions and spices from the port wine liquid. Fill the

jars as instructed in the Introduction. Leave a head-space of 1 inch. Pour the wine marinade into the jars. Remove any air spaces, clean the rims, and seal. Process the jars for 10 minutes. Remove the jars from the canner, and set out to cool in a draft-free location. After 24 hours, test the seals. Any unsealed product must be used immediately, or it may be reprocessed. Store the jars in a cool, dark, airy location. Serve port wine onions with fondue or with steaks and chops.

Crackling Rings
(Illustrated below)

1 1/2 pounds (750 g) large onions, cut into 1/4-inch
    thick slices separated into rings
3 tablespoons flour
    Vegetable oil
    Salt and pepper to taste

Pat the onion rings dry with paper towels. Dust them with flour. Heat fat in a deep fryer to 350 F. Fill the basket no more than 2/3 full. Fry each batch for about 3 to 4 minutes; then drain them on paper towels. Sprinkle with salt and pepper. Serve with wine.

Caramel and Cinnamon Onions
(Illustrated below)

2 tablespoons vegetable oil
1 pound (500 g) small onions, peeled
    Salt
1/4 cup plus 2 tablespoons brown sugar
3/4 cup plus 4 teaspoons (200 ml) red wine
6 tablespoons red wine vinegar
2 tablespoons tomato puree
2 teaspoons ground cinnamon
    Cayenne pepper to taste
    Vinegar and cinnamon to taste

In a large skillet, heat the oil, add the onions, and sauté until translucent. Season the onions with salt; then sprinkle with the brown sugar, cooking gently until the sugar caramelizes. In a small mixing bowl, combine the wine, vinegar, and tomato puree. Pour mixture over the onions, mix well, and cook until the liquid evaporates and thickens. Season with cinnamon and cayenne pepper. Cover, and simmer for about 15 minutes more, stirring occasionally. Remove the onions from the pan, and simmer the liquid, uncovered, for about 10 minutes until it thickens. Return the onions to the pan, and heat through. Season to taste with vinegar and ground cinnamon. Serve immediately. Serve with lamb, game or fondue.

Onion Soup with Cheese Croutons

(Illustrated this page)

5 tablespoons (75 g) butter *or* margarine
2 1/4 pounds (1 kg) onions, quartered and sliced
3-4 cups (3/4-1 liter) meat stock
1 cup (250 ml) white wine
   Salt and pepper to taste
   Cheese Croutons (see recipe below)

In a dutch oven, heat the butter, add the onions, and sauté until translucent. Add the stock and wine, and season to taste. Bring to a boil, cover, and simmer for about 10 minutes. Prepare the Cheese Croutons. Pour the soup into 6 soup dishes. Shortly before serving, top each portion with 2 croutons, or serve them separately.

Cheese Croutons

6 slices bread
1 cup (3 1/4 ounces) grated medium-ripe Gouda
   cheese

Preheat the broiler. Cut the bread slices into triangles; place on a cookie sheet, and toast on one side only. Sprinkle the untoasted sides with the cheese, return the triangles to the broiler for about 2 minutes, or until cheese has melted.

Onion Strudel
Onion Strudel Filling

   Strudel Dough
1/3 cup (80 g) butter *or* margarine
1/4 pound (100 g) lean bacon, diced
3 1/2 pounds (1 1/2 kg) onions, thinly sliced, and
   divided
   Salt and pepper to taste
2 teaspoons caraway seed
   Butter *or* margarine
1 egg yolk
2 teaspoons vegetable oil
2 tablespoons butter, melted

Preheat the oven to 350° F. Prepare the Strudel Dough. In a large skillet, melt the butter, and sauté the bacon until crisp and brown. Add 3 1/4 pounds of onions, and sauté them together for 10 to 15

minutes. Season to taste. Stir in the caraway seed, and allow the onion slices to cool. On a large floured cloth, roll out the dough into a sheet, so thin that you can almost see through it. Shape it with your hands into a rectangle about 20 by 28 inches. If the edges are too thick, trim them away. Spread the filling over the dough (leaving about 1 inch uncovered at the edges). Fold the uncovered edges over the filling, to the center of the dough. Then, using the cloth to turn the strudel, roll it from the bottom to the top. Press the ends together well, and lay it in a greased baking tray. In a small mixing bowl, combine the egg yolk with the oil, and brush the mixture over the strudel. Bake for 35 to 40 minutes, until golden. In a small skillet, melt the butter, sauté the remaining onion slices until the rings are brown, and use as a garnish.

Strudel Dough

2 cups flour
$^1/_3$ cup plus 1 tablespoon (100 ml) lukewarm water
1 small egg
3 tablespoons vegetable oil
  Salt to taste

Sift the flour onto a pastry board. Make a hollow in the middle, and add the water, egg, and vegetable oil. Sprinkle salt over the top. With your hands, work the ingredients into a thick paste with some of the flour, then cover the paste with more of the flour, and, working from the center outwards, quickly knead it to a smooth dough. Cut a piece of waxed paper to fit the bottom and sides of a small saucepan. Coat the paper with oil. Warm oven to 200° F; turn heat off. Place the prepared paper inside, and place the dough on the paper. Cover the saucepan, and let stand in warmed oven for about 30 minutes.

Pureed Onions

1 tablespoon butter
4 slices (75 g) lean bacon
2 1/4 pounds (1 kg) large onions, sliced
    Salt to taste
1/2 cup (125 ml) water
6 tablespoons cream
    Salt and cayenne pepper to taste

In a large skillet, melt the butter, and sauté the bacon until crisp and brown; remove the bacon and set aside. Add the onions, and sauté until translucent. Season with salt. Add the water slowly. Bring to a boil, cover, and simmer for about 15 minutes. Puree the onions, return puree to skillet, and heat to boiling. Stir in the cream. Add salt and cayenne pepper to taste; heat through. Crumble the bacon, and use it for a garnish. Serve Pureed Onions with roast mutton.

Onions in Cream

1 tablespoon butter
6 strips (150 g) lean bacon, diced
2 1/4 pounds (1 kg) onions, quartered and sliced
    Salt and pepper to taste
6 tablespoons cream
2 tablespoons chopped parsley

In a large skillet, melt the butter; sauté the bacon until crisp and brown. Add the onions; season to taste. Cover, and simmer for about 5 minutes. Stir in the cream; simmer uncovered for an additional 5 minutes, stirring occasionally. Season to taste; stir in the parsley. Serve immediately. Serve with chops or roasts.

Onion Chutney

2 1/4 pounds (1 kg) onions, diced
2 1/4 pounds (1 kg) apples, peeled, cored, and sliced
1/2 cup dried currants
1 1/2 cups (350 g) cane sugar
1 cup (250 ml) white wine vinegar
1 teaspoon turmeric
1 teaspoon ground pimiento
1/2 teaspoon ground cinnamon
1/2 teaspoon ground cloves
1/2 teaspoon curry powder
1 pinch cayenne pepper
1/2 teaspoon salt
4-5 pieces dried ginger

Prepare the jars for canning as instructed in the Introduction. Fill the water-bath canner 2/3 full, and begin heating the water. In a large dutch oven or cooking kettle, combine the ingredients. Bring to a boil, cover, and simmer slowly for 1 1/4 hours, stirring occasionally. Fill the jars as instructed in the Introduction. Leave a headspace of 1 inch. Remove any air spaces, clean the rims, and seal. Process the jars for 15 minutes. Remove the jars from the

canner, and set out to cool in a draft-free location. After 24 hours, test the seals. Any unsealed product must be used immediately, or it may be reprocessed. Store the jars in a cool, dark, airy location.

Onion Cake with Tomato
(Illustrated this page)

Onion-Tomato Topping

Yeast Dough (see recipe below)
1 tablespoon vegetable oil
6 slices (150 g) lean bacon, diced
3 1/4-4 1/2 pounds (1 1/2-2 kg) onions, quartered and sliced
   Salt and pepper to taste
2 eggs
6 ounces (150 g) sour cream
1 pound (500 g) tomatoes, sliced
1-2 tablespoons thyme leaves
1-2 tablespoons finely chopped chives
5 ounces (150 g) Swiss Emmenthal cheese, grated

Preheat the oven to 325° F. Prepare the Yeast Dough; set aside. In a large skillet, heat the oil, and sauté the bacon until crisp and brown. Add the onions, season with salt and pepper, cover, and simmer for about 10 minutes. If any liquid forms, drain the onion mixture. Set the mixture aside for 5 minutes to cool. Add the eggs and the sour cream,

and season to taste. Spread the onion mixture smoothly over the pastry dough. Place tomato slices on top, and sprinkle with pepper, thyme and chives. Spread the cheese on top; bake for 40 to 45 minutes.

Yeast Dough

2 1/2 cups (350 g) flour
1 packet dried yeast
3/4 cup plus 4 teaspoons (200 ml) lukewarm water
3 1/3 tablespoons (50 g) melted lukewarm butter
1 teaspoon salt
1 teaspoon sugar
   Flour

Carefully mix the flour and dried yeast. Add the water, butter, salt, and sugar. Stir carefully until mixed, then beat the dough until bubbles form. Should the dough become sticky, add a little flour (not too much, as the dough must remain soft). Grease the inside of a medium mixing bowl, set the dough inside, and put it in a warm place until it has risen to about twice its size. Punch down the dough, and knead it well. Place the dough on a greased roasting pan, and press it out to fit the pan. Shape ridges around the edges of the rectangle.

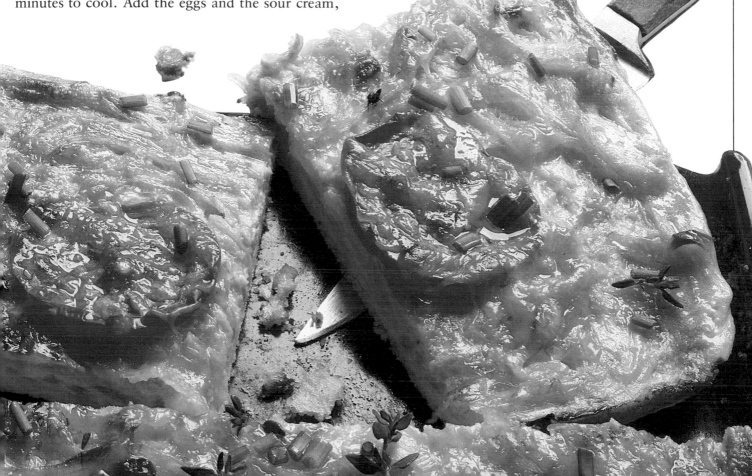

Pickled Pearl Onions

2 teaspoons salt
6 ¹/₂ pounds (3 kg) pearl onions, peeled
5-6 cloves garlic, peeled
4 cups (1 liter) dry white wine
2 cups (500 ml) white wine vinegar
1 cup (250 ml) water
2 cups plus 4 teaspoons (500 g) sugar
3-4 level tablespoons salt
5-6 small bay leaves
1 tablespoon black peppercorns
1-2 teaspoons mustard seeds
6-8 sprigs tarragon, rinsed and patted dry

Prepare the jars for canning as instructed in the Introduction. Fill the water-bath canner ²/₃ full, and begin heating the water. Fill a dutch oven half full with water, add salt, and bring to a boil. Add the onions and garlic, cover, return to a boil, and cook for 5 minutes. Set aside to cool. In a clean dutch oven, combine all remaining ingredients except tarragon. Bring to a boil, and continue boiling until the sugar and salt have dissolved. Pack the onions and garlic cloves in the jars as instructed in the Introduction. Add one or two sprigs of tarragon to each jar. Pour the wine mixture over the vegetables, leaving a headspace of 1 inch. Remove any air spaces, clean the rims, and seal. Process the jars for 10 minutes. Remove the jars from the canner, and set out to cool in a draft-free location. After 24 hours, test the seals. Any unsealed product must be used immediately, or it may be reprocessed. Store the jars in a cool, dark, draft-free location. Serve pickled pearl onions with grilled meat or with sandwiches.

Shallots in Their Skins

¹/₂ cup (4 ounces) butter *or* margarine
1 ¹/₄ pounds (600 g) small shallots, rinsed and patted dry
2-5 cloves garlic, peeled
   Salt and white pepper to taste

Remove any loose skin from the shallots, but don't pull off any excess layers. In a large skillet, melt the butter, and sauté the shallots and garlic about 10 minutes, turning often. Season to taste with salt and white pepper. Serve as a side dish with lamb chops.

Rump Steaks with Shallots

2 ²/₃ tablespoons (40 g) butter
1 ¹/₂ pounds (750 g) shallots, peeled and halved if large
4 tablespoons white wine
1 teaspoon green peppercorns
   Salt and pepper to taste
2 tablespoons vegetable oil
1 tablespoon butter
4 rump steaks, edges scored
2 tablespoons white wine
   Tomato wedges and parsley for garnish

In a large skillet, melt the butter until very hot. Remove the skillet from the heat, add the shallots, and set aside to draw out liquids. Return the skillet to the stove. Add the wine and peppercorns, and season with salt and pepper. Bring to a boil, cover, and simmer for about 10 minutes, stirring occasionally. In a large skillet, heat the oil and butter; sauté the steaks for about 3 minutes on each side. Sprinkle with salt and pepper, and arrange on a warm plate. Add wine to pan juices, and bring to a boil. Pour this over the steaks, and garnish with tomato wedges and parsley. Arrange the onions on the plate with the steaks, or serve separately. Serve with roast potatoes.

Glazed Onions

2 ²/₃ tablespoons (40 g) butter
1 rounded tablespoon sugar
4 tablespoons water
2 ¹/₄ pounds (1 kg) pearl onions, peeled
   Salt to taste

In a large skillet, melt the butter, add sugar, and caramelize, stirring constantly. Add water, stirring until the water and caramel are combined. Add the onions, and season with salt. Cover, and cook for 10 to 15 minutes, stirring and turning occasionally to glaze the onions well. Serve glazed onions with tongue, ragout, smoked pork, or boiled beef.

Beef with Shallots and Wine Sauce

2 tablespoons vegetable oil
5 ounces (150 g) lean bacon, diced
2 1/4 pounds (1 kg) beef, cut into 5 or 6 large pieces
    Salt and pepper to taste
1 pound (500 g) shallots, peeled
1 rounded tablespoon flour
3-5 sprigs thyme, rinsed and patted dry
2 cups (500 ml) red wine
1/2 cup (125 ml) red wine
2 tablespoons sour cream

In a large skillet, heat the oil, and sauté the bacon until crisp and brown. Add the meat, and sauté well on all sides, turning frequently. Season with salt and pepper. Add shallots to the beef mixture, and heat through. Dust flour over the surface, mix well, and cook through. Add thyme and wine. Stir well, cover, and simmer for 1 1/2 hours. If the mixture becomes too dry, add another 1/2 cup red wine. Before serving, remove the thyme sprigs, and stir in 2 tablespoons sour cream. Season to taste. Serve immediately. Serve with small fried potatoes and bean salad.

Onion Salad with Oranges
(Illustrated alongside)

2/3 pounds (300 g) red onions, sliced
3 medium oranges, peeled, and sliced
    Wine-Sherry Sauce (see recipe below)
1 tablespoon chopped dill

Mix the onions and orange slices in a medium serving bowl. Prepare the Wine-Sherry Sauce. Pour over the onion mixture, cover, and refrigerate for 1/2 hour. Sprinkle with dill, and serve immediately.

Wine-Sherry Sauce

3 tablespoons salad oil
1 tablespoon white wine vinegar
2 tablespoons cream sherry
1 teaspoon honey
    Salt and pepper to taste

In a small mixing bowl, combine all ingredients.

Cheese Soup with Spring Onions

(Illustrated this page)

4 tablespoons butter, divided
1/4 cup (40 g) flour
4 cups (1 liter) meat stock
1/2 pound (200 g) Gouda cheese, diced
2 tablespoons sour cream
 Salt, pepper, and grated nutmeg to taste
1 bunch spring onions, rinsed, trimmed, and cut to
 about 4 inches of green, sliced, and separated into
 rings

In a medium skillet, melt 3 tablespoons butter, add the flour, and heat, stirring until it is light yellow in color. Add the meat stock, and whisk the mixture, taking care that no lumps form. Bring the mixture to a boil, cover, and simmer for about 5 minutes. Add the cheese, along with sour cream. Bring to a boil while stirring, and continue stirring until the cheese has melted. Season with salt, pepper, and grated nutmeg. In a large skillet, melt 1 tablespoon butter, and sauté the onion rings for 3 to 5 minutes. Add the onions to the cheese soup just before serving.

Spring Onion Salad with Fried Chicken Breast

(Illustrated this page)

6 ounces (200 g) boneless chicken breast, rinsed and
 patted dry
 Salt and pepper to taste
2 tablespoons vegetable oil
2 bunches spring onions (about 1 pound), rinsed,
 trimmed, and cut into rings, green and bulbs separated
1 teaspoon salt
1 bunch radishes, trimmed, rinsed, and sliced
1 large onion, sliced
 Herb Vinegar Dressing
6 ounces (150 g) sour cream
1-2 tablespoons chopped herbs (parsley, chives, tarragon, lemon mint)
 Salt and pepper to taste

Season the chicken with salt and pepper. In a large skillet, heat the oil, and brown the chicken breasts

for about 3 minutes on each side. Remove them from the pan, cool, and slice. Fill a medium saucepan half full with water, add salt, and bring to a boil. Add the bulbs, return to a boil, cover, and simmer for about 1 minute. Drain the onions through a colander, rinse with cold water, and set aside to drain. Combine the vegetables in a large serving bowl. Prepare the Herb Vinegar Dressing. Pour over the vegetables, cover, and refrigerate for ¹/₂ hour. Season to taste, and arrange on a platter, topped with the sliced chicken. In a small mixing bowl, combine the sour cream, herbs, salt, and pepper. Serve as a salad topping.

Herb Vinegar Dressing

2 tablespoons salad oil
2 tablespoons herb vinegar
   Salt, pepper, and sugar to taste

In a small bowl, combine the salad oil, herb vinegar, salt, pepper, and sugar.

Garlic Chops with Pearl Onions

4 pork chops (about ¹/₂ pound each)
4 cloves garlic, peeled and crushed
   Salt, pepper, and sweet paprika to taste
2 tablespoons butter *or* margarine
¹/₂ pound (250 g) pearl onions, peeled
4 tablespoons white wine *or* water
2 tablespoons sour cream

Rub both sides of the chops with the crushed garlic. Cover, and let stand for about 30 minutes. Sprinkle with salt, pepper, and sweet paprika. In a large skillet, melt the butter, and sauté the chops and onions together for about 10 minutes, turning the chops several times. Remove the chops from the pan; keep warm. Add the wine to the juices in the pan. Stir in the sour cream, and simmer until warmed through. Add salt, pepper, and paprika to taste. Pour the sauce over the chops, or serve separately. Serve with boiled potatoes and butter beans.

Young Garlic in Vinegar

4 cups (1 liter) water
1 teaspoon salt
²/₃ pound (300 g) very young garlic plants, with green included, rinsed, and roots trimmed (bulbs barely formed)
3-4 large sprigs pickling dill, rinsed and patted dry
3-4 sprigs savory, rinsed and patted dry
1 cup (250 ml) white wine
¹/₂ cup (125 ml) vinegar
1 tablespoon salt
1 teaspoon sugar
¹/₂ cup (125 ml) olive oil

Prepare two jars for canning as instructed in the Introduction. Fill the water-bath canner ²/₃ full, and begin heating the water. In a large saucepan, combine the water and salt, and bring to a boil. Add the young garlic, return to a boil. Drain garlic, rinse with cold water, and set aside to drain. In a large saucepan, combine the wine, vinegar, salt, sugar, and oil; bring to a boil. Continue boiling and stirring until salt and sugar have dissolved. Pack the garlic and herbs into the jars as instructed in the Introduction. Pour the boiling liquid over the garlic, leaving a 1-inch headspace. Remove any air spaces, clean the rims, and seal. Process the jars for 10 minutes. Remove the jars from the canner, and set out to cool in a draft-free location. After 24 hours, test the seals. Any unsealed product must be used immediately, or it may be reprocessed. Store the jars in a cool, dark, airy location.

Aioli

(Illustrated opposite page)

1 egg yolk
2 teaspoons mustard
1 tablespoon vinegar
  Salt to taste
1 teaspoon sugar
¹/₂ cup (125 ml) vegetable oil
4-5 cloves garlic, minced
  Cayenne pepper and lemon juice to taste

Beat together the egg yolk, mustard, vinegar, salt, and sugar until thick. Gradually beat in vegetable oil; then mix the sauce with the garlic. Season to taste with cayenne pepper and lemon juice.

Garlic Yeast Ring

¹/₂ pound (250 g) potatoes, rinsed
1 teaspoon salt
6 cloves garlic, crushed
2 ⁵/₈ cups (375 g) flour
4 ounces (125 g) coarse-ground rye
1 packet (42 g) fresh yeast
1 teaspoon sugar
1 cup (250 ml) lukewarm milk
1 egg
1 level tablespoon salt
1 ¹/₂ ounces (50 g) soft pork drippings or shortening
  Flour
  Water

Preheat the oven at 325° F. Place the potatoes in a medium saucepan, and add enough water to cover. Add the salt, and bring to a boil. Cover, and simmer for about 20 minutes. Pour off the water, and skin the potatoes. In a large mixing bowl, mash the potatoes while they are still hot. Set aside to cool. Add the garlic cloves to the potatoes. Sift the flour, and add it and the rye to the potato mixture. Mix all the ingredients with a fork, and shape a hollow in the center. Combine the yeast and the sugar in a small bowl. Stir in a small portion of the lukewarm milk, cover with a tea towel, and let stand in a warm place for about 15 minutes. Add some of the potato mixture, and mix into a paste. Add egg, salt, pork drippings and the remaining milk; add to the potato mixture, either by hand or with a dough hook in an electric mixer, using the lowest and then the highest setting. Knead the dough until it forms fine blisters, cover, and set aside in a warm place until it has doubled in size. Punch down the dough, and knead again. If it becomes sticky, work in a little plain flour. Halve the dough, and form it into 2 long rolls about 15 inches long. Twist them together, and form into a ring. Lay the ring on a greased baking tray, cover, and leave it in a warm place until the ring has doubled. Brush the ring with water, and bake for about 30 minutes, or until golden brown.

Lettuce and Leaf Vegetables

Walnut-y Green Salad
(Illustrated above)

2 heads lettuce, rinsed and drained
2 cooking apples, rinsed, peeled and sliced
  Lemon juice
  Nut Dressing (see recipe below)
2 tablespoons coarsely chopped walnuts

Place large inner lettuce leaves on salad plates. Sprinkle the apple slices with lemon juice; place on lettuce leaves. Prepare the Nut Dressing; pour over salad. Top with walnuts, and serve immediately.

Nut Dressing

2 tablespoons walnut oil
1 $^1/_2$ tablespoons white wine vinegar
1 teaspoon orange *or* apple juice
  Salt and white pepper to taste

In a small mixing bowl, combine the oil, vinegar, juice, salt, and pepper.

Potpourri Salad
(Illustrated above)

  Herb-Oil Dressing
3 small onions, sliced
1 $^1/_2$ ounces (50 g) button mushrooms, rinsed, trimmed, and sliced
1 bunch radishes, rinsed, trimmed, and sliced
1 red apple, rinsed, cored, and sliced
2 hard-boiled eggs, diced
8 ounces canned mandarin orange segments, drained
1 head lettuce (prepare last), rinsed, drained, and trimmed

Prepare the Herb-Oil Dressing, and combine it with the onions, mushrooms, radishes, apple, eggs, and mandarin segments. Cover, and refrigerate for at least an hour. Just before serving, break the head lettuce. Split the leaves that are large, and leave the heart leaves whole. Wash the leaves, and use them to line individual salad dishes. Top with the vegetables, and serve immediately with dressing.

Herb-Oil Dressing

4 tablespoons olive oil
3 tablespoons lemon juice
  Salt, pepper, and sugar to taste
3 tablespoons chopped herbs (chervil, tarragon, lovage, basil)

Mix the olive oil, lemon juice, salt, pepper, and sugar. Add the chopped herbs. Pour over the salad vegetables.

Green and Yellow Salad

(Illustrated above)

  Herb-Egg Dressing (see recipe below)
1 head lettuce, rinsed, broken, and drained
1 yellow sweet pepper, rinsed, cored, and cut into fine strips
7 1/4 ounces (225 g) cooked sweet corn kernels, drained

Prepare the Herb-Egg Dressing. Place the lettuce leaves in a medium salad bowl, and sprinkle with a little dressing. Spread the vegetables over the lettuce, top with remaining dressing, and serve immediately. If desired, sprinkle the salad with chopped parsley.

Herb-Egg Dressing

4 tablespoons olive oil
3 tablespoons red wine vinegar
1 clove garlic, crushed
1/2 teaspoon sugar
1 teaspoon mustard
  Finely chopped chives
  Chopped basil leaves
  Chopped marjoram leaves
  Chopped lovage leaves
1 hard-boiled egg, diced

In a small mixing bowl, combine the olive oil, vinegar, garlic, sugar, and mustard. Stir in the chives, basil, marjoram, and lovage leaves. Add the diced egg. Set aside until ready to serve.

277

Cress Soup with Trout Puffs
(Illustrated this page)

Cress Soup

2 bunches watercress, cleaned, trimmed, and rinsed
4 cups (1 liter) concentrated chicken broth
1/2 cup (125 ml) cream
3 egg yolks
3 tablespoons sour cream
    Trout Puffs (see recipe below)

Remove any yellow leaves and thick ribs from the cress. Reserve a few leaves for garnish, and puree the rest. In a medium saucepan, bring the broth to a boil; remove from the heat. Beat together the cream and the egg yolks; add to the broth, along with the sour cream. Under a low flame, heat, stirring constantly, until the soup thickens. Add the puree, stirring continually. Heat through. Keep warm while preparing the Trout Puffs. Ladle the soup into warmed individual soup bowls, add the trout, and sprinkle with the reserved cress leaves.

Trout Puffs

1/2 pound (250 g) trout fillets, rinsed, patted dry, and cut into chunks
1 egg
3 tablespoons sour cream
    Salt, pepper, and grated nutmeg to taste
1 teaspoon salt

Puree the fillets, egg, sour cream, salt, pepper, and grated nutmeg. With a teaspoon or melon ball cutter, shape the puree into small balls, about 1 inch in diameter. Fill a medium saucepan half full with water, add the salt, and bring to a boil. Spoon in the trout balls, return to a boil, and simmer for about 10 minutes. Control the heat; a heavy boil will break up the balls. Remove with a slotted spoon, and add to the Cress Soup.

Watercress Salad with Marinated Beef

(Illustrated this page)

Lemon Marinade (see recipe below)
²/₃ pound (300 g) beef tenderloin
2 bunches watercress (about 9 ¹/₂ ounces), rinsed
    and drained
1 clove garlic, halved
¹/₂ pound (250 g) button mushrooms, rinsed,
    drained, and sliced
1 tablespoon hot mustard
2-3 tablespoons lemon juice, optional
    Grated lemon rind

Prepare the Lemon Marinade. Freeze the beef for a short time; then slice into paper-thin slices. Lay the slices of meat in the marinade, cover, and marinate in refrigerator for about 1 hour. Remove the yellow leaves and the thicker stalks from the watercress. Rub the garlic over the inside of a medium serving bowl. Remove the beef slices from the marinade, and arrange them in the bowl with the cress and mushrooms. Add the hot mustard to the marinade. If desired, add lemon juice. Pour the marinade over the salad, and garnish with grated lemon rind. Serve immediately.

Lemon Marinade

1 lemon
4 tablespoons sunflower oil
    Salt, pepper, and sugar to taste

Grate the lemon rind, then squeeze the lemon. In a small bowl, mix the rind and juice with sunflower oil, salt, pepper, and sugar. Pour over the meat slices.

Poached Eggs in Ham with Cress Sauce

4 cups (1 liter) water
1 teaspoon salt
2 tablespoons vinegar
4 eggs
4 slices boiled ham
  Tomato wedges
  Cress leaves
  Cress Sauce (see recipe below)

In a medium saucepan, bring the water, salt, and vinegar to a boil. Carefully break each egg individually into a soup ladle; then lay them carefully into the boiling water. Reduce heat to low. After 3 or 4 minutes, remove the eggs with a slotted spoon, and place them in a bowl of cold water until cool. Wrap each egg in a slice of boiled ham, and arrange on individual plates. Prepare the Cress Sauce. Garnish each plate with tomato wedges and cress leaves. Pour sauce over salad. Serve with toast or French bread.

Cress Sauce

1 egg yolk
1 tablespoon vinegar
$^1/_2$ teaspoon salt
1 level teaspoon sugar
  Dash of pepper
$^1/_2$ cup (125 ml) vegetable oil
2 tablespoons yogurt
1 $^1/_2$ ounces (50 g) garden cress, cleaned, trimmed, and patted dry
  Salt and pepper to taste

Beat the egg yolk, vinegar, salt, sugar, and pepper until thick. Gradually beat in the vegetable oil. Stir in the yogurt. Strip the watercress leaves from the stalks, and chop; stir into the sauce. Season to taste with salt and pepper.

Summer Salad

(Illustrated this page)

3 $^1/_4$-5 ounces (100-150 g) garden cress, trimmed, rinsed, and patted dry
4 tomatoes, rinsed and sliced
  Salt and pepper to taste
1 bunch radishes, rinsed and sliced

1-2 hard-boiled eggs, chopped, optional
  Vinegar Dressing (see recipe below)

Strip the watercress leaves from the stalks, and line a shallow dish or plate with them. Arrange the tomatoes on top of the cress, in a circle around the plate. Sprinkle with salt and pepper. Add the radish slices. Prepare the Vinegar Dressing, and pour over the vegetables. If desired, garnish with chopped eggs.

Vinegar Dressing

3 tablespoons vegetable oil
3 tablespoons vinegar
1 teaspoon sugar

In a small mixing bowl, combine the ingredients. Pour over the vegetables.

Herb Cream Cheese in a Bed of Cress

1/4 cup (75 g) butter *or* margarine
7 1/4 ounces (200 g) Boursin *or* cream cheese
1 tablespoon sour cream
  Pinch of grated lemon rind
1 small clove garlic, crushed
1 teaspoon thyme leaves
1 tablespoon chopped parsley
1 tablespoon chopped dill
1 tablespoon finely chopped chives
1 tablespoon chopped borage leaves
1 tablespoon chopped lemon mint leaves
1 tablespoon chopped basil leaves
  Salt and pepper to taste
1-1 1/4 ounces (30-40 g) garden cress, trimmed, rinsed, and patted dry

In a small saucepan, melt butter. In a medium mixing bowl, cream the butter with the Boursin. Stir in the sour cream and grated lemon rind. Stir in the garlic, thyme leaves, chopped parsley, dill, chives, borage, lemon mint, and basil leaves. Season with salt and pepper. Cover, and refrigerate for 4 to 5 hours. Use the cress to line a plate. Shape the chilled cream cheese into a ball, and place on top of cress leaves. Serve with garlic bread.

Head Lettuce Gisela

6 ounces (150 g) button mushrooms, trimmed,
  rinsed, and sliced very thinly
1-2 tablespoons lemon juice
1 cooking apple, peeled, cored, and diced
1 leek, rinsed, trimmed to 3 inches of green, and cut
  into very thin strips
4 ounces (125 g) boiled ham, sliced
¹/₂ head lettuce, trimmed, broken, rinsed, and
  drained
  Mixed Herb Dressing (see recipe below)
  Salt, pepper, and vinegar to taste
1 hard-boiled egg, sliced

Place the mushroom slices in a medium mixing
bowl, and sprinkle with lemon juice. Add apple to
the mushrooms, and toss. Add the leek and ham
slices. Toss. Prepare the Mixed Herb Dressing. Mix
the dressing with the salad ingredients, cover, and
set aside for 10 minutes. Line a medium serving
bowl with lettuce, and place the vegetables on top.
Season to taste with salt, pepper, and vinegar.
Garnish with slices of egg. Serve with French bread
and butter.

Mixed Herb Dressing

4 tablespoons vegetable oil
3 tablespoons herb vinegar
  Salt, pepper, and sugar to taste
2 tablespoons chopped herbs (parsley, chervil, dill,
  lemon mint)

In a small mixing bowl, combine the oil, vinegar,
salt, pepper, and sugar. Stir in the chopped herbs;
pour over the vegetables.

Head Lettuce with Fruit

(Illustrated this page)

¹/₂ head lettuce, rinsed, broken, and drained
1 grapefruit, peeled and sliced
1 orange, peeled and sliced
2 kiwis, peeled and sliced
  Walnut halves
  Walnut Dressing (see recipe below)

Arrange the salad ingredients in a medium serving
bowl. Prepare Walnut Dressing; pour over salad.
Garnish with walnut halves, and serve immediately.

Walnut Dressing

4 tablespoons vegetable oil
3 tablespoons lemon juice
2 tablespoons vinegar
2 tablespoons sugar
  Salt and lemon pepper to taste
¹/₄ cup (50 g) coarsely chopped walnuts

In a small mixing bowl, combine all the ingredients.

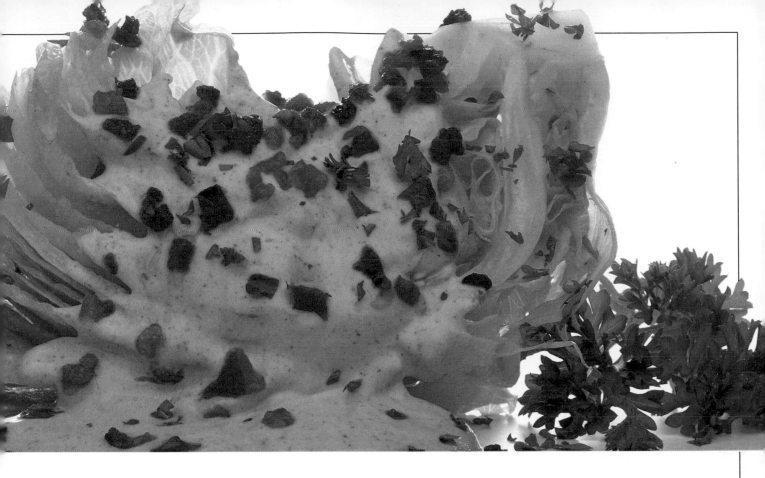

Head Lettuce with Apple

2 medium cooking apples, peeled, cored, and diced
  Lemon juice
$^1/_2$ head lettuce, rinsed, broken, and drained
2-3 sticks celery (about $^1/_2$ pound), rinsed and diced
  Hazelnut Dressing (see recipe below)

Sprinkle apple with lemon juice. Combine all ingredients in a medium serving bowl. Prepare the Hazelnut Dressing, and pour it over the salad. Serve immediately.

Hazelnut Dressing

5 tablespoons sour cream
2-3 tablespoons lemon juice
4 tablespoons orange juice
  Salt, white pepper, sugar, and ground ginger
  to taste
1 tablespoon coarsely chopped hazelnuts

In a small mixing bowl, combine all the ingredients.

Head Lettuce with Bacon

(Illustrated above)

1 head lettuce, cut into serving-size wedges, rinsed, and drained
  Lemony Sour Cream Dressing (see recipe below)
  Margarine *or* butter
1 onion, minced
3 slices (100 g) lean bacon, minced

Place the wedges on individual salad plates. Prepare the Lemony Sour Cream Dressing; pour over the lettuce wedges. In a medium skillet, melt the margarine, and sauté onion and bacon until bacon is brown. Spread over salad, and serve immediately.

Lemony Sour Cream Dressing

2 tablespoons vegetable oil
6 tablespoons sour cream
2 tablespoons lemon juice
  Salt, pepper, sugar, and sweet paprika to taste
2 tablespoons chopped parsley

In a small mixing bowl, combine all ingredients.

Arrange salad ingredients in a large serving bowl. Prepare the Oil-Vinegar Dressing, and pour it over the vegetables. Prepare the Parsleyed Cream Cheese. Drop the cheese mixture in balls onto the salad, or serve as a side dish. Garnish with radish slices. Serve immediately.

Oil-Vinegar Dressing

2 tablespoons vegetable oil
3 tablespoons vinegar
   Salt, pepper, and sugar to taste

In a small mixing bowl, combine all the ingredients.

Parsleyed Cream Cheese

1 ³/₄ ounces (50 g) cream cheese, softened
1 teaspoon mixed herbs
6 ounces (150 g) sour cream
1 tablespoon chopped parsley
   Salt and pepper to taste

In a small bowl, combine cream cheese with herbs; stir in the sour cream and parsley. Season to taste.

Boston Lettuce with Walnut Sauce

6 ¹/₂-8 ounces (150-200 g) Boston lettuce, cleaned, broken, rinsed, and drained
   Walnut Sauce (see recipe below)
   Salt, pepper, and vinegar to taste

Place the lettuce into a medium serving bowl. Prepare the Walnut Sauce, and pour it over the lettuce. If necessary, season to taste with salt, pepper, and vinegar. Serve immediately.

Walnut Sauce

1 small red onion, sliced
3 tablespoons walnut oil
2 tablespoons white wine vinegar
¹/₄ cup (50 g) coarsely chopped walnuts
   Salt, pepper, and sugar to taste

In a small mixing bowl, combine all the ingredients.

Colorful Romaine with Cream Cheese

(Illustrated above)

1 head romaine lettuce, rinsed, drained and torn
   into pieces
1 bunch radishes, trimmed, rinsed, and sliced
1 tomato, peeled and sliced into wedges
1 red onion, halved and sliced
2-3 sticks celery (about ¹/₂ pound), cleaned, rinsed,
   and cut into strips
4 ounces (100 g) fresh button mushrooms
   Oil-Vinegar Dressing
   Parsleyed Cream Cheese
   Radish slices

Stuffed Swiss Chard Leaves

(Illustrated this page)

Cheese-Mushroom Filling (see recipe below)
1 teaspoon salt
16 large Swiss chard leaves (about 2 plants), stalks removed and rinsed
3 ¹/₃ tablespoons (50 g) butter *or* margarine

Preheat the oven to 375° F. Prepare the Cheese-Mushroom Filling. Fill a large saucepan half full with water, add salt, and bring to a boil. Add the Swiss Chard, return to a boil, cover, and simmer for about 2 to 3 minutes. Drain. Lay the leaves side by side, and place about 1 tablespoon of filling on each one. Fold the edges of the leaves over the filling, roll them up, and lay them side by side in a well-greased, medium baking dish. Melt the butter, and sprinkle it over the leaves. Cover the dish, and bake for about 30 minutes.

Cheese-Mushroom Filling

1 tablespoon butter *or* margarine
1 onion, diced
1 clove garlic, minced
¹/₂ pound (250 g) mushrooms, cleaned, rinsed, and diced
Salt and pepper to taste
6 ounces (200 g) boiled ham, diced
¹/₄ pound (125 g) Gouda cheese, diced
3 tablespoons chopped herbs (parsley, chervil, tarragon, burnet)
2 eggs
2 tablespoons fine bread crumbs

In a large skillet, melt the butter, and sauté the onion and garlic until the onion is translucent. Add the mushrooms, and season with salt and pepper. Cover, and cook over a low heat for about 5 minutes. Add the boiled ham, and heat through. Remove from heat, and add cheese, herbs, eggs, and bread crumbs. Season to taste with salt and pepper.

Rich Sorrel Soup

3 tablespoons butter *or* margarine
2 slices white bread, cut into cubes
4 cups (1 liter) water
1 carrot, peeled and diced
1 stick celery, peeled and diced
2 leeks, rinsed, trimmed to about 4 inches of green, and diced
2 tablespoons (30 g) butter *or* margarine
1 tablespoon flour
3 ¹/₄ ounces (100 g) sorrel, cleaned, stalks removed, rinsed, drained, and cut into strips
1 clove garlic, minced
2 shallots *or* 1 small onion, minced
1 tablespoon finely chopped chives
1 tablespoon chopped parsley
Salt, pepper, and grated nutmeg to taste
1 egg yolk
1 tablespoon cream

Poached Eggs with Sorrel Cream

(Illustrated this page)

Poached Eggs

Sorrel Cream (see recipe below)
4 cups (1 liter) water
4-6 tablespoons vinegar
4 eggs
Coarsely grated pepper
Sorrel leaves

Prepare Sorrel Cream. In a medium saucepan, heat the water and vinegar to boiling. Break the eggs individually into a soup ladle, and carefully place them in the boiling water. Reduce heat to low, cover, and simmer. After 3 to 4 minutes, remove the eggs with a slotted spoon, and put them into a bowl full of cold water for a short time. When ready to serve, arrange eggs on a serving platter, along with the Sorrel Cream. Sprinkle with grated pepper, and garnish with sorrel leaves.

Sorrel Cream

1 tablespoon butter *or* margarine
3 shallots, minced
2 ¹/₂ ounces (70 g) sorrel, stalks removed, rinsed, drained, and cut into strips
1 egg yolk
1 teaspoon lemon juice
Salt and white pepper to taste
¹/₂ cup (125 ml) vegetable oil
1 tablespoon cream

In a large skillet, melt the butter, and sauté the shallots for about 5 minutes. Set aside a few sorrel strips, and add the remaining sorrel to the shallots. Cover, and simmer for 5 more minutes; remove from heat, and allow to cool. In a large mixing bowl, beat together egg yolk, lemon juice, salt, and white pepper until thick. Gradually beat in the oil. Add the cooked sorrel, the reserved sorrel, and puree. Stir in the cream.

In a small skillet, melt the butter, and sauté the bread cubes until golden yellow. Put bread cubes into 4 soup bowls, and set aside. In a large saucepan, place the water and the vegetables. Bring to a boil, cover, and simmer for about 30 minutes. Drain the vegetables in a colander, reserving the cooking water. In a small skillet, melt the butter, add flour, and heat until it becomes a light yellow, stirring constantly. Slowly add the reserved vegetable water, beating continuously with a wire whisk, so that no lumps form. Bring the mixture back to a boil. Add the garlic, sorrel, shallots, chives, and parsley. Simmer for about 10 to 15 minutes, until the mixture thickens somewhat. Season to taste with salt, pepper, and grated nutmeg. In a small mixing bowl, combine the egg yolk and cream; stir the mixture into the soup. Heat through, but do not boil. Pour soup over the bread cubes, and serve immediately.

Radicchio and Asparagus Salad

(Illustrated below)

2 cups (500 ml) water
1 teaspoon salt
1 pound (500 g) asparagus, woody parts
    trimmed away
    Olive-Lemon Dressing
²/₃ pound (300 g) radicchio, trimmed, cleaned, and
    separated (split the larger leaves)
1 red onion, halved and thinly sliced
4 ounces (100 g) fresh button mushrooms,
    trimmed, rinsed, and sliced
    Dill to taste

In a medium saucepan, combine the water and salt, and bring to a boil. Add the asparagus, return to a boil, cover, and simmer for about 5 minutes. Pour off the water, and plunge the asparagus immediately into cold running water. Drain. Prepare the Olive-Lemon Dressing. Arrange the vegetables on a medium serving platter, and pour the dressing over them. Garnish with dill.

Olive-Lemon Dressing

3 tablespoons olive oil
3 tablespoons lemon juice
    Salt and pepper to taste

In a small mixing bowl, combine all the ingredients.

Radicchio with Bacon Sauce

    Oil and Vinegar Dressing
    Bacon Sauce
¹/₂ pound (250 g) radicchio, trimmed, cleaned, and
    separated (split the larger leaves)

Prepare the Oil and Vinegar Dressing and the Bacon Sauce. Place the radicchio in a medium serving bowl. Pour the dressing over the radicchio, and toss. Top with the Bacon Sauce, and serve immediately.

Oil and Vinegar Dressing

1 tablespoon vegetable oil
1 tablespoon vinegar
  Salt, pepper, and sugar to taste

In a small mixing bowl, combine the ingredients.

Bacon Sauce

2 tablespoons (30 g) margarine
2 onions, diced
4 slices (80 g) lean bacon, diced
¼ cup (35 g) flour
1 cup (250 ml) meat stock, heated
1 cup (250 ml) hot milk
  Salt to taste

In a large skillet, melt the butter, add the onion and bacon, and sauté until the onions are translucent. Stir in the flour, and continue cooking, stirring constantly, until the flour becomes a light yellow. Slowly add the stock and milk, and continue stirring so that no lumps form as you bring the mixture back to a boil. Reduce heat to low and cook for about 10 minutes, and season to taste with salt. Pour over the radicchio.

Spinach Salad

(Illustrated this page)

Tangy Cream Dressing (see recipe below)
1/2 pound (250 g) spinach, trimmed, separated, rinsed, and drained
5 tomatoes, rinsed and cut into wedges
3 hard-boiled eggs, sliced
Chives, finely chopped, to taste

Prepare the Tangy Cream Dressing. Arrange the salad ingredients in a medium serving bowl, and pour the dressing over them. Garnish with chives.

Tangy Cream Dressing

1 onion, minced
3 tablespoons vegetable oil
3 tablespoons vinegar
1-2 tablespoons cream
1 teaspoon grated horseradish
1 teaspoon sugar
Salt and pepper to taste

In a small mixing bowl, combine all the ingredients.

Delicate Spinach Leaves

2 1/4 pounds (1 kg) spinach, trimmed and rinsed
1 tablespoon butter *or* margarine
8 slices (150 g) lean bacon, diced
1 onion, diced
Salt, pepper, and grated nutmeg to taste

Place the spinach, while still dripping wet, into a medium saucepan. Cover, and braise until the leaves disintegrate; then drain. In a large skillet, melt the butter, add the bacon, and sauté until crisp and brown. Add the onion and the spinach. Season with salt, pepper, and grated nutmeg. Cover, and cook for about 5 minutes. Remove the cover, and cook an additional 2 or 3 minutes. Season again to taste. Serve with roast pork or veal.

remain soft. Cover the bowl, and set in a warm location until it has doubled. Punch the dough down, and knead well. Roll out into a circle, and lay it on a baking tray. Prepare the Spinach Topping; spread over dough. Sprinkle with salt, pepper, and marjoram. Top with cheese. Place the pan in a warm place, and let the dough rise for about 20 minutes. Bake for 25 to 30 minutes, or until cheese is golden brown.

Spinach Topping

2 tablespoons vegetable oil
4 slices (75 g) lean bacon, diced
3-4 slices (75 g) boiled ham, diced
1 medium onion, diced
1 pound (500 g) spinach, trimmed and rinsed
2 cloves garlic, minced
   Salt, grated nutmeg, and lemon juice to taste

In a medium skillet, heat the oil, add the bacon, and sauté until crisp and brown. Add the ham and onion, cover, and continue to sauté for 2 to 3 minutes. Put the spinach, while still dripping wet, into a medium saucepan. Cover, and cook until the leaves disintegrate; drain. Mix with the onion, ham, and bacon. Add the garlic, and season with salt, grated nutmeg, and lemon juice.

Spinach Pizza
(Illustrated this page)

Pizza Dough

1 3/4 cup (175 g) flour
1/2 packet dry yeast
1 2/3 tablespoons (25 g) melted butter *or* margarine
1/2 teaspoon sugar
   Salt and pepper to taste
1/2 cup (125 ml) lukewarm milk
   Spinach Topping
2 tablespoons chopped marjoram leaves
5 ounces (150 g) Gouda cheese, coarsely grated

Preheat the oven to 350° F. Sift the flour into a medium mixing bowl, and add the yeast, butter, sugar, salt, pepper, and milk. Mix until the ingredients are thoroughly combined (or use an electric mixer with a dough hook, first on low, and then on high settings, for a total of 5 minutes). Should the dough become sticky, add a little more flour, but not too much, since the dough must

Endive and Apple Salad
(Illustrated below)

Cider Vinegar Dressing (see recipe below)
1 medium endive, trimmed,
   halved, cut into strips, rinsed, and drained
2 cooking apples, peeled and sliced

Prepare the Cider Vinegar Dressing. In a medium serving bowl, combine the endive and apples; toss. Pour the dressing over the salad, toss, and serve immediately.

Cider Vinegar Dressing

4-5 tablespoons vegetable oil
2 teaspoons cider vinegar
4 teaspoons water
   Salt, pepper, and sugar to taste

In a small mixing bowl, combine the ingredients.

Bulgarian Endive Salad
(Illustrated below)

1 large endive, trimmed, halved, cut into strips,
   rinsed, and drained
2 ounces (75 g) feta cheese, crumbled

Sliced olives, optional
Tangy Sour Cream and Yogurt Dressing
(see recipe below)

In a large serving bowl, combine the endive, cheese, and olives, if desired. Prepare the Tangy Sour Cream and Yogurt Dressing. Pour over the salad, toss, and serve immediately.

Tangy Sour Cream and Yogurt Dressing

2 tablespoons vegetable oil
1 tablespoon vinegar
3 tablespoons sour cream
3 tablespoons plain yogurt
   Salt, pepper, and cayenne pepper to taste
2 tablespoons chopped chives
1 teaspoon chopped basil leaves

In a small mixing bowl, combine the oil, vinegar, sour cream, yogurt, salt, pepper, and cayenne pepper. Add the chives and basil.

Endive Salad with Mushrooms

(Illustrated below)

1/2 head endive, trimmed, cut into strips, rinsed, and drained

2-3 sticks celery (about 1/2 pound), trimmed, rinsed, and chopped

6 ounces (200 g) fresh button mushrooms, trimmed, rinsed, and sliced
    Nutty Anchovy Dressing (see recipe below)
    Anchovy fillets

In a large serving bowl, combine the endive, celery, and mushrooms; toss. Prepare the Nutty Anchovy Dressing, and pour over the salad. Toss, garnish with anchovy fillets, and serve immediately.

Nutty Anchovy Dressing

4 anchovy fillets, flaked

3 tablespoons vegetable oil

2 tablespoons wine vinegar

1 tablespoon cream
    Pepper to taste

1 tablespoon grated hazelnuts

In a small mixing bowl, combine the ingredients.

Spanish Endive and Sweet Pepper Salad

(Illustrated below)

1 head endive, trimmed, halved, cut into strips, rinsed, and drained

2 sweet peppers, seeded, rinsed, and cut into fine strips

10 stuffed green olives, sliced
    Onion-Egg Dressing (see recipe below)
    Hard-boiled egg white, diced

In a large serving bowl, combine the endive, peppers, and olives; toss. Prepare the Onion-Egg Dressing. Pour the dressing over the vegetables; toss. Garnish with the reserved egg white, and serve immediately.

Onion-Egg Dressing

1 hard-boiled egg, separated

1 onion, minced

4 tablespoons olive oil

3 tablespoons vinegar
    Salt, pepper, sugar, mustard, and paprika to taste

Mash the egg yolk; reserve the white for a garnish. In a small mixing bowl, combine the ingredients.

293

Belgian Endive Soup

(Illustrated next page)

3 cups (750 ml) chicken stock
1 pound (500 g) Belgian endive, withered leaves and
  stalk removed, rinsed, and cut into strips
2 egg yolks
1/2 cup (125 ml) cream
  Salt, pepper, and grated nutmeg to taste
  Croutons
1 tablespoon chopped parsley

In a large saucepan, bring the chicken stock to a
boil. Add the Belgian endive strips, return to a boil,
cover, and simmer for about 5 minutes. Remove 3
tablespoons of cooked endive, and set aside. Puree
remaining endive and stock in a blender or food
processor. In a small mixing bowl, combine the egg
yolks and cream. Return the puree to the saucepan,
and add egg yolk mixture and reserved endive. Heat
through, stirring constantly, but do not boil. Season
to taste with salt, pepper, and nutmeg. Ladle the
soup into individual serving bowls, garnish with
croutons and parsley, and serve immediately.

Baked Belgian Endive

(Illustrated next page)

2 tablespoons vegetable oil
1/2 pound (250 g) ground beef
1/2 pound (250 g) ground pork
2 onions, minced
2 ounces (70 g) tomato puree
1 cup (250 g) cooked long grain rice
  Salt, pepper, and sweet paprika to taste
1 teaspoon salt
1 1/4 pounds (600 g) Belgian endive, withered
  leaves removed, cut into wedges, and rinsed
  Creamy Cheese Sauce
8 strips (150 g) bacon
2 tablespoons fine bread crumbs
  Butter *or* margarine

Preheat the oven to 350° F. In a large skillet, heat
the oil, add the ground meats, and sauté until all
pinkness is gone. Add the onions to the meat, and
sauté until translucent. Add the tomato puree and
rice, and season to taste. Place the mixture in a
large baking pan. Fill a medium saucepan half full
with water, add salt, and bring to a boil. Add the
Belgian endive, return to a boil, cover, and simmer

for about 2 to 3 minutes. Drain, and lay on top of
the meat mixture. Prepare the Creamy Cheese
Sauce, and pour over the endive. Arrange the bacon
slices on top, and sprinkle the bread crumbs over
all. Dot with butter, and bake for about 30 minutes, or until the crumbs are golden.

Creamy Cheese Sauce

6 ounces (150 g) sour cream
1 6-ounce carton (150 g) plain yogurt
  Salt, pepper, and sweet paprika to taste
3 tablespoons chopped herbs (tarragon, parsley,
  burnet)
1 cup (3 1/4 ounces) grated Gouda cheese

In a small mixing bowl, combine the sour cream,
yogurt, salt, pepper, and paprika. Add the herbs
and cheese.

Beef Rolls with Belgian Endive

(Illustrated next page)

  Salt, pepper, and sweet paprika to taste
4 slices beef (each about 6 ounces)
4 strips lean bacon
4 small Belgian endives withered leaves and stalk
  removed, rinsed, and patted dry
4 tablespoons vegetable oil
1 cup (250 ml) white wine
3 tomatoes, peeled, and quartered
2 teaspoons flour
2 tablespoons cream
  Salt, pepper, sugar, and Worcestershire
  sauce to taste

Season the beef slices with salt, pepper, and paprika. Place one slice of bacon, then one endive on
each slice. Roll up each slice, from the narrowest to
the broadest end, and tie with kitchen string or
small wooden skewers. In a large skillet, heat the
oil, and sauté the beef rolls well on all sides. Add
1/2 cup of the wine, cover, and simmer for about
1 1/2 hours, adding remaining wine as needed.
Continue simmering until the rolls are tender. Puree
the tomatoes, and add to the pan juices. In a small
mixing bowl, combine the flour and cream. Stir
into the cooking juices, and heat, stirring constantly, until thickened. Season to taste. Serve immediately. Serve with dumplings or boiled potatoes.

Fruity Belgian Endive Salad

³/₄ pound (400 g) Belgian endive, withered leaves
   and stalk removed, rinsed, and cut into strips
1 apple, peeled and sliced
1 orange, peeled, separated, and thinly sliced
1 banana, peeled and sliced
¹/₃ cup (50 g) hazelnuts, sliced (reserve half for
   garnish)
   Creamy Citrus Dressing

Place the Belgian endive, apple, orange, banana,
and nuts in a large serving bowl; toss. Prepare the
Creamy Citrus Dressing. Pour the dressing over the
salad, toss, cover, and set aside for about 30
minutes. Garnish with reserved hazelnuts, and serve
immediately.

Creamy Citrus Dressing

¹/₂ cup (125 ml) cream
2 tablespoons mayonnaise
   Juice of ¹/₂ orange
2-3 tablespoons lemon juice
   Salt, pepper, and sugar to taste

In a small mixing bowl, combine all the ingredients.

Lamb's Lettuce Dusseldorf

(Illustrated above)

6 ounces (200 g) lamb's lettuce, trimmed, separated
   (split the larger leaves), rinsed, and drained
2 medium oranges, peeled, divided into segments,
   sliced, and halved
1 bunch spring onions (about $^1/_2$ pound), trimmed
   to about 5 inches of green, peeled (if necessary),
   rinsed, and sliced
   Creamy Lemon Dressing (see recipe below)

Arrange the lamb's lettuce, oranges, and onions on
individual serving dishes. Prepare the Creamy
Lemon Dressing. Pour the dressing over the salads,
and serve immediately.

Creamy Lemon Dressing

$^1/_2$ cup (125 ml) sour cream
1 tablespoon vegetable oil
3 tablespoons lemon juice
   Salt, pepper, and sugar to taste
   Ground ginger or Tabasco or Worcestershire
   sauce to taste

In a small mixing bowl, combine the ingredients.

Nussli Salad

(Illustrated above)
$^1/_2$ pound (250 g) lamb's lettuce, trimmed, separated (split the larger leaves), rinsed, and drained
2 hard-boiled eggs, quartered
   Onion and Chive Dressing (see recipe below)

Arrange the lettuce and hard-boiled eggs on individual serving plates. Prepare the Onion and Chive
Dressing. Pour the dressing over the salads, and
serve immediately.

Onion and Chive Dressing

1 clove garlic, halved
1 shallot or 1 small onion, minced
3 tablespoons vegetable oil
1 tablespoon wine vinegar
   Salt and pepper to taste
2-3 tablespoons finely chopped chives

Rub the cut side of the garlic pieces over the inside
of a small mixing bowl. Add the shallot, oil,
vinegar, salt, pepper, and chives, and mix well.

Lamb's Lettuce with Tomato and Mushrooms

(Illustrated above)

Lemon juice
6 ounces (150 g) fresh button mushrooms,
  trimmed, rinsed, and sliced
1 ripe avocado, peeled, cored, and thinly sliced
6 ounces (150 g) lamb's lettuce, trimmed, separated
  (split the larger leaves), rinsed, and drained
3 medium tomatoes, rinsed, dried, and sliced
  Herb Vinegar and Onion Dressing (see recipe
  below)

Sprinkle the lemon juice over the mushrooms and avocado slices. Arrange the mushrooms, avocado, lamb's lettuce, and tomatoes on individual serving dishes. Prepare the Herb Vinegar and Onion Dressing. Pour over the salads, and serve immediately.

Herb Vinegar and Onion Dressing

2 onions, minced
4 tablespoons vegetable oil
3 tablespoons herb vinegar
  Salt and white pepper to taste

In a small mixing bowl, combine the ingredients.

Lamb's Lettuce with Onions and Bacon

(Illustrated above)

1 teaspoon butter *or* margarine
4 slices (75 g) bacon
9 ounces (300 g) lamb's lettuce, trimmed, separated
  (split the larger leaves), rinsed, and drained
2 onions, sliced
  Mustard and Herb Vinegar Dressing (see recipe
  below)

In a small skillet, melt the butter, and sauté the bacon slices for a few minutes. Arrange the bacon, lamb's lettuce, and onions on individual serving dishes. Prepare the Mustard and Herb Vinegar Dressing, pour over the salads, and serve immediately.

Mustard and Herb Vinegar Dressing

4 tablespoons olive oil
3 tablespoons herb vinegar
1 tablespoon mustard
  Salt, pepper, and sweet paprika to taste

In a small mixing bowl, combine all the ingredients.

297

Root Vegetables

To sink your teeth into

Vegetable and Seafood Fritters

(Illustrated on pp. 298-299)

6-8 young, thin carrots, peeled, rinsed, and patted dry
6-8 young, thin parsley roots, trimmed, rinsed, and patted dry
2 fennel bulbs, (about 1 pound *or* 500 g), trimmed, rinsed, patted dry, and quartered
4 large raw scampi, shelled, rinsed, and patted dry
6 ounces (200 g) oven-ready squid, rinsed, patted dry, and cut into rings
  Lemon juice
  Oil *or* shortening for deep-fat frying
  Deep-fat Batter (see recipe below)
  Lemon wedges

Place the carrots, parsley, fennel, scampi, and squid in individual bowls; sprinkle with lemon juice. Let stand for about 15 minutes; then pat dry. Fill a deep-fat fryer according to the manufacturer's directions, and heat the oil to 350° F. Prepare the Deep-fat Batter. Dip the vegetables, parsley, and seafood in the batter, and fry to a golden brown. (Vegetables will take about 10 to 12 minutes, and seafood will require about 3 to 5 minutes.) Drain on paper towels, and sprinkle with salt. Garnish with lemon wedges, and serve immediately.

Deep-fat Batter

1 ³/₄ cups (250 g) flour
1 cup (250 ml) light beer
1 egg
  Salt and pepper to taste

Sift the flour into a medium mixing bowl. Make a hollow in the center, and add a little of the beer. Working from the center out, work the beer into the flour. Add the remaining beer and the egg; stir into a smooth batter, taking care that no lumps form. Season with salt and pepper.

Cream of Carrot Soup

1-2 tablespoons butter
2-3 onions, peeled and diced
³/₄ pound (400 g) carrots, peeled and diced
2 large potatoes (about 175 g), peeled and diced
1 piece root celery *or* 2 stalks celery, peeled and diced
4 cups (1 liter) water

2 teaspoons salt
  Pepper to taste
3 ounces sour cream
  Salt and pepper to taste
1 tablespoon chopped dill
  Butter

In a dutch oven, melt the butter, add the onions, and sauté until translucent. Add the carrots, potatoes, and celery, and sauté for another 3 to 5 minutes. Add the water, salt, and pepper. Bring to a boil, cover, and simmer for about 12 minutes. Puree in a blender or food processor. Return the puree to the dutch oven. Add the sour cream, season to taste, and add the dill. Ladle into individual serving bowls, dot with butter, and serve immediately.

Carrot Croquettes

1 pound (500 g) potatoes, rinsed
1 teaspoon salt
2-3 tablespoons butter *or* margarine
¹/₂ pound (250 g) carrots, peeled and diced
¹/₂ cup (125 ml) meat stock
1 teaspoon salt
1 egg yolk
2-3 tablespoons chopped parsley
2-3 tablespoons semolina
  Grated nutmeg to taste
3-4 tablespoons fine bread crumbs
  Melted butter

Place the potatoes in a medium saucepan, add the salt and enough water to cover, and bring to a boil. Cover, and simmer for 20 to 25 minutes, or until fork-tender. Drain, allow the steam to evaporate, and peel while still hot. Puree in a blender or food processor. In a dutch oven, melt the butter, add the carrots, and sauté for 5 minutes. Add the stock and salt, bring to a boil, cover, and simmer for 15 minutes. Drain, and puree in a blender or food processor. In a large mixing bowl, combine the two purees. Add the egg yolk, parsley, semolina, and nutmeg. Shape the mixture into rolls, about an inch thick and 2 or 3 inches long, and roll them in bread crumbs. In a large skillet, melt the butter, and fry the croquettes until golden brown. Add more butte. as needed. Serve with steaks or chops.

Glazed Carrots

(Illustrated this page)

1 teaspoon salt
1 pound (500 g) young carrots, peeled and rinsed
3 ¹/₃ tablespoons (50 g) butter
3 tablespoons sugar
  Pepper to taste
  Mint leaves, chopped

Fill a medium saucepan half full with water, add salt, and bring to a boil. Add the carrots, return to a boil, cover, and simmer for about 7 minutes. Drain. In a large skillet, melt butter, add the carrots, and braise for about 5 minutes. Add the sugar, and continue braising carrots, stirring occasionally, for about 10 minutes, or until fork-tender. Turn carrots into a medium serving bowl, sprinkle with pepper and mint, and serve immediately.

Carrot and Apple Cream

(Illustrated above)

2 cups (500 ml) cream
  Juice of 1 lemon
2 tablespoons sugar
1 cooking apple, peeled, cored, and grated
1 carrot, peeled, rinsed, and grated
  Cress leaves, optional
1-2 carrots, peeled rinsed, and patted dry

In a small serving bowl, combine the cream, lemon juice, and sugar. Refrigerate for 30 minutes. Add the grated apple and carrot to the cream, stir well, and pour into individual glasses. Garnish with cress, if desired. Cut the carrots into spirals with a potato peeler, and use for a garnish.

Carrot Flakes

(Illustrated above)

  Lemon juice
$^1/_2$ pound (250 g) carrots, peeled, rinsed, and grated
2 tablespoons cream
1 tablespoon sugar
5 tablespoons regular oatmeal (not quick-cooking)

In a medium mixing bowl, sprinkle the grated carrot with lemon juice. In a small mixing bowl, combine the cream and sugar. Combine the oatmeal with the carrots, and pour the cream mixture over the carrot mixture. Serve in individual cereal bowls.

Carrot and Walnut Salad

1 ¹/₂ pounds (750 g) carrots, peeled, rinsed, and
  grated
5-6 tablespoons lime *or* lemon juice
4 tablespoons walnut oil
2-3 tablespoons sugar
  Salt and pepper to taste
¹/₂ cup (75 g) walnuts, chopped coarsely
  Lettuce leaves, rinsed and shaken dry
  Lemon *or* lime slices

In a large mixing bowl, combine the carrots, lime
juice, walnut oil, sugar, salt, and pepper. Toss well.
Add the walnuts, and toss. Cover, and refrigerate
for about 15 minutes. Arrange the lettuce leaves on
individual serving plates, divide the salad between
the dishes, and garnish with lemon slices.

Carrot Drink

(Illustrated above)

²/₃ pound (300 g) carrots, peeled, rinsed, and diced
¹/₂ red sweet pepper, seeded, rinsed, and diced
  Juice of ¹/₂ lemon
  Juice of 2 oranges
  Salt, pepper, and celery salt to taste
  Celery sticks
  Celery leaves

Puree the carrots and red pepper in a blender or
food processor. Add the lemon juice and orange
juice, and mix well. Season with salt, pepper, and
celery salt. Pour into individual glasses, garnish
with celery sticks and celery leaves, and serve immediately.

Carrot Stew

(Illustrated this page)

$^1/_4$ pound (100 g) dried beans
3 cups (750 ml) water
2 tablespoons butter *or* margarine
$^1/_2$ pound (250 g) salt pork *or* jowl bacon, diced
1 pound (500 g) sirloin
2 medium onions, diced
  Salt and pepper to taste
3 cups (750 ml) hot water
2 $^1/_4$ pounds (1 kg) carrots, peeled, rinsed, and
  minced
1 pound (500 g) potatoes, rinsed, peeled, and minced
1 piece root celery (3 $^1/_4$ ounces) *or* 3 stalks celery,
  rinsed, peeled, and diced
$^1/_2$ pound (250 g) apples, peeled, cored, and sliced
2 tablespoons chopped mixed herbs (smooth parsley,
  chervil, burnet)

In a large saucepan, soak the beans in the water
overnight. In a dutch oven, heat the butter, and
sauté the meats until they are beginning to brown
on all sides. Add the onions, and continue to sauté
until the meat is brown on all sides. Season with
salt and pepper. Add the water. Drain the dried
beans, and add them to the meat mixture. Bring to
a boil, cover, and simmer for about 15 minutes.
Add the carrots, potatoes, and celery, return to a
boil, cover, and simmer for an additional 10 minutes. Add the apples, return to a boil, cover, and
simmer for about 10 minutes more. Remove the
sirloin, bone it, and dice the meat. Return the meat
to the dutch oven; season with salt and pepper. Stir
in the mixed herbs, and serve immediately.

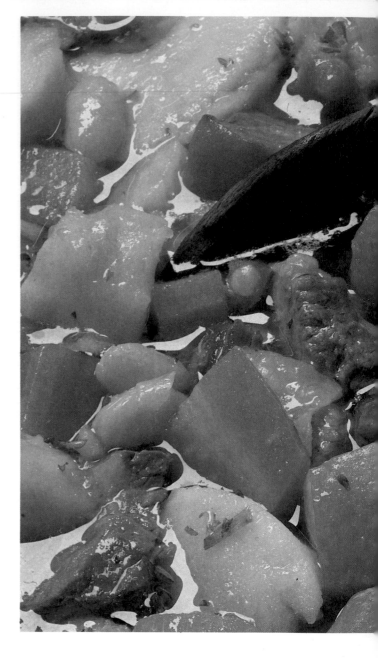

Carrot and Potato Puree

1 teaspoon salt
1 $^1/_2$ pounds (750 g) carrots, peeled, rinsed,
  and diced
$^3/_4$-1 pound (375-500 g) potatoes, peeled, rinsed,
  and diced
3-6 ounces (75-150 g) sour cream
  Salt, pepper, and grated nutmeg to taste
2 tablespoons chopped parsley

Fill a large saucepan half full with water, add salt,
and bring to a boil. Add the carrots and potatoes,
return to a boil, cover, and simmer for about 10 to
15 minutes, or until fork-tender. Drain, and puree
in a blender or food processor. Stir in the sour
cream; season with salt, pepper, and grated nutmeg.
Add the parsley, and serve immediately.

Carrot-Nut Cake

1 1/4 cups (250 g) ground hazelnuts
6 egg yolks
5 ounces (150 g) brown sugar
  Grated rind of 1 lemon
3 tablespoons lemon juice
1/2 to 1 teaspoon anise seed
2/3 pound (300 g) carrots, peeled, rinsed, and grated
1/3 cup (50 g) almonds, ground
3/8 cup (50 g) flour
1/2 cup (50 g) fine bread crumbs
1 rounded teaspoon baking powder
6 egg whites
3 1/4 ounces (100 g) sugar
2 tablespoons apricot jam
2 tablespoons water
3-4 ounces (100-125 g) powdered sugar
1 1/2-2 tablespoons lemon juice
1/4 cup (40 g) peeled, chopped hazelnuts
  Whipped cream

Preheat the oven at 350° F. Spread the ground
hazelnuts over a clean baking sheet, and roast for 5
minutes. Cool. In a large mixing bowl, cream the
egg yolks and brown sugar. Add the lemon rind,
lemon juice, and anise seed, and mix well. Add the
hazelnuts, carrots, and almonds. Set aside. Sift the
flour into a small mixing bowl, and add the bread
crumbs and baking powder. Mix well, and add to
the carrot mixture. Set aside. In a small mixing
bowl, combine egg whites and sugar, and whip
until they form stiff peaks. Stir half of the whipped
egg whites into the carrot mixture, then fold in the
second half. Grease and flour a 9-inch cake pan,
and insert a sheet of waxed paper cut to fit the
bottom of the pan. Turn the carrot mixture into the
pan, smoothing the top. Bake for 50 to 55 minutes,
or until golden brown. Remove the cake from the
pan, remove the waxed paper, and set the cake on a
rack to cool. Rub the apricot jam through a sieve
and into a small saucepan. Add water, and heat to
boiling. As soon as it boils, remove it from the
heat, and spread it over the cake. Set the cake aside
for 15 minutes to cool. In a small mixing bowl, sift
the powdered sugar. Add the lemon juice, and
spread over the cake. Sprinkle with the hazelnuts.
Serve with whipped cream.

Carrots in Juice

3 1/3 tablespoons (50 g) butter *or* margarine
1 1/2 pounds (750 g) carrots, peeled, rinsed, and
  diced
  Salt and pepper to taste
1/2 cup (125 ml) water
4 tablespoons chopped parsley

In a large skillet, melt the butter, and add the
carrots. Cover, and cook until tender. Season with
salt and pepper. Add the water, cover, and sweat the
carrots for about 10 minutes, stirring occasionally.
Add the parsley, and serve immediately.

Radish Sandwich

(Illustrated below)

4 slices whole-wheat bread
   Butter *or* margarine
2 2/3 ounces (80 g) Boursin *or* cream cheese
   with herbs
2 hard-boiled eggs, sliced
1-2 bunches radishes, trimmed, rinsed, and sliced
2 tablespoons finely chopped chives
   Salt and pepper to taste

Spread each slice of bread with butter. Then spread the Boursin over each slice; layer egg slices over cheese. Place radishes in overlapping slices on top of the Boursin, sprinkle with chives, salt, and pepper, and serve.

Radish Salad

(Illustrated below)

3 bunches radishes, trimmed, rinsed, and sliced
5 young spring onions, cleaned, trimmed to about 4
   inches of green, rinsed, and sliced
1 apple, peeled, cored, and sliced
   Chive and Parsley Dressing (see recipe below)

In a medium serving bowl, combine the radishes, onions, and apple slices. Prepare the Chive and Parsley Dressing. Pour the dressing over the salad, toss, and set aside for 15 minutes before serving.

Chive and Parsley Dressing

3 tablespoons salad oil
3 tablespoons herb vinegar
   Salt, pepper, and sugar to taste
1 tablespoon chopped parsley
1 tablespoon finely chopped chives

In a small serving bowl, combine the oil, vinegar, salt, pepper, and sugar. Add the parsley and chives.

Radish Sour Cream

(Illustrated below)

2 cups (500 g) half & half
6 ounces (150 g) sour cream
  Salt and pepper to taste
3 bunches radishes, trimmed, rinsed, and sliced
1 tablespoon chopped dill
1 tablespoon chopped basil leaves
1-2 teaspoons pickle relish
  Radish slices

In a small serving bowl, combine the half-and-half and the sour cream. Season to taste. Add the radishes, dill, basil, and pickle relish. Season to taste. Garnish with radish slices. Serve with baked potatoes or whole-wheat bread and butter.

Roast Beef Rolls with Radish Cream

  Radish Cream (see recipe below)
4-6 slices roast beef

Prepare the Radish Cream. Spread the cream over the beef slices, roll, and slice into appetizer-size pieces. If necessary, secure with toothpicks.

Radish Cream

1 bunch radishes, trimmed, rinsed, and diced
6 ounces (150 g) sour cream
2-3 tablespoons chopped garden cress
  Herb salt to taste

Puree the radishes in a blender or food processor. Place the puree into a fine-mesh sieve, and drain for 30 minutes. In a small mixing bowl, combine sour cream, cress and herb salt. Mix well. Add the radish puree and mix well.

Beets with Horseradish

(Illustrated this page)

2 tablespoons butter
2 onions (about 3 1/4 ounces), diced
3 large beets, trimmed, scrubbed with a soft brush,
    peeled, and grated or thinly sliced
    Salt
3 tablespoons sour cream
1 tablespoon grated horseradish
1 teaspoon mustard
1 pinch ground ginger
1 teaspoon sugar
    Grated cheese, optional

In a large skillet, melt the butter, and sauté the
onions until translucent. Add the beets, and sauté
for another 5 minutes. Season with salt. Add a little
water, bring to a boil, cover, and simmer for about
30 minutes, or until tender. Remove from heat. In a
small bowl, combine the sour cream, horseradish,
mustard, ginger, and sugar. Combine the sour
cream mixture with the beet mixture, cover, and set
aside for about 45 minutes. Reheat, and serve. If
desired, turn the beets into a baking dish, sprinkle
with grated cheese, and brown under a broiler.

Stuffed Beets

(Illustrated on right)

1 teaspoon salt
4 equal-sized beets, trimmed and scrubbed with a
    soft brush
    Meat and Parmesan Filling (see recipe below)
2 tablespoons cornstarch
2 tablespoons water
1 cup (250 ml) cream
    Butter or margarine

Preheat the oven to 350° F. Fill a medium saucepan
half full with water, add salt, and bring to a boil.
Add beets, return to a boil, cover, and simmer for
about 45 minutes, or until fork-tender. Pour off the
boiling water, and immediately plunge the beets into
cold water. (This will make them easier to peel.)
Peel, and hollow them out, leaving a shell about 1
inch thick. Puree the flesh; reserve for filling. Prepare the Meat and Parmesan Filling. Fill the beet
shells, and place side by side in a well-greased
soufflé dish. In a small mixing bowl, combine the
cornstarch, water, and cream. Mix well, and pour

into the soufflé dish around the beets. Dot the filling with butter, and bake for about 30 minutes, or
until brown.

Meat and Parmesan Filling

2 tablespoons butter or margarine
1 onion, minced
1 clove garlic, minced
1/4 pound (125 g) ground beef
1/4 pound (125 g) ground pork
1/2 teaspoon sweet paprika
    Salt and pepper to taste
    Reserved beet puree
3 tablespoons grated Parmesan cheese

In a large skillet, melt the butter, and sauté the
onion and garlic until translucent. Cool. In a large
mixing bowl, combine the cooked onion and garlic
with ground beef and pork. Season with paprika,
salt, and pepper. Add the reserved beet puree and
Parmesan cheese.

Spicy Pickled Beets

(Illustrated below)

1 teaspoon salt
4 large beets (about 2 1/4 pounds) trimmed and
    scrubbed with a soft brush
    Sugar-Vinegar Solution (see recipe below)
5 onions, sliced
2 bay leaves

Prepare the jars for canning as instructed in the
Introduction. Fill the water-bath canner 2/3 full,
and begin heating the water. Fill a medium saucepan half full with water, add salt, and bring to a
boil. Add the beets, return to a boil, cover, and simmer for about 45 minutes, or until fork-tender.
Pour off the water, and immediately plunge the
beets into cold water. (This will make them easier
to peel.) Peel the beets, and slice. Halve if necessary.
Prepare the Sugar-Vinegar Solution. Layer the beets,
onions, and bay leaves in the prepared canning jars
as instructed in the Introduction. Pour the hot solution over the vegetables, leaving a headspace of 1/2

inch. Remove any air spaces, clean the rims, and
seal. Process the jars for 30 minutes (add 1 minute
for every 1,000 feet above sea level). Remove the
jars from the canner, and set out to cool in a draft-
free location. After 24 hours, test the seals. Any
unsealed product must be used immediately, or it
may be reprocessed. Store the jars in a cool, dark
location

Sugar-Vinegar Solution

2 cups (500 ml) water
1/4 cup plus 1 tablespoon (75 g) sugar
1 teaspoon salt
1 cup (250 ml) wine vinegar

In a large saucepan, combine the water, sugar, and
salt, and bring them to a boil. Remove from the
heat, and add the wine vinegar.

Grilled Salsify

(Illustrated this page)

4 cups (1 liter) cold water
2 tablespoons flour
4 tablespoons vinegar, divided
2 ¹/₄ pounds (1 kg) salsify, trimmed and scrubbed
   with a soft brush
1 ¹/₂ cups (375 ml) water
4-8 ham slices (about 400 g)
   Creamed Dill Sauce (see recipe below)
¹/₂ cup (50 g) grated medium-ripe Gouda cheese

To retain the white salsify color, combine the water,
flour, and 2 tablespoons vinegar in a large mixing
bowl. Immerse the salsify, cover, and set aside for 3
hours. Preheat the oven at 350° F. Drain the salsify
and halve the roots lengthwise. In a large saucepan,
combine the water and 2 tablespoons vinegar, and
bring to a boil. Add the salsify, return to a boil,
cover, and simmer for about 10 minutes. Remove
the salsify with a slotted spoon, and reserve 1 ¹/₂
cups of the cooking liquid. Wrap the salsify roots in
the ham slices, and lay them in a greased baking
dish. Prepare the Creamed Dill Sauce, and pour it
over the salsify. Sprinkle the cheese over the top,
and bake for 20 to 25 minutes, or until the cheese
is golden brown. Serve with boiled potatoes or rice.

Creamed Dill Sauce

2 ²/₃ tablespoons (40 g) butter *or* margarine
¹/₄ cup (40 g) flour
1 ¹/₂ cups (375 ml) cooking liquid, reserved
¹/₂ cup (125 ml) milk *or* cream
   Salt, pepper, and grated nutmeg to taste
2-3 tablespoons chopped dill

In a medium skillet, melt the butter, add the flour,
and sauté until it is light yellow. Add the reserved
cooking liquid and milk, stirring constantly with a
wire whisk, so that no lumps form. Bring the milk
mixture to a boil. Season with salt, pepper, and
grated nutmeg. Stir in the dill.

Salsify in Herb Cream

2 ¹/₄ pounds (1 kg) salsify, trimmed and scrubbed
   with a soft brush
4 cups (1 liter) cold water
2 level tablespoons flour
6 tablespoons vinegar, divided
1 ¹/₂ cups (375 ml) water
1 teaspoon salt
   Creamy Herb Sauce (see recipe below)
   Lettuce leaves, rinsed and patted dry
   Tomato wedges
   Parsley

To retain the white salsify color, combine the water, flour, and 2 tablespoons vinegar in a large mixing bowl, and immerse the salsify in the liquid. Cover, and set aside for 3 hours. Drain the salsify, and halve the roots lengthwise, or quarter them, and cut them into 2-inch pieces. In a large saucepan, combine water, salt, and 2 tablespoons vinegar, and bring to a boil. Add the salsify, return to a boil, cover, and simmer for about 10 minutes. Remove from the heat, add 2 tablespoons vinegar, and set aside to cool in the liquid. When completely cooled, drain. Prepare the Creamy Herb Sauce. Line a large serving platter with lettuce leaves, and arrange the salsify on top. Spread the sauce over the salsify, garnish with tomato wedges and parsley, and serve. Serve with whole-wheat bread and butter.

Creamy Herb Sauce

2 yolks of hard-boiled eggs
2 tablespoons vegetable oil
2 tablespoons half-and-half
6 ounces (150 g) sour cream
2 tablespoons chopped parsley
2 tablespoons chopped chervil leaves
1 tablespoon chopped dill
1 tablespoon chopped lemon mint leaves
1 tablespoon chopped basil leaves
1 tablespoon chopped tarragon leaves
1 tablespoon finely chopped chives
1-2 shallots, peeled and minced
   Salt and pepper to taste

In a medium mixing bowl, combine the yolks, oil, half-and-half, and sour cream. Add the remaining ingredients.

Celeriac Slices with Onions and Marrow Bone Slices

(Illustrated next page)

1 teaspoon salt
1-2 celeriac (about 1 ¹/₂ pounds), peeled, rinsed, and sliced
4 marrow bones, rinsed, and dipped in hot water or grilled in an oven for 2 minutes
   Sautéed Onions (see recipe below)
   Chopped parsley

Fill a medium saucepan half full with water, add salt, and bring to a boil. Add the celeriac, return to a boil, cover, and simmer for about 12 minutes. Drain. Remove the marrow from the bones, and cut into 3 slices. Prepare the Sautéed Onions. Spread the celeriac slices with the onions, and top each with a slice of marrow. Place the slices on a baking sheet, and broil for about 5 minutes, or until the marrow is browned. Sprinkle the slices with parsley, and serve immediately.

Sautéed Onions

7 tablespoons (3 ¹/₄ ounces or 100 g) butter or margarine
1 ¹/₂ pounds (750 g) onions, minced

In a large skillet, melt the butter. Add the onions, and sauté, stirring constantly, until they form a smooth consistency. Don't let them become too brown.

Vegetables Au Gratin a la Wallis

(Illustrated this page)

   Salt
2 celeriac (about 700 g), peeled, rinsed, and thinly sliced
2 medium red onions, thinly sliced
¹/₂ head savoy cabbage, rinsed, drained, and cut into thin strips
4-5 sticks celery (about 1 pound), trimmed, rinsed, and diced
8 slices (200 g) thin-sliced bacon
   Salt, pepper, grated nutmeg, and mace to taste
³/₄ cup plus 4 teaspoons (200 ml) cream
4 tablespoons grated Gruyere cheese

Fill a medium saucepan half full with water, add 1 teaspoon salt, and bring to a boil. Add the celeriac,

return to a boil, cover, and simmer for about 8 minutes. Drain. Fill a medium saucepan half full with water, add 1 teaspoon salt, and bring to a boil. Add the onions, savoy, and celery, return to a boil, cover, and simmer for about 8 minutes. Pour the onion mixture into a colander, rinse with cold water, and drain well. Preheat the oven at 350° F. Grease a soufflé dish. Beginning and ending with celeriac slices, layer the celeriac, onion mixture, and bacon in the dish, sprinkling each layer with salt, pepper, nutmeg, and mace, and a dash of the cream and cheese. Top the dish with the remaining cream and cheese, and bake for about 45 minutes, or until the ingredients are fork-tender and the cheese is browned.

Stuffed Celeriac

(Illustrated next page)

1 teaspoon salt
2 celeriac (each about 600 g), peeled, rinsed, and halved horizontally
2 tablespoons lemon juice
   Pork and Mushroom Stuffing (see recipe below)
   Creamy Wine Sauce (see recipe below)
8 strips bacon

Fill a medium saucepan half full with water, add salt, and bring to a boil. Add the celeriac and lemon juice, return to a boil, cover, and simmer for about 30 minutes, or until fork-tender. Drain, and reserve 2 tablespoons of the cooking water. Carefully hollow out the celeriac halves, leaving a shell about 1/2 inch thick. Preheat the oven at 325° F. Puree the celeriac meat, set aside and prepare the Pork and Mushroom Stuffing. Prepare the Creamy Wine Sauce. Fill the celeriac shells with the stuffing. Grease a soufflé dish, and set the filled shells inside. Pour the sauce over the shells. Top each shell with 2 slices of bacon. Cover, and bake for about 40 minutes. Serve with mashed potatoes.

Pork and Mushroom Stuffing

4 slices (100 g) bacon, minced
1 onion, minced
6 fresh mushrooms (200 g), trimmed, and diced
Salt, pepper, and celery salt to taste
6 ounces (175 g) ground pork
    Pureed celeriac meat, reserved
1 egg

In a large skillet, sauté the bacon until brown. Add the onion, and sauté until translucent. Add the mushrooms, and continue to sauté for another 5 to 6 minutes. Season with salt, pepper, and celery salt. Set aside to cool. When completely cool, combine the mushroom mixture and the pork; mix well. Add the reserved celeriac meat and the egg; mix well.

Creamy Wine Sauce

2 tablespoons white wine
6 tablespoons cream
2 tablespoons reserved cooking water
    Salt, pepper, and celery salt to taste

In a small mixing bowl, combine all the ingredients. Set aside until ready to pour over the filled shells.

Celery with Tomatoes

(Illustrated this page)

1 teaspoon salt
5-6 sticks celery (about 600 g), trimmed, rinsed, and
   halved lengthwise
1-2 tablespoons butter *or* margarine
6 young spring onions, trimmed to about 4 inches of
   green, rinsed, and sliced
1 clove garlic, minced
1 pound (500 g) tomatoes, peeled and halved
   Salt and pepper to taste
1-2 tablespoons chopped basil leaves

Fill a medium saucepan half full with water, add
salt, and bring to a boil. Add the celery stalks, return to a boil, cover, and simmer for about 8 to 10
minutes. Drain, place them on a warmed medium
serving platter, and keep warm. In a large skillet,
heat the butter, and sauté the onions and garlic until translucent. Add the tomatoes, season to taste,
cover, and simmer for about 3 minutes. Remove
tomatoes, place around the celery stalks, and top
with the onion mixture. Sprinkle with basil, and
serve immediately. Serve with roast pork or beef, or
with pork chops.

Celery and Fruit Salad

(Illustrated this page)

2 cooking apples, peeled and sliced
   Juice of 1 lemon
2-3 sticks celery, trimmed, rinsed, drained, and cut
   into thin strips
1 large mango, peeled, stone removed, and cut into
   strips
2 kiwis, peeled and sliced
   Roquefort and Yogurt Dressing (see recipe below)

Sprinkle the apple slices with the lemon juice. In a
large serving bowl, combine the apples, celery,
mango, and kiwis. Prepare the Roquefort and
Yogurt Dressing, and pour it over the salad. Serve
immediately.

Roquefort and Yogurt Dressing

2 ²/₃ ounces (80 g) Roquefort cheese, finely crumbled
6 ounces (150 g) yogurt
   Sugar, salt, white pepper, and ground ginger to
   taste

In a small mixing bowl, combine all the ingredients.

Piquant Filled Celery
(Illustrated this page)

4-6 stalks celery, trimmed, rinsed, and patted dry
Pineapple and Ham Filling (see recipe below)
   Celery leaves, optional
   Sliced pineapple, halved

Cut the celery stalks into pieces about 7 inches long. Prepare the Pineapple and Ham Filling. Place the filling in a frosting bag, and fill the celery stalks. On a large serving platter, arrange the filled stalks on celery leaves, if desired. Garnish with sliced pineapple halves.

Pineapple and Ham Filling

8 ounces (200 g) Boursin *or* cream cheese
1 tablespoon yogurt
3 tablespoons cream
2 tablespoons pineapple juice
2-3 slices canned pineapple, minced
2-3 slices boiled ham, minced
   Salt and pepper to taste

In a medium mixing bowl, combine the Boursin, yogurt, cream, and pineapple juice. Mix in the pineapple and ham, and season to taste.

Celery Stalks with Cottage Cheese

12 ounces (340 g) dry cottage cheese
1 green sweet pepper, seeded, cut into strips, and rinsed
1 red sweet pepper, seeded, cut into strips, and rinsed
4 ounces (100 g) cooked corn, drained
2 tablespoons minced onion
2 tablespoons minced chives
   Salt and pepper to taste
4 sticks celery (about 9 ounces *or* 300 g), trimmed, rinsed, and cut into pieces about 2 1/2 inches long
   Tomato wedges

Place the cottage cheese into a large mixing bowl, and break it apart. Add the peppers, corn, onions, and chives, and mix well. Arrange the celery sticks on a platter, and top with the cottage cheese mixture. Garnish with tomato wedges, and serve.

Potatoes Chantilly

3 cups mashed potatoes
1/2 cup whipping cream, beaten until stiff
   Salt and white pepper to taste
1/2 cup grated cheddar cheese

Preheat oven to 375 F. Mound mashed potatoes in the center of a cookie sheet. Combine beaten whipping cream with salt, pepper, and cheese. Spread over mounded potatoes. Bake for 10 to 15 minutes or until cheese has melted and potatoes are light brown.

Piquant Turnip Casserole

(Illustrated below)

1 pound turnips, washed, peeled and cubed
   Salt to taste
2 cups water
2 tablespoons butter *or* margarine
2 tablespoons minced fresh parsley
3 tablespoons lemon juice
1 teaspoon sugar
2 teaspoons minced onion

Place turnips in a saucepan with salt and water; bring to a boil. Cook for 10 to 20 minutes or until tender. Remove from heat; drain. Toss with remaining ingredients.

Stewed Potatoes

1 onion thinly sliced
2 tablespoons butter *or* margarine
2 cups diced potatoes
   Salt and pepper to taste
2 teaspoons minced fresh parsley
3/4 cup boiling water
1 tablespoon water
1 tablespoon flour

Place onion and butter in a large skillet; cook for 5 minutes or until onion is tender. Add potatoes; season with salt and pepper. Sprinkle with parsley. Cover with boiling water. Cook for about 20 minutes or until potatoes are tender. Mix water and flour in a small container; stir into potatoes. Bring to a boil; cook for 2 to 3 minutes.

Stuffed Turnips

4 large turnips
2 tablespoons butter *or* margarine
1/8 cup finely minced onion
1/4 cup cooked green peas
    Salt and pepper to taste
1/4 cup bread crumbs
1/2 cup milk
1/2 cup parmesan cheese

Preheat oven to 350 F. Hollow out turnips; finely chop pulp and set aside. In a small skillet, melt butter and saute onion and peas for 3 to 5 minutes. Season with salt and pepper. Stir in bread crumbs and reserved turnip pulp. Fill hollowed-out turnips with mixture. Place in a greased baking dish; pour milk around turnips. Bake for 15 minutes. Remove from oven; top with cheese. Return to oven for 5 minutes or until cheese is lightly browned.

Scalloped Potatoes and Ham
(Illustrated below)

1/2 pound thick-cut ham slices,
    cut into 8 pieces
2 pounds potatoes, peeled and thickly cut
1 small onion, minced
    Salt and pepper to taste
1/3 cup flour
2 cups milk
1/8 cup bread crumbs
2 tablespoons butter *or* margarine, melted

Preheat oven to 350 F. Place 4 slices of ham in an ovenproof casserole. Cover with half the potatoes and half the onion. Season with salt and pepper; sprinkle with half the flour. Repeat layers. Pour milk gently over the casserole. Cover casserole with foil or lid. Bake for 60 to 80 minutes or until potatoes are almost tender. Combine bread crumbs and butter; spread over top of casserole. Return to oven; bake for 15 to 20 minutes or until potatoes are tender.

Herbs

Full of flavoring power

Tarragon Vinegar

(Illustrated on pp. 318-319)

2 sprigs tarragon, rinsed and patted dry
2 cups (500 ml) white wine vinegar

Place the herbs in a clean, sterilized jar. Pour the vinegar over the herbs, and seal the bottle. Store for about 14 days in a cool, dark location before using. Use tarragon vinegar for salad dressings and flavoring fish dishes.

Dill Vinegar

(Illustrated on pp. 318-319)

2 large sprigs dill blossoms, rinsed and patted dry
2 cups (500 ml) white wine vinegar

Place the herbs in a clean, sterilized jar. Pour the vinegar over the herbs, and seal the bottle. Store for about 14 days in a cool, dark location before using.

Lemon Mint and Lavender Vinegar

(Illustrated on pp. 318-319)

2 large sprigs lemon mint, rinsed and patted dry
1-2 sprigs lavender, rinsed and patted dry
2 cups (500 ml) white wine vinegar

Place the herbs in a clean, sterilized jar. Pour the vinegar over the herbs, and seal the bottle. Store for about 14 days in a cool, dark location before using. Use lemon mint and lavender vinegar for salad dressings.

Rosemary Oil

(Illustrated on pp. 318-319)

2 large or 3-4 small sprigs rosemary, rinsed and patted dry
3 cups (750 ml) vegetable oil

Hang the rosemary sprigs in a cool, airy location for about 3 days to dry. Place the herbs in a clean, sterilized jar. Pour the oil over the herbs, and seal

the bottle. Store for about 14 days in a cool, dark location before using. Use rosemary oil for sautéing lamb, or for basting, broiling, or barbecuing meat.

Green Sauce

(Illustrated this page)

4 hard-boiled eggs, separated; chop the white, and mash the yolk
2 tablespoons vegetable oil
6 ounces (150 g) sour cream
10 spinach leaves, rinsed
1 onion, minced

3 tablespoons finely chopped chives
1 tablespoon chopped lemon mint leaves
1 tablespoon chopped burnet leaves
1 tablespoon chopped borage leaves
1 tablespoon chopped dill
1 tablespoon chopped chervil leaves
1 tablespoon chopped tarragon leaves
1 tablespoon chopped basil leaves
1 tablespoon chopped parsley
1 teaspoon mustard
4-6 tablespoons cream
1-2 tablespoons vinegar
  Salt and pepper to taste

In a large mixing bowl, combine the mashed egg yolk and vegetable oil. Stir in the sour cream; set aside. Fill a medium saucepan half full with water, and bring to a boil. Add the spinach leaves, return to a boil, cover, and simmer for about 2-3 minutes. Drain, and mince. Add the spinach, onions, chives, lemon mint, burnet, borage, dill, chervil, tarragon, basil, and parsley to the egg mixture; mix well. Add the mustard and cream; mix well. Stir in the chopped egg white and vinegar. Season to taste with salt and pepper. Serve Green Sauce with pot roast or with poached eggs and salad.

Beef Roast in Lovage Brew

(Illustrated above)

4 1/2 to 5 pounds beef roast
2 1/2 quarts water
2 teaspoons salt
2 carrots, rinsed, peeled, and diced
2 leeks, trimmed, halved, rinsed, and diced
1 piece celery, complete with leaves, rinsed and diced
1 onion, peeled
4 springs lovage, rinsed and patted dry
2 bay leaves
2 cloves
Peppercorns

In a large kettle, place the roast, water, and salt. Bring to a boil, and skim off the foam. Add all the remaining ingredients to the kettle; return to a boil, cover, and simmer for about 2 1/2 to 3 hours, replacing evaporated water as necessary with hot water. Remove the cooked meat from the kettle, and cut it into slices. Arrange the meat slices on a warm plate. Strain the liquid through a colander, and pour a little of it over the meat. Serve the remaining liquid as a broth.

Chervil Sauce

2 hard-boiled eggs, whites chopped, yolks riced
1 raw egg yolk
. Salt to taste
1/2 cup vegetable oil
1 tablespoon vinegar
1 teaspoon mustard
1 tablespoon sour cream
3-4 tablespoons chopped chervil leaves
   Salt and pepper to taste

In a medium mixing bowl, combine the riced yolks, raw yolk, and salt. While beating continually, add 1/4 cup vegetable oil, drop by drop. When the mixture is fairly stiff, add vinegar, mustard and remaining oil. Stir in sour cream, chervil leaves and chopped egg whites. Season with salt and pepper. Serve chervil sauce with beef or pork roasts, hot or cold, or with boiled eggs.

Bean Salad with Savory

3-4 springs savory, rinsed
2 cups water
1 teaspoon salt
1 1/2 pounds green beans, cut into 1/2 inch pieces
1-2 onions, diced
   oil and herb vinegar dressing (see recipe below)
   Salt, pepper, and herb vinegar to taste
2 tablespoons chopped parsley

In a medium saucepan, combine the savory, water, and salt; bring to a boil. Add the beans; return to a boil, cover and simmer for 15 minutes or until tender-crisp. Pour off the water and remove savory. Add the onions to the beans. Prepare the oil and herb vinegar dressing; pour over the beans. Cover and set aside for 2 hours. Season to taste with salt, pepper and herb vinegar. Stir in parsley, and serve immediately.

Oil and Herb Vinegar Dressing

4 tablespoons vegetable oil
3 tablespoons herb vinegar
   Salt, pepper, and sugar to taste

In a small mixing bowl, combine the oil, herb vinegar, salt, pepper, and sugar.

Eggs with Tarragon Sauce

(Illustrated above)

Tarragon sauce (see recipe below)
6 boiled eggs, halved
Tarragon leaves

Prepare the tarragon sauce. Arrange the eggs on a medium serving platter. Pour the sauce over them, and garnish with tarragon leaves. Serve immediately.

Tarragon Sauce

3 1/3 tablespoons butter
2 tablespoons flour
1 cup cream
4 egg yolks
3 tablespoons cold milk
   Salt and pepper to taste
1-2 tablespoons finely chopped tarragon leaves

In a medium saucepan, melt the butter. Add flour and heat, stirring constantly, until flour is a light yellow. Add cream while beating constantly with a whisk, to be sure no lumps form. Bring the mixture to a boil, and simmer for about 5 minutes. In a small mixing bowl, combine the egg yolks and cold milk; stir into flour mixture. Simmer until thickened. Season to taste; add tarragon.

Chervil Soup

(Illustrated below)

1 spring onion, trimmed to about 4 inches of green,
and rinsed
2 tablespoons butter *or* margarine
1 cup chopped celery with leaves
1 quart (1 liter) meat stock
2-3 tablespoons cornstarch
4-5 tablespoons cold water
6 ounces (150 g) sour cream
4-5 tablespoons chopped chervil leaves
2 tablespoons chopped parsley
Salt and pepper to taste

Cut the green of the onion into fine strips, and set
aside. Mince the bulb. In a dutch oven, melt butter,
and sauté the diced onion and celery lightly. Add
the stock, bring to a boil, cover, and simmer for
about 15 minutes. In a small mixing bowl, combine
the cornstarch and cold water; add to the soup,
stirring to thicken. Add the sour cream, chervil, and
parsley. Season with salt and pepper, and add the
reserved green onion top. Serve immediately.

Colorful Stew with Savory

(Illustrated below)

3 tablespoons vegetable oil
1/2 pound (250 g) stewing beef, cut into 1-inch cubes
1/2 pound (250 g) stewing pork, cut into 1-inch cubes
2 large onions, diced
Salt, pepper, and sweet paprika to taste
3 cups (750 ml) water
1 pound (500 g) potatoes, rinsed, peeled, and diced
1 pound (500 g) young green beans, rinsed, and broken or cut into 1-inch pieces
1 small red sweet pepper, rinsed, seeded, and cut into
fine strips
3-4 sprigs savory, rinsed and patted dry
1/2 pound (250 g) mushrooms, trimmed, rinsed,
drained, and diced
1/2 pound (250 g) tomatoes, peeled and quartered
2 tablespoons chopped parsley

In a dutch oven, heat vegetable oil, and brown the beef and pork on all sides for about 10 minutes. Add the onions, and season with salt, pepper, and sweet paprika. Add the water, stir, and bring to a boil. Cover, and simmer for about 30 minutes. Add the potatoes, return to a boil, cover, and simmer for about 5 minutes. Add the beans, sweet pepper, and savory, return to a boil, cover, and simmer for about 15 minutes. Add the mushrooms, return to a boil, cover, and simmer for about 2 to 3 minutes. Add the tomatoes, heat through, and season to taste with salt, pepper, and paprika. Sprinkle with chopped parsley, and serve immediately.

Saltimbocca Rolls
(Illustrated this page)

8 small thin veal cutlets (each 3-4 ounces), rinsed,
    patted dry, and pounded flat
1 tablespoon lemon juice
    Salt and pepper
8 sage leaves, rinsed and patted dry
8 small slices ham
3 $^1/_3$ tablespoons (50 g) butter *or* margarine
$^1/_2$ cup (125 ml) water
$^1/_2$ cup (125 ml) Marsala *or* white wine
2 tablespoons sour cream
1 teaspoon flour mixed with 1 teaspoon cold water,
    optional
    Salt and pepper to taste
    Mushroom soy sauce (available in health food
    stores)
    Sage leaves

Sprinkle the cutlets with the lemon juice, salt, and
pepper. Lay one sage leaf on each cutlet. Top with
slices of ham, roll up, and fasten the rolls with
small wooden skewers. In a pressure cooker, melt
the butter, and sauté the rolls on all sides. Add the
water and Marsala. Seal the pressure cooker, and
cook the rolls for about 6 minutes. Remove the
skewers, and place the rolls in a warm dish. Keep
warm. Add the sour cream to the cooking juices. If
desired, thicken the juices with the flour mixture.
Season to taste with salt, pepper, and mushroom
soy sauce. Pour sour cream sauce over the rolls,
garnish with sage leaves, and serve. Serve with rice
or buttered noodles and salad.

Burnet Salad Dressing

(Illustrated below)

3 tablespoons vegetable oil
3 tablespoons vinegar
1 teaspoon medium-hot mustard
  Salt, pepper, and sugar to taste
2-3 tablespoons finely chopped burnet leaves
  Burnet leaves

In a small mixing bowl, combine the oil, vinegar, mustard, salt, pepper, and sugar. Add the chopped burnet. Before serving, sprinkle the top of the dressing with a few burnet leaves. This sauce is suitable for all lettuces.

Pan-Fried Liver with Mushrooms, Onions, and Sage

1 ¼ pounds (600 g) beef liver
  Flour
2 tablespoons vegetable oil
¼ pound (125 g) bacon, diced
10-15 sage leaves, rinsed and patted dry
  Salt, pepper, and sweet paprika to taste
⅓ pound (150 g) onions, diced
½ pound (250 g) mushrooms, trimmed, rinsed, and thinly sliced
½ cup (125 ml) red wine
6 ounces (150 g) sour cream

Dredge the liver slices in flour. In a large skillet, heat the oil, and sauté the bacon until crisp and brown. Add the sage leaves and the liver, and sauté for about 3 minutes, turning constantly. Season with salt, pepper, and sweet paprika. Add the onions, and cook through; then add the mushrooms and red wine. Bring to a boil, cover, and simmer for about 5 minutes. Stir in sour cream, and season to taste with salt, pepper and sweet paprika. Serve immediately.

Cold Apple Dish with Borage
(Illustrated above)

1 pound (500 g) cooking apples, peeled, cored, and
   sliced
1 cup (250 ml) white wine
$^1/_2$ cup (125 ml) lemon juice
1 cup (250 ml) water
$^1/_2$ cup plus 2 tablespoons (150 g) sugar
2 teaspoons cornstarch mixed with 2 teaspoons
   cold water
   Small borage leaves, rinsed and patted dry
   Borage flowers, rinsed and patted dry

In a large saucepan, combine the apple slices, wine;
lemon juice, and water. Simmer the apple slices for
a few minutes, and remove them with a slotted
spoon before they have become soft. Set the slices
aside. Add the sugar to the apple juices. Stir well,
and bring to a boil. Add the cornstarch mixture,
stirring constantly, to thicken. Remove the soup
from the stove and cool; add the apple slices, and
refrigerate for several hours. Sprinkle the borage
leaves and flowers over the cold soup, and serve
immediately.

Dill and Cucumber Salad

Dill and Yogurt Dressing (see recipe below)
1 cucumber (about 1 $^1/_5$ pounds), peeled, rinsed, and
   thinly sliced or grated
   Salt, pepper, and sugar to taste

Prepare the Dill and Yogurt Dressing. In a small
serving bowl, combine the cucumber and the
dressing. Cover, and set aside for at least 20
minutes. If necessary, season to taste with salt,
pepper, and sugar.

Dill and Yogurt Dressing

1 onion, diced
1 6-ounce carton (200 g) plain yogurt
1 tablespoon tarragon vinegar
1 teaspoon medium-hot mustard
   Salt, pepper, and sugar to taste
4-5 tablespoons chopped dill

In a small mixing bowl, combine all ingredients.

White Herring in Dill
(Illustrated above)

Bay Vinegar
10 white herring fillets, rinsed and patted dry

2-3 red onions (about 150 g), peeled and sliced
5-6 tablespoons chopped dill

Prepare the Bay Vinegar. In a clean, sterile glass jar, place alternate layers of fillets, onions, and dill. Pour the cold marinade over the fish, seal the jar, and store in a cool place (not in the refrigerator) for about 2 days. Serve with farmhouse bread and butter.

Bay Vinegar

1 ¹/₂ cups (375 ml) red wine vinegar
¹/₂ cup plus 2 tablespoons (150 g) sugar
2 bay leaves

In a medium saucepan, combine the ingredients, and bring them to a boil. Simmer, stirring constantly, until the sugar has dissolved. Set aside to cool.

Potato Pancakes with Dill Cream

Potato Pancakes

Dill Cream
2 ¹/₄ pounds (1 kg) potatoes, rinsed, peeled, and grated

1 onion, minced
2 eggs
2 tablespoons flour
Salt to taste
Vegetable oil

Prepare the Dill Cream. In a large mixing bowl, combine the potatoes, onion, eggs, flour, and salt. In a medium skillet, heat the oil, and add the batter, one spoonful at a time. Press each pancake flat, and sauté on both sides for 6 to 8 minutes, until the pancakes are crispy brown. Keep the finished potato pancakes warm until all have been made. Serve with the Dill Cream.

Dill Cream

6 ounces (150 g) sour cream
2 ounces Boursin *or* cream cheese
3-4 tablespoons chopped dill
Salt, garlic powder, and grated lemon rind to taste

In a small mixing bowl, combine the sour cream and Boursin. Mix in chopped dill, and season to taste with salt, garlic powder, and grated lemon rind. Cover, and refrigerate until ready to use.

Cod with Parsley Stuffing

1 oven-ready cod (about 3 ¹/₄ pounds), rinsed and
   patted dry
   Lemon juice
   Salt and pepper to taste
   Parsley Stuffing (see recipe below)
   Tomato slices

Preheat the oven to 375° F. Sprinkle the cod with
lemon juice, and let stand for about 30 minutes. Pat
dry, and season inside and out with salt and pepper.
Prepare the Parsley Stuffing. Cover a baking sheet
with aluminum foil, and place the fish on foil. Fill
the cavity with the Parsley Stuffing, and put a little
of the stuffing over the fish. Lay the tomato slices
on top of the fish, and sprinkle with salt and
pepper. Fold the foil over the fish, sealing it well,
and bake for about 45 minutes, or until the fish
flakes with a fork. Serve with buttered potatoes and
green salad.

Parsley Stuffing

3 ¹/₃ tablespoons butter *or* margarine
1 bunch spring onions (about 250 g), sliced
2-3 tablespoons chopped smooth parsley
2-3 tablespoons chopped crinkly parsley
   Salt, pepper, and Worcestershire sauce to taste

In a medium skillet, melt the butter, and sauté the
onions until almost cooked. Add the two parsleys,
and sauté together. Season with salt, pepper, and
Worcestershire sauce.

Tomatoes with Scrambled Egg and Chives

(Illustrated this page)

2 large tomatoes, rinsed, halved horizontally, and
   hollowed out
   Salt and pepper to taste
   Scrambled Eggs and Chives

Sprinkle tomatoes inside with salt and pepper. Prepare the Scrambled Eggs and Chives. Fill the tomato halves with the scrambled eggs, and serve
immediately.

Scrambled Eggs and Chives

3 eggs
3 tablespoons milk
   Salt
1-2 tablespoons finely chopped chives
1 tablespoon butter *or* margarine

In a small mixing bowl, combine the eggs, milk, and salt. Stir in finely chopped chives. In a large skillet, melt the butter, and add the egg mixture. As soon as the mixture begins to set, stir it with a spoon so it doesn't stick to the bottom of the pan. Continue cooking until eggs are no longer runny.

Colorful Sour Cream and Chives

1 pint (500 g) half-and-half
6 ounces (150 g) sour cream
2 bunches radishes, trimmed, rinsed, and sliced
2 hard-boiled eggs, diced
3-4 tablespoons finely chopped chives
   Salt and pepper to taste
2 hard-boiled eggs, halved
   Finely chopped chives, optional

In a large mixing bowl, combine the half-and-half and sour cream. Add the radishes, diced eggs, and chives. Season with salt and pepper, and turn into a medium serving bowl. Garnish with the halved hard-boiled eggs. If desired, sprinkle the top with chives. Serve with baked potatoes, butter, and salt.

Marinated Feta Cheese

(Illustrated below)

2 ¹/₄ pounds (1 kg) feta cheese cut into chunks
  Salt
2 sprigs thyme, rinsed and patted dry
2 sprigs rosemary, rinsed and patted dry
2 sprigs lavender, rinsed and patted dry
2-3 sage leaves, rinsed and patted dry
4 cloves garlic, halved
2 bay leaves
  Black peppercorns
2 ounces walnut halves
6 ¹/₄ cups (1 ¹/₂ liter) olive oil

Rub the cut edges of the cheese with salt. Put the cheese, herbs, and garlic into a large, clean, sterile glass jar with bay leaves, peppercorns, and walnuts. Add enough olive oil to cover the cheese. Seal the jar, and store it in a cool and dark location (not the refrigerator). Let the cheese marinate for about 2 weeks. Eat the cheese within 2 to 3 weeks. Use the leftover oil for savory salad dressings.

Lavender Blossom Jelly

5 tablespoons lavender blossoms
6 tablespoons spirits of wine (96% alcohol from a pharmacist)
1 bottle (700 ml) white wine (Riesling)
1 packet pectin
3 ¹/₃ cups (800 g) sugar
  Juice of 1 lemon

Marinate the lavender blossoms in spirits of wine for 4 to 5 hours; then strain through a fine tea-strainer, crushing the softened blossoms somewhat with a spoon. Put the extract into a large saucepan, and add the white wine. Add the pectin. With the heat on high, bring the liquid to the boil, stirring constantly and working out any lumps. As soon as the mixture reaches a rolling boil, stir in 3¹/₃ cups sugar (no less). Return to a boil. When you have again reached a rolling boil, allow to boil for another ¹/₂ minute (by the clock), stirring constantly. Remove from the heat, and add the lemon juice. To bottle and store jelly see the Introduction.

Pesto

(Illustrated below)

3-4 cloves garlic, peeled
1 teaspoon salt
2 ounces pine nuts
8 tablespoons chopped basil leaves
2 ounces grated Pecorino cheese
2 *or* 4 tablespoons grated Parmesan cheese
³/₄ cup plus 4 teaspoons (200 ml) olive oil

With a mortar and pestle, work the garlic cloves, salt, pine nuts, and basil until they have a creamy consistency. Add the grated cheese, and work it into the mixture. Stir in the oil. Serve Pesto with noodle dishes or with vegetable soup. If you do not have a pestle and mortar, puree the ingredients in a blender or a food processor, and then complete the recipe.

Duck with Thyme

(Illustrated this page)

1 teaspoon salt
2 1/4 pounds (1 kg) small potatoes
3 tablespoons thyme leaves
1 teaspoon chopped rosemary leaves
  Salt
1 tablespoon olive oil
1 oven-ready duck (about 4 1/2 pounds), rinsed and
  patted dry
2 medium onions, quartered
  Rosemary *or* thyme sprigs

Preheat the oven to 350° F. In a medium saucepan, add the salt, potatoes, and enough water to cover. Bring to a boil, cover, and simmer for 15 to 20 minutes. Pour off the water, and peel them at once. Sprinkle with thyme, rosemary, salt, and olive oil, and set aside. Rub the duck with salt, inside and out. Stuff it with a few of the herb potatoes, and set the rest aside. Lay the duck on its back in a baking pan that has been rinsed out with water, place the onions alongside it, and bake for 1 3/4 hours. While it is baking, prick the duck under the wings and legs occasionally, so that the fat can escape. After about 30 minutes, skim off the collected fat. As soon as the cooking juices become brown, add a little hot water, and baste the duck with the juices occasionally. Replace any liquid that evaporates, as necessary. Add the remaining potatoes to the pan 15 minutes before the end of the roasting period. Cut the roast duck into portions, and arrange on a warm plate with the potatoes. Garnish with rosemary or thyme sprigs. Serve the juices separately.

Calf Sweetbreads with Thyme

1 ¹/₂ pounds (750 g) calf sweetbreads
2 cups (500 ml) water
1 teaspoon salt
2 tablespoons butter *or* margarine
2 shallots, minced
  Salt and pepper to taste
1 cup (250 ml) cream
2 tablespoons white wine
2 tablespoons finely chopped thyme leaves
1 teaspoon chopped rosemary leaves

Soak the sweetbreads in water for several hours to blanch. Rinse first with boiling water and then cold water to set the sweetbreads and to make it easier to remove the blood vessels. Fill a medium saucepan half full with water, add salt, and bring to a boil. Add the sweetbreads, return to a boil, cover, and simmer for about 15 minutes. Remove from the water, and chop. In a medium skillet, melt the butter, and sauté the shallots to a golden yellow. Add the sweetbreads, and sauté for about 5 minutes. Season with salt and pepper. Gradually stir in cream and white wine, and cook for a few minutes to thicken the liquid somewhat. Add the thyme and rosemary, and serve immediately. Serve with bread and a mixed salad.

Marjoram Kebabs

(Illustrated above)

1 bread roll, torn into pieces
1 large onion, minced
$^1/_2$ pound (250 g) ground beef
$^1/_2$ pound (250 g) ground pork
1 egg
$^1/_2$ tablespoon finely chopped marjoram leaves
  Salt, pepper, and sweet paprika to taste
1 red sweet pepper, seeded, rinsed, and cut into strips
1 bunch spring onions (about 250 g), washed and
  trimmed to about 4 inches of green, and cut into
  1 $^1/_2$-inch pieces
  Bay leaves (fresh)
3 $^1/_3$ tablespoons shortening
  Marjoram sprigs

Soak the bread pieces in cold water; squeeze out the excess water. Mix bread with onions, ground meats, egg, and marjoram. Season with salt, pepper, and sweet paprika. Mix well, and form into small meatballs. Thread the meatballs, pepper strips, onion pieces, and bay leaves alternately onto skewers. In a large skillet, heat vegetable oil, and sauté the kebabs, turning them constantly, for 5 to 8 minutes, until they are brown on all sides. Baste them occasionally with the oil, and replenish as needed. Arrange them on a warm plate, and garnish with marjoram sprigs.

Marjoram Potatoes

1 $^1/_2$ pounds potatoes, peeled, rinsed, and thinly
  sliced
1 teaspoon salt
1 cup (250 ml) cream
2-3 tablespoons finely chopped marjoram leaves
2 egg yolks
  Salt and pepper to taste
3 ounces salt pork *or* jowl bacon, minced
2 tablespoons butter *or* margarine

Preheat the oven to 375° F. Put the potatoes into a medium saucepan, add the salt, and add enough water to cover. Bring to a boil, cover, and simmer for 4 to 5 minutes. Drain well. In a small mixing

bowl, combine the cream, marjoram, and egg yolks. Season with salt and pepper. Layer half of the potatoes, then half of the bacon in a well-greased medium casserole. Sprinkle with salt and pepper. Add the remaining potatoes on top. Spread the remaining bacon and the marjoram over the top, and dot with butter. Bake for 30 to 35 minutes, or until the potatoes are a golden yellow.

Marjoram Chicken with Vegetables

2 whole chickens (each about 2 pounds), rinsed, patted dry, and quartered
  Salt and pepper to taste
2 cloves garlic, minced
3 $^1/_3$ tablespoons soft butter *or* margarine
2-3 tablespoons chopped marjoram leaves
1 cup (250 ml) white wine
1-2 green sweet peppers (about $^1/_2$ pound), seeded, rinsed, and cut into strips
1-2 yellow sweet peppers (about $^1/_2$ pound), seeded, rinsed, and cut into strips

1 pound (500 g) fleshy tomatoes
1-2 tablespoons chopped marjoram leaves

Preheat the oven to 350° F. Rub the chicken pieces with salt and pepper. In a small bowl, combine the garlic and butter, and spread this over the chicken pieces. Place the chicken and the marjoram in a well-greased large casserole, and bake. After about 20 minutes baking time, add some of the white wine. Continue to replace any liquid that has evaporated. After about 40 minutes, add the sweet peppers. Add the tomatoes 5 minutes later. Bake for 10 minutes more. (Total baking time is about 1 hour.) Sprinkle the marjoram leaves over the chicken, and serve immediately.

Marjoram Meat

3 1/3 tablespoons pork drippings *or* shortening
1 pound (500 g) stewing pork
3/4 pound (375 g) onions, sliced
2-3 tablespoons chopped marjoram leaves
1 cup (250 ml) meat stock
9 ounces sour cream
  Salt and pepper to taste

In a large skillet, melt the pork drippings, and sauté the meat, turning it often, until it is browned on all sides. Add the onions, and sauté for about 5 minutes. Add about half of the marjoram leaves, and sauté for about 5 minutes. Add the meat stock, bring to a boil, cover, and simmer for about 20 minutes. Stir in the sour cream. Continue cooking for a few more minutes, to thicken the juices. Add the remaining marjoram leaves, and season with salt and pepper to taste. Serve with spaghetti and green salad.

Rosemary and Tomatoes

  Olive oil
6 medium tomatoes (about 2 1/4 pounds), rinsed and patted dry
3 small sprigs rosemary, rinsed, patted dry, leaves stripped off the stalks, and chopped
3 cloves garlic, crushed
3 tablespoons chopped parsley
2 tablespoons olive oil
  Salt and pepper to taste

Preheat the oven to 350° F. Grease a medium baking dish with olive oil. In the top of each tomato make several crosswise cuts. Place them in the baking dish. In a small mixing bowl, combine the rosemary, garlic, chopped parsley, olive oil, salt, and pepper. Press open the cut tomato edges, and fill with the rosemary mixture. Bake for about 25 minutes. Serve these tomatoes with French bread as an appetizer, or as a side dish with steaks or leg of lamb.

Saddle of Lamb with Rosemary

(Illustrated above)

3 3/4-4 1/2 pounds (1 3/4-2 kg) saddle of lamb, fat and skin removed, rinsed, and patted dry
  Salt and pepper to taste
3 cloves garlic, crushed
3 tomatoes, rinsed and cut into chunks
2 onions, cut into eighths
3 tablespoons vegetable oil
3 tablespoons rosemary leaves
2-3 tablespoons chopped parsley
1 tablespoon chopped rosemary leaves

1 egg
2-3 slices toasted bread, cut into croutons

Preheat the oven to 350° F. Sprinkle the lamb with salt and pepper, then spread the crushed garlic over the meat. Place half of the rosemary leaves in a well-greased casserole. Lay the meat on top of the rosemary, add the tomato and onion pieces, and sprinkle with the remaining rosemary leaves. Bake for 1 1/2 hours. As soon as the cooking juices brown, add a little hot water. Baste the lamb occasionally, and replace any liquid that evaporates. After roasting for about 1 1/4 hours, in a small mixing bowl, combine the parsley, rosemary leaves, and egg. Season with salt and pepper, and spread on the meat. Place the croutons on the herb mixture, pressing firmly into place, and roast for 15 minutes more. Carefully loosen the meat from the bone, and arrange the bone on a serving platter. Place the meat on top of the bone. Rub the juices and the vegetables through a sieve, and season to taste with salt and pepper. Place sieved vegetables atop meat. Serve with roast potatoes, grilled tomatoes, and broccoli.

Lemon Mint Dressing

(Illustrated below)

1 6-ounce carton (200 g) plain yogurt
3 tablespoons lemon juice
Sugar to taste
2-3 tablespoons finely chopped lemon mint leaves
    Lemon mint leaves

In a small mixing bowl, combine the yogurt, lemon juice, and sugar. Add the finely chopped lemon mint leaves. Garnish with whole leaves. Serve as a salad dressing with leaf salads.

Green Widow

(Illustrated below)

3 teaspoons mint leaves
$3/4$ cup plus 4 teaspoons (200 ml) boiling water
    Ice cubes
1 teaspoon lemon juice
1 tablespoon peppermint liqueur
1 slice lemon
1 sprig mint

Place the mint leaves in a small mixing bowl, and pour the boiling water over them. Cover, and steep for about 8 minutes, then strain through a colander, and cool. Fill a tall glass with ice, add the lemon juice and peppermint liqueur, and pour in the cooled mint tea. Garnish with a lemon slice and a mint sprig.

Lemon Mint Jelly

4-5 tablespoons minced lemon mint leaves
$^1/_4$ cup plus 1 tablespoon (75 ml) gin
1 bottle (700 ml) light grape juice
1 packet pectin
3 $^1/_3$ cups (800 g) sugar
  Juice of 1 lemon

Sterilize the jelly jars according to the directions in the Introduction. Prepare the lids according to the manufacturer's directions. Leave both jars and lids in the water until ready to use. Steep the lemon mint leaves in the gin for about 4 to 5 hours. Then place the mixture in a large saucepan, and add the grape juice and pectin. Bring the mixture quickly to a boil, stirring constantly so that no lumps form. As soon as the mixture reaches a rolling boil, stir in

the sugar (do not use less). Return to a rolling boil, and continue to boil for $^1/_2$ minute (by the clock), stirring constantly. Remove from the heat, and stir in the lemon juice. Fill the jars to within $^1/_4$ to $^1/_8$ inch of the top. Immediately after filling, clean the rims, and apply the lids. Invert the jars. After 5 minutes, turn the jars upright again, and let cool for 24 hours. Test the seals. Any product that is not sealed must be used immediately. Store the jars in a cool, dark, dry location.

Lemon Mint Punch

6-8 sprigs lemon mint, rinsed and patted dry
2 bottles well-chilled Riesling wine
1 lemon *or* lime sliced
  Lemon peel
  Sugar, optional
  Well-chilled champagne to taste

Tie the lemon mint sprigs together. Pour the wine into a large punch bowl, and hang the lemon mint so the leaves are immersed in the wine. Add the lemon slices and the lemon peel to the wine. Chill the punch in the refrigerator for about 2 hours. Before serving, if desired, sweeten with sugar, and pour in champagne.

Cold Mint Sauce
(Illustrated this page)

1 cup (250 ml) apple wine
1 cup (250 ml) orange juice
$^1/_2$ cup (125 ml) water
3-4 sprigs mint with blossoms, rinsed
1 tablespoon lemon juice
$^1/_2$ cup minus 4 teaspoons (100 g) sugar
2 tablespoons cornstarch, dissolved in 4 tablespoons cold water
1 sprig mint, rinsed and patted dry

In a large saucepan, bring the wine, orange juice, and water to a boil. Add the mint sprigs with blossoms to the liquid, and return to a boil. Add the lemon juice, and steep for 3 to 4 minutes. Remove the mint. Add the sugar, and heat. Add the cornstarch mixture, and heat, stirring constantly, until the liquid thickens. Cool, garnish with a mint sprig, and serve.

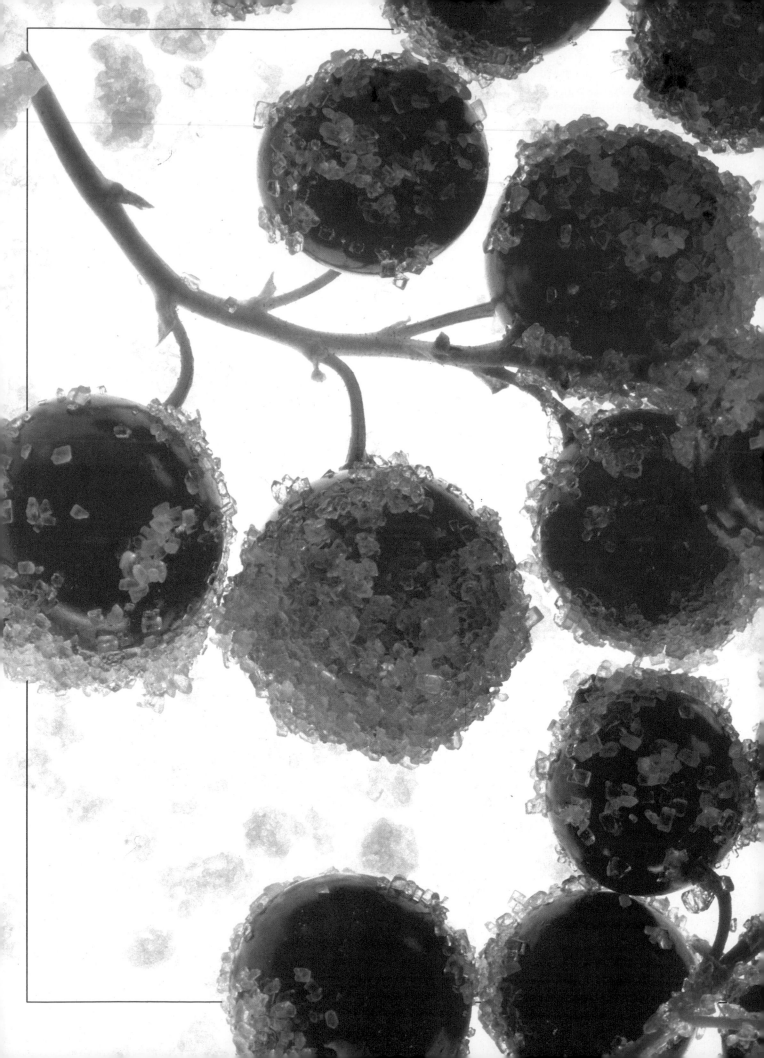

Berries
Fruits: a way to pamper yourself

Strawberry Jam/Preserves

2 pounds (1 kg) strawberries (weighed after being prepared)
1 packet pectin
4 $^1/_2$ cups plus 3 tablespoons (1 $^1/_8$ kg) sugar
  Grated rind of 1 orange
4 tablespoons orange liqueur

Sterilize the jelly jars according to the directions in the Introduction. Prepare the lids according to the manufacturer's directions. Leave both jars and lids in the water until ready to use. To prepare the strawberries, carefully wash them, and drain well. Remove the stems; halve larger berries, if necessary. Place them into a large saucepan or a dutch oven. Stir in the pectin. With the heat on high, bring the berries to a boil, stirring constantly, until the mixture reaches a rolling boil. Add the sugar (do not use less) and orange rind. Over high heat, return to a boil, and when the boil is rolling begin timing 1 minute by the clock, stirring constantly. Remove from heat, and add the orange liqueur. Fill the jars to within $^1/_4$ to $^1/_8$ inch of the top. Wipe the rims clean, and apply the lids. Invert the jars for 5 minutes; then set them upright and let them cool in a draft-free location for 24 hours. Test the seals. Any unsealed product must be used immediately or be reprocessed. Store the jars in a dark, cool, dry location.

Currant and Orange Jelly

2 pounds (1 kg) light currants (weighed when prepared)
1 cup (250 ml) water

6 ounces (175 g) frozen concentrated orange juice, thawed
1 packet pectin
4 ¹/₂ cups plus 3 tablespoons (1 ¹/₈ kg) sugar

Sterilize the jelly jars according to the directions in the Introduction. Prepare the lids according to the manufacturer's directions. Leave both jars and lids in the water until ready to use. To prepare currants, look them over for any that are spoiled or damaged; then rinse, and drain well. (Do not remove the stalks.) Place them into a large saucepan or a dutch oven. Crush the fruit, preferably with a wooden mallet. Add the water. Stirring constantly, heat the currants until almost ready to boil to draw out the juice. Do not boil. Pour the fruit into a jelly bag suspended over a saucepan or mixing bowl, and drain. Once the mixture has cooled, squeeze the

juice bag firmly to remove all the juice. Add the orange juice concentrate to the currant juice, and measure. Add enough water to create 4 cups of liquid. Place the currant mixture into a large saucepan or dutch oven, and add the pectin. Over high heat, bring the mixture to a boil, stirring constantly, and taking care that no lumps form. As soon as the mixture reaches a rolling boil, stir in the sugar (do not use less), and return to a boil. When the boil is rolling again, begin timing, while stirring, 30 seconds by the clock. Remove from the heat. Fill the jars to within ¹/₄ to ¹/₈ inch of the top. Wipe the rims clean, and apply the lids. Invert the jars for 5 minutes; then set them upright, and let them cool in a draft-frcc location for 24 hours. Test the seals. Any unsealed product must be used immediately or be reprocessed. Store the jars in a dark, cool, dry location.

Blackberry Liqueur

1/2 pound (250 g) blackberries, cleaned, rinsed, and
    drained
1 cup minus 1 tablespoon (150 g) brown sugar
1 piece cinnamon stick
2 pieces lemon peel
2 crushed juniper berries
1 bottle (0.7 liter) juniper spirits

Place the blackberries in a clean, sterilized,
wide-necked bottle. Add the brown sugar, cinnamon
stick, lemon peel, juniper berries, and juniper
spirits. Seal the bottle, and let it stand in a sunny
spot for 6 to 8 weeks, shaking it up occasionally.
Then pour the liqueur through filter paper into a
carafe or other decorative bottle. Serve with ice
cream, vanilla blanc mange, or sour cream.

Gooseberry Preserves with Gin

2 3/4 pounds (1 3/8 kg) ripe green gooseberries
    (weighed when prepared)
2-3 pieces lemon peel
1 packet pectin
6 1/4 cups (1 1/2 kg) sugar
5 tablespoons gin

Sterilize the jelly jars according to the directions in
the Introduction. Prepare the lids according to the
manufacturer's directions. Leave both jars and lids
in the water until ready to use. To prepare the
gooseberries, stem the berries; rinse, and drain well.
Put the berries through a grinder, or quarter them.
Place in a large saucepan or a dutch oven. Add the
lemon peel and pectin. Over high heat, bring the
fruit to a boil, stirring constantly. As soon as it
reaches a rolling boil, stir in the sugar, and return
to a boil. When the boil is rolling again, begin
timing for 1 minute by the clock, stirring
constantly. Remove from the heat. Remove the
lemon peel, and add the gin. Fill the jars to within
1/4 to 1/8 inch of the top. Wipe the rims clean, and
apply the lids. Invert the jars for 5 minutes; then set
them upright, and let them cool in a draft-free
location for 24 hours. Test the seals. Any unsealed
product must be used immediately or be
reprocessed. Store the jars in a dark, cool, dry
location.

Blackberry and Elderberry Jam/Preserve

1 pound (500 g) blackberries (weighed after
    preparation)
1 pound (500 g) ripe elderberries (weighed after
    preparation)
1 packet pectin
4 1/2 cups plus 3 tablespoons (1 1/8 kg) sugar
    Grated rind of 1 lemon
4-5 tablespoons blackberry liqueur

Sterilize the jelly jars according to the directions in
the Introduction. Prepare the lids according to the
manufacturer's directions. Leave both jars and lids
in the water until ready to use. To prepare the
blackberries, go through them to remove any
spoiled or green ones; then rinse, and drain well.
Crush them, and set aside. To prepare the
elderberries, rinse the berry clusters, and drain.
Then strip the berries from the stems. Place the
fruit in a large saucepan or dutch oven, and add the
pectin. Over high heat, bring the berries to a boil,
stirring constantly. As soon as it reaches a rolling
boil, stir in the sugar and grated lemon rind. Still
over high heat, return to a boil, and then begin
timing 1 minute by the clock, stirring constantly.
Remove from the heat, and add the liqueur. Fill the
jars to within 1/4 to 1/8 inch of the top. Wipe the
rims clean, and apply the lids. Invert the jars for 5
minutes; then set them upright, and let them cool
in a draft-free location for 24 hours. Test the seals.
Any unsealed product must be used immediately or
be reprocessed. Store the jars in a dark, cool, dry
location.

Raspberry Parfait

(Illustrated opposite page)

1 pound (500 g) raspberries, cleaned, rinsed, and
    drained
2 egg yolks
1/2 cup plus 1 teaspoon (125 g) sugar
2 tablespoons lemon juice
2 egg whites
2 cups (500 ml) cream
    Peeled, chopped almonds, optional

Puree the raspberries, and rub them through a sieve.
In a small mixing bowl, cream the egg yolks and
sugar. Add the lemon juice, and set aside. In a

medium mixing bowl, whip the egg whites until they form stiff peaks. Set aside. In a medium mixing bowl, whip the cream until stiff. Fold the egg whites and the cream into the egg yolk mixture, and carefully blend with the puree. Put into individual bowls or into a large mold, cover with aluminum foil, and freeze for 3 to 4 hours. Just before serving, place the mold in hot water for a minute or so, run a knife along the upper edge of the parfait, and turn onto a plate. Sprinkle with peeled, chopped almonds.

Gooseberry Delight

2 ¹/₄ pounds (1 kg) red gooseberries, trimmed and rinsed
1 cup (250 ml) water
  Lemon peel
1 piece cinnamon stick
1 cup plus 3 tablespoons (275 ml) red wine
¹/₂ cup plus 2 tablespoons (150 g) sugar
  Whipped Topping

In a large saucepan, combine the gooseberries with water, lemon peel, and cinnamon stick. Bring to a boil, and simmer for about 8 minutes, until berries are soft. Remove the lemon peel and cinnamon. Rub the gooseberries through a sieve, and return to the saucepan. Add the wine and sugar, and bring the mixture quickly to a boil. Cool, then refrigerate for about 4 hours. Serve with whipped topping.

Swiss Rice with Berries
(Illustrated this page)

1 cup (250 ml) cream
1 cup (250 ml) water
  Salt to taste
1 vanilla bean pod *or* 1 teaspoon vanilla
1 cup plus 1 tablespoon (250 g) raw rice
6 tablespoons sugar
4 tablespoons raspberry liqueur
Grated rind of 1 lemon
1 cup (250 ml) cream
1 pound (500 g) berries (gooseberries, currants, and
  blackberries), cleaned, trimmed, rinsed, and
  drained
  Sugar, optional

In a medium saucepan, bring the cream, water, and
salt to a boil. Halve the vanilla pod lengthwise, and
scrape out the pith. Add it, and the rice to the
cream mixture. Bring to a boil, and simmer for
about 25 minutes. Remove from the heat. Stir in the
sugar, raspberry liqueur, and grated lemon rind, and
cool. In a medium mixing bowl, whip the cream
until stiff. Fold it into the rice mixture, and set
aside in the refrigerator. If desired, sprinkle with
sugar. Top rice mixture with the fruit.

Strawberry Confections

4 ounces (125 g) semi-sweet baking chocolate
1 pound (500 g) large strawberries with stems, rinsed
  and drained on paper towels (strawberries must be
  completely dry)

Melt the chocolate in a double boiler, stirring
constantly until it becomes creamy. Dip the
strawberries into the chocolate so that they are 2/3
covered. Store in the refrigerator until just before
serving.

Crepes with Strawberries
(Illustrated next page)

Strawberry Filling

  Crepes Batter (see recipe below)
1 pound (500 g) strawberries, rinsed, drained,
  stemmed, and halved
1 teaspoon vanilla
1/4 cup sugar
4 tablespoons brandy

2-3 tablespoons red currant jelly
¼ cup (30 g) peeled, chopped, roasted almonds,
  optional

Prepare the Crepes Batter. In a medium mixing bowl, combine the strawberries and vanilla, and sprinkle with sugar. In a small skillet, warm the brandy, light it, and pour it over the strawberries while still flaming. In a small saucepan, warm the currant jelly, and carefully pour it over the strawberries. Place the strawberries along the center of the crepes, and fold them over. If desired, sprinkle with almonds.

Crepes Batter

1 ¾ cups (250 g) flour
1 tablespoon sugar
  Salt to taste
  Grated rind of 1 lemon
½ cup (125 ml) milk
1 egg
1 egg yolk
4 tablespoons (60 g) butter

In a medium mixing bowl, combine the flour, sugar, salt, and grated lemon rind. Add the milk, and set aside for 15 minutes. Then add the egg and egg yolk. In a small skillet, melt the butter. Pour in a thin layer of batter, and cook to a golden yellow on both sides. Repeat 5 more times. Keep them warm until ready to serve.

Iced Raspberry Tea

1 pound (400 g) raspberries, cleaned, trimmed,
  rinsed, and drained
3-4 tablespoons sugar
4 tablespoons (4 cl) raspberry liqueur
1 ½ cups (375 ml) cold tea
⅓ cup plus 1 tablespoon (100 ml) cream
1 teaspoon sugar
  Lemon juice
  Wafers

Place the raspberries in 4 chilled glasses. Sprinkle each glass with about a tablespoon of sugar and a tablespoon of raspberry liqueur. Divide the tea between the 4 glasses, and refrigerate for at least 30 minutes. In a small mixing bowl, combine the cream, sugar, and lemon juice. Whip the mixture until it forms stiff peaks. Top the tea with a dollop of the cream, and serve with wafers.

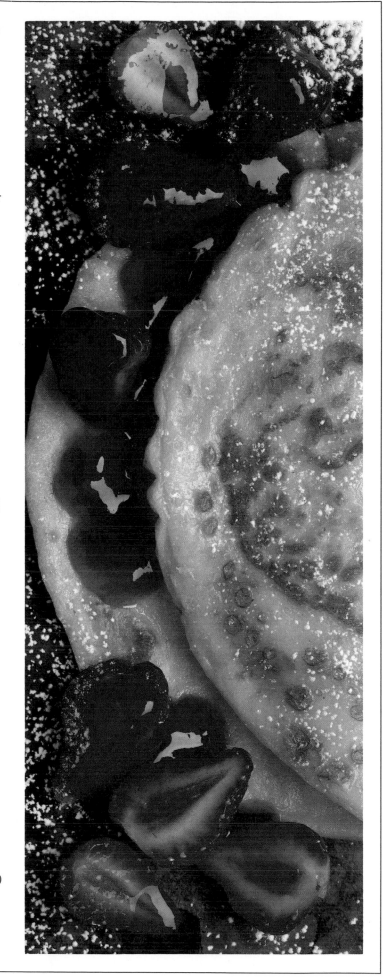

Gooseberry Sorbet

1/2 pound (250 g) ripe green gooseberries, cleaned, trimmed, rinsed, drained, and sliced
6 tablespoons water
1/4 cup (60 g) sugar
   Mint leaves, rinsed and patted dry
1-2 tablespoons peppermint liqueur

Freeze the gooseberries for about 1 hour. In a large saucepan, heat the water and sugar, stirring constantly, until sugar has dissolved. Cool. Add mint leaves and gooseberries to the liquid. Puree the mixture in a blender or a food processor, and rub it through a sieve. Add the peppermint liqueur. Freeze for 1 to 1 1/2 hours, stirring it every 15 minutes. As soon as the mixture has frozen to a thick consistency and holds its shape in a spoon, put into well-chilled glasses. Garnish with mint leaves, and serve immediately.

Currant and Peach Sorbet

8 ounces (200 g) light currants, cleaned, trimmed, rinsed, and drained
8 ounces (200 g) peaches (about 1 or 2 peaches), peeled and diced
8 tablespoons white wine
1/4 cup minus 2 teaspoons (50 g) sugar

In a large mixing bowl, combine the currants and peaches, and freeze for about 1 hour. In a small saucepan, heat the wine and sugar, stirring constantly, until sugar has dissolved. Cool. Add the frozen fruit to the liquid, puree the mixture in a blender or a food processor, and rub it through a sieve. Freeze for 1 to 1 1/2 hours, stirring every 15 minutes. As soon as it has frozen to a thick consistency and holds its shape in a spoon, put it into well-chilled glasses, and serve immediately.

Blackberry and Huckleberry Sorbet

8 ounces (200 g) blackberries, cleaned, trimmed, rinsed, drained, and slightly crushed
8 ounces (200 g) huckleberries
6 tablespoons water
1/4 cup (60 g) sugar
Juice and peel from 1/2 lime, peel cut into slivers

In a medium mixing bowl, combine the fruit, and freeze for about 1 hour. In a small saucepan, heat the water and sugar, stirring constantly, until the sugar dissolves. Add the lime peel, return to a boil, and simmer for 1 to 2 minutes. Cool, and strain the liquid through a sieve into a large mixing bowl. Add the frozen fruit and the lime juice, puree the mixture in a blender or a food processor, and rub it through a sieve. Freeze the mixture for another 1 to 1 1/2 hours, stirring it every 15 minutes. As soon as it has frozen to a thick consistency and holds its shape in a spoon, put it into well-chilled glasses, and serve immediately.

Currant Sorbet

1 pound (400 g) red currants cleaned, trimmed, rinsed, and drained
5 tablespoons grenadine syrup
Red currants, trimmed and rinsed

In a medium mixing bowl, freeze the currants for about 1 hour. Add the grenadine, puree the mixture in a blender or a food processor, and rub through a sieve back into the mixing bowl. Freeze the mixture for another 1 to 1 1/2 hours, stirring every 15 minutes. As soon as it has frozen to a thick consistency and holds its shape in a spoon, place it into well-chilled glasses. Garnish with red currants, and serve immediately.

Champagne and Currant Sorbet

2 cups light currant juice (recipe on p. 353)
1 3/4 cup plus 1 teaspoon (250 g) sifted powdered sugar
1 bottle champagne
2 egg whites
1 tablespoon sugar

In a large mixing bowl, combine the currant juice, powdered sugar, and half of the champagne. Stir until the sugar is entirely dissolved. In a large mixing bowl, quickly beat together the egg whites and sugar; this mixture should remain fairly thick. Add the champagne mixture. Freeze for about 1 1/2 hours, stirring it every 15 minutes. As soon as it freezes to a thick consistency and holds its shape in a spoon, put into well-chilled glasses, and serve immediately.

Currant Gateau

(Illustrated above)

Gateau Cake

1 cup (250 g) butter *or* margarine
1 cup plus 4 teaspoons (200 g) sugar
1 teaspoon vanilla
4 egg yolks
   Salt to taste
1 ³/₄ cups (250 g) flour
2 level teaspoons (6 g) baking powder
   Gateau Topping (see recipe below)
   Gateau Filling (see recipe below)
   Red currants, cleaned, trimmed, rinsed, and
   drained

Preheat the oven to 350° F. In a large mixing bowl, cream the butter. Gradually add the sugar, vanilla, egg yolks, and salt. Mix well. Sift the flour and baking powder, and add to the butter mixture one spoonful at a time. Divide the dough into 4 equal portions, and spread each portion into a greased 10-inch cake pan. (Be sure that the dough is not too thin at the edges, so that it does not become too dark). Prepare the Gateau Topping, and sprinkle it over the cake batter. Bake for 15 to 20 minutes, or

until golden brown. Remove immediately from the pans, and cool on a wire rack. Prepare the Gateau Filling and spread 3 of the 4 layers with it. Sandwich the layers together to make a gateau, with the fourth layer on top. Garnish with red currants.

Gateau Filling

2 cups sour cream
1 teaspoon vanilla
³/₄ cup (100 g) sifted powdered sugar
1 pound (500 g) red currants, cleaned, trimmed,
   rinsed, and drained

In a medium mixing bowl, whip the sour cream for about ¹/₂ minute. Add vanilla and powdered sugar. Whip the mixture until it forms stiff peaks; then stir in the red currants.

Gateau Topping

4 egg whites
¹/₂ cup minus 2 teaspoons (50 g) sugar
1 teaspoon vanilla
1 level teaspoon ground cinnamon
³/₄ cup (100 g) peeled, chopped almonds

In a medium mixing bowl, whip the egg whites until they form stiff peaks. Spread $1/4$ of it evenly onto each cake base. In a small mixing bowl, combine the sugar, vanilla, cinnamon, and almonds. Sprinkle the mixture over the layers.

Strawberry Flan

Strawberry Flan Topping

Flan Cake (see recipe below)
6 ounces (150 g) red currant jelly
1 $1/2$ pounds (750 g) strawberries, cleaned, trimmed, rinsed, drained, and halved
4 tablespoons orange liqueur

Prepare the Flan Cake, and set aside on a wire rack to cool. In a small saucepan, stirring constantly, bring the currant jelly to a boil, reduce heat, and continue to simmer for about 5 minutes, until it thickens somewhat. Spread about half of the melted jelly over the baked flan base. Place the strawberry halves on the flan base so that they overlap. Warm the remaining jelly, and add the liqueur. Spread the jelly mixture evenly over the strawberries.

Flan Cake

1 $1/2$ cups (200 g) flour
1 egg yolk
2 tablespoons very cold water
10 tablespoons (150 g) cold butter
  Salt and sugar to taste

Preheat the oven to 350° F. Sift the flour onto a pastry board. Make a hollow in the middle, and add the egg yolk and cold water. Work these into the flour to form a thick paste. Cut the butter into pieces, and add to the paste. Sprinkle salt and sugar over the top, and knead all the ingredients quickly to a smooth dough, working from the middle out. Chill the dough for about 30 minutes. Dust the work surface with flour, and roll out the dough to the size of a flan pan or a pan with a diameter of about 12 inches. Place the dough into the pan, and make a 1 $1/4$-inch ridge around the edge. Cut the edges smooth, and prick the base several times with a fork. Bake for about 20 to 25 minutes.

353

Strawberry Juice

6 pounds (3 kg) strawberries, cleaned, trimmed,
    rinsed, and drained
4 cups water
8 1/3 cups (2 kg) sugar
    Fruit preservative, optional

Prepare the jars for canning as instructed in the
Introduction. Fill the water-bath canner 2/3 full,
and begin heating the water. Place the strawberries
in a large saucepan or dutch oven, and crush them,
preferably with a wooden mallet. Add the water,
and bring them to a boil. Pour the mixture into a
jelly bag suspended over a large saucepan. Drain
well. Weigh the juice obtained, and add 3/4 to 1
pound of sugar for every pound of juice. Bring the
mixture to a boil, and skim off the foam. If desired,
add the preservative according to the manufacturer's
directions. Pour the juice into the prepared jars,
leaving 1/2 inch headspace. Remove any air spaces,
clean the rims, and seal. Process the jars for 5
minutes. Remove the jars from the canner, and set
out to cool in a draft-free location. After 24 hours,
test the seals. Any unsealed product must be used
immediately or be reprocessed. Store the jars in a
cool, dark, airy location.

Currant Juice

8 pounds (4 kg) red *or* light currants, cleaned,
    trimmed, rinsed, and drained
8 cups water
8 1/3 cups sugar
    Fruit preservative, optional

Prepare the jars for canning as instructed in the
Introduction. Fill the water-bath canner 2/3 full,
and begin heating the water. Place the currants in a
large saucepan or a dutch oven, and crush them,
preferably with a wooden mallet. Add the water,
and bring the mixture to a boil. Remove from heat;
strain mixture through a jelly bag suspended over a
large saucepan. Measure the juice, and add the
sugar. (For every quart of juice add no more than
2/3 pound of sugar, or the juice may turn into jelly!)
Bring the mixture to a boil, remove from heat and
skim off the foam. If desired, add the fruit
preservative according to the manufacturer's
directions. Pour the juice into the prepared jars,
leaving 1/2-inch headspace. Remove any air spaces,

clean the rims, and seal. Process the jars for 5
minutes. Remove the jars from the canner, and set
out to cool in a draft-free location. After 24 hours,
test the seals. Any unsealed product must be used
immediately or be reprocessed. Store the jars in a
cool, dark, airy location.

Blackberry Juice

5 pounds (2 1/2 kg) blackberries cleaned, trimmed,
    rinsed, and drained
5 tablespoons (50 g) citric acid, dissolved in 6 cups
    water
8 1/3 cups (about 2 kg) sugar
    Fruit preservative, optional
1 teaspoon sugar

Prepare the jars for canning as instructed in the
Introduction. Fill the water-bath canner 2/3 full,
and begin heating the water. Place the blackberries
in a china or earthenware bowl, and crush them,
preferably with a wooden mallet. Pour the citric
acid mixture over the blackberries. Cover, and
refrigerate for 24 hours, stirring frequently. Strain
the mixture through a jelly bag suspended over a
large saucepan or dutch oven. Measure the juice,
and stir in about 3/4 to 1 pound of sugar for every
1 quart of juice. If desired, in a small mixing bowl,
combine the fruit preservative and sugar. Add 1
tablespoon of the juice, and mix well. Add the
sugar mixture to the remaining juice. When the
sugar has completely dissolved, pour the juice into
the prepared jars, leaving 1/2-inch headspace.
Remove any air spaces, clean the rims, and seal.
Process the jars for 5 minutes. Remove the jars from
the canner, and set out to cool in a draft-free
location. After 24 hours, test the seals. Any
unsealed product must be used immediately or be
reprocessed. Store the jars in a cool, dark, airy
location.

Raspberry Milk

4 ounces (100 g) raspberries, cleaned, trimmed,
   rinsed, and drained
1 cup (250 ml) buttermilk
2 tablespoons cream
1/3 cup plus 1 tablespoon (100 ml) white wine
2 teaspoons sugar

Puree the raspberries in a blender or a food
processor. In a medium mixing bowl, combine them
with the buttermilk, cream, wine, and sugar. If
desired, add more sugar to taste. Serve well chilled.

Blackberries with Spicy Cream

1 pound (500 g) blackberries, cleaned, trimmed,
   rinsed, and drained
   Sugar
4 tablespoons blackberry liqueur
6 ounces (150 g) sour cream
   Sugar, vanilla, and cinnamon to taste
   Ladyfingers

In a medium mixing bowl, sprinkle the blackberries
with sugar, and set aside for about an hour. Divide
them between 4 glasses, and add 1 tablespoon of
blackberry liqueur to each. In a small mixing bowl,
combine the sour cream, sugar, vanilla, and ground
cinnamon to taste, and top each serving with a
dollop of the mixture. Refrigerate for at least 2
hours before serving. Garnish with ladyfingers.

Red Wine Punch with Raspberries

(Illustrated opposite page)

1 1/2 pounds (750 g) raspberries, cleaned, trimmed,
   rinsed, and drained
3 bottles red wine (Beaujolais)

Put the raspberries into a punch bowl. Add the
Beaujolais. Refrigerate for at least 2 hours. Serve
well chilled.

Strawberry Liqueur

1/2 pound (250 g) small strawberries, cleaned,
   trimmed, rinsed, and drained
1 cup plus 2 teaspoons (150 g) powdered sugar
1 vanilla bean pod
1 bottle fruit schnapps

In a sterilized, wide-necked quart bottle, combine
the strawberries with the powdered sugar and the
vanilla pod. Fill with the schnapps. Seal the bottle,
and set aside in a sunny place for about 14 days.
Then, pour the liquid through a filter paper, and
pour it into a sterilized decorative flask. Seal, and
set aside for another 4 to 6 weeks. Serve with ice
cream or cream dishes.

Cassis Punch

(Illustrated opposite page)

3/4 pound (375 g) black currants, rinsed and drained
1/2 cup (125 ml) Cassis (black currant liqueur)
2 bottles burgundy wine
1 bottle extra-dry champagne

Strip 1/2 pound berries from the stems. Combine
the berries, the liqueur, and 1 bottle of burgundy in
a large serving bowl or punch bowl. Seal the container, and refrigerate for 2 to 3 hours, then pour it
through a colander into a punch bowl. Strip the
remaining berries from the stalks, and add them to
the bowl. Add the second bottle of wine and the
champagne. Serve well chilled.

Gooseberries and Cream with Flaked Oats

(Illustrated this page)

$^1/_2$ cup (125 ml) white wine
$^1/_4$ cup plus 1 tablespoon (75 g) sugar
    Grated rind of 1 lemon
$^2/_3$ pound (300 g) ripe green gooseberries, cleaned, trimmed, rinsed, and drained
$^1/_4$ to $^1/_2$ cup (75-100 g) regular oatmeal (not quick-cooking)
3 $^1/_2$ tablespoons cornstarch
5-6 tablespoons cream
2 tablespoons lemon juice
$^1/_4$ cup minus 2 teaspoons (50 g) sugar
$^1/_2$ vanilla bean pod

In a large saucepan, combine the wine, sugar, and grated lemon rind. Bring to a boil, add the gooseberries, return to a boil, cover, and simmer for about 5 minutes (the berries must not disintegrate). Remove the berries with a slotted spoon, and place them in a large mixing bowl. Continue to simmer the juice until it thickens; then pour it over the berries. Cool. In a large, ungreased skillet, brown the oatmeal to a golden brown. Cool. In a small mixing bowl, combine the cornstarch, cream, lemon juice, sugar, and the vanilla pith from $^1/_2$ of the vanilla pod. Cover, and refrigerate for at least 30 minutes, or until ready to serve. Reserve a few berries for garnish. Divide the remaining gooseberries and the roasted oatmeal between serving dishes, and top with a dollop of the cream mixture. Garnish with the reserved berries.

Raspberry Foam with Vanilla Ice Cream

1 vanilla bean pod
$^1/_2$ pound (250 g) raspberries, cleaned, trimmed, rinsed, and drained
3 tablespoons port wine
2 heaping tablespoons sugar
1 tablespoon raspberry liqueur
2 eggs
1 tablespoon sugar
1 quart vanilla ice cream, cut into small cubes

Halve the vanilla pod lengthwise, and scrape out the pith. In a medium saucepan, combine the pith, raspberries, wine, and sugar. Bring to a boil, and simmer for 4 to 5 minutes. Rub the mixture through a sieve into a large mixing bowl. Add the raspberry liqueur, eggs, and sugar. Set the bowl in a cold-water bath, and whip for 10 to 15 minutes until the mixture is a thick foam. Divide the ice cream between individual serving dishes or glasses, and pour the raspberry foam over the ice cream. Serve immediately.

Berry Salad with Champagne Sabayon

(Illustrated above)

$^{1}/_{2}$ pound (250 g) raspberries, rinsed and drained
$^{1}/_{2}$ pound (250 g) currants, rinsed and drained
   Sugar to taste
Champagne Sabayon (see recipe below)
   $^{1}/_{2}$ cup (125 ml) medium-dry champagne

Set some berries aside for garnishing, and remove the stems from the remaining berries. Place them in individual serving dishes, and sprinkle sugar over each serving. Refrigerate until ready to serve. Prepare the Champagne Sabayon. Pour the champagne over the fruit. Top with the warm sabayon, garnish with the reserved berries, and serve immediately.

Champagne Sabayon

2 egg yolks
1 egg
2 tablespoons sugar
1 tablespoon lemon juice
$^{1}/_{2}$ cup (125 ml) medium-dry champagne

Combine all the ingredients in a small mixing bowl. In a cold-water bath, whip the mixture for about 7 minutes, until creamy.

Strawberry Tapioca with Vanilla Cream

(Illustrated this page)

2 1/2 pounds (1 1/4 kg) strawberries, cleaned, trimmed, rinsed, and drained
4 cups water
3-4 pieces lemon peel
1/2 cup plus 2 tablespoons (150 g) sugar
1 cup (120 g) pearl sago *or* tapioca
  Sugar to taste, optional
  Vanilla Cream (see recipe below)

Set 1/4 of the strawberries aside. In a medium saucepan, combine the remaining berries and the water, and bring to a boil. Strain the mixture through a jelly bag suspended over a large bowl. Once the fruit is cool, squeeze the bag tightly to be sure you have all the juice. Measure the juice, and add enough water to equal 5 cups. In a dutch oven, combine the juice, lemon peel, and sugar. Begin to heat the mixture, and sprinkle the sago over the top, stirring constantly. Bring the mixture to a boil, cover, and simmer for about 20 minutes. Remove the lemon peel. Add the reserved berries, return to a boil, cover, and simmer for about 1 to 2 minutes. If desired, add sugar to taste. Turn the mixture out into a medium serving bowl, and cool before serving. Prepare the Vanilla Cream, and serve as a side dish with the tapioca.

Vanilla Cream

1/2 vanilla bean pod
1 cup (250 ml) cream
  Sugar to taste

Scrape the pith from the vanilla pod, and combine with the cream and sugar to taste.

Gooseberry Pudding with Vanilla and Cream Sauce

1 pound (500 g) ripe green gooseberries, cleaned, trimmed, rinsed, and drained
1 cup (250 ml) white wine
³/₄ cup sugar
1 teaspoon vanilla
1 piece cinnamon stick
2-3 pieces lemon peel
¹/₄ cup (30 g) cornstarch dissolved in 3 tablespoons cold water
2-3 tablespoons lemon juice
Vanilla and Cream Sauce (see recipe below)

In a dutch oven, combine the gooseberries, wine, sugar, vanilla, cinnamon stick, and lemon peel. Bring to a boil, cover, and simmer for 3 to 5 minutes. Remove the cinnamon stick and lemon peel. Add the cornstarch mixture to gooseberries. Quickly return to a boil. Add the lemon juice. Turn the mixture into a glass serving bowl, and refrigerate until ready to serve. Prepare the Vanilla and Cream Sauce. Divide the gooseberries into separate serving dishes, top with the sauce, and serve.

Vanilla and Cream Sauce

1 package custard powder
2 level tablespoons sugar
2 cups (500 ml) milk
¹/₂ cup (125 ml) cream

In a medium mixing bowl, combine the custard powder, sugar, and 2 or 3 tablespoons of the milk. In a small saucepan, bring the remaining milk to a boil, and remove from the heat. Stirring constantly, add the custard mixture, and bring quickly to a boil. Then cool, stirring occasionally. In a small mixing bowl, whip the cream until it forms stiff peaks. Fold it into the lukewarm vanilla custard. Refrigerate until ready to serve.

Venison Medallions with Blackberry Sauce
(Illustrated this page)

Blackberry Sauce (see recipe below)
8 slices bacon
8 venison medallions (about 1/8 pound each)
Salt and pepper to taste
Butter *or* margarine
Blackberries
Orange peel, cut into strips

Prepare the Blackberry Sauce. Wrap each medallion with a bacon slice, and secure with kitchen twine. Season the meat with salt and pepper. In a large skillet, melt the butter, and sauté the medallions on both sides for about 2 minutes. Remove the twine. Garnish the medallions with blackberries and strips of orange peel. Serve with Blackberry Sauce.

Blackberry Sauce

1/2 pound (250 g) blackberries, cleaned, trimmed, rinsed, and drained
1/3 cup plus 1 tablespoon (100 ml) burgundy wine

1 tablespoon sugar
1/2 teaspoon mustard powder
  Grated rind of 1/4 orange
  Ground pimiento
  Brandy to taste
  Angostura bitters to taste

In a medium saucepan, combine the berries with a little water, heat for a minute or so, and rub through a fine sieve. Return the berries to the saucepan, add the wine, sugar, mustard powder, grated orange rind, and ground pimiento. Heat the mixture, but do not boil. Add the brandy and bitters to taste. Keep warm until ready to serve.

Breast of Duck with Currant Sauce

(Illustrated opposite page)

3 1/2 tablespoons (50 g) butter *or* margarine
2 pounds (1 kg) breast of duck fillets (with skin), rinsed and patted dry
2-3 onions, minced
1 1/2 ounces (50 g) red currants, cleaned, trimmed, rinsed, and drained
1 1/2 ounces (50 g) black currants, cleaned, trimmed, rinsed, and drained
4 tablespoons cream
1/2 cup (125 ml) meat stock
1 tablespoon brandy
  Salt and cayenne pepper to taste
  Currants

In a large skillet, melt the butter, and sauté the fillets on both sides for about 4 minutes. Remove them from the skillet, wrap them in aluminum foil, and keep warm. Add the onions, and sauté until translucent. Add half of the currants, and sauté for about 5 minutes. Add the cream, meat stock, and brandy, and bring to a boil. Rub the currant mixture through a sieve, and return to the skillet. Bring to a boil, and simmer until the mixture thickens somewhat. Season to taste with salt and cayenne pepper. Add the remaining berries to the sauce, and heat. Serve the duck breasts with the sauce, and garnish with currants. Serve with potato croquettes.

Strawberry and Chicken Salad

(Illustrated opposite page)

3/4-1 pound (about 400 g) chicken breast fillets, rinsed and patted dry
  Salt to taste
2 tablespoons cooking oil
  Chopped tarragon leaves
  Coarsely ground white pepper
1-2 tablespoons lemon juice
  Wine Marinade
2 bunches spring onions (each about 250 g), trimmed to about 4 inches of green, rinsed, and sliced
1 pound (500 g) strawberries, cleaned, trimmed, rinsed, drained, and halved

Sprinkle the chicken breasts with salt. In a large skillet, heat the oil, and sauté the breasts on both sides for about 4 minutes, until they are a golden brown. Remove the meat, cool, and cut into slices. Sprinkle the slices with chopped tarragon leaves, white pepper and lemon juice. Prepare the Wine Marinade. Add the chicken slices to the marinade, and steep for 20 minutes. Remove the slices, and arrange them on a medium serving platter. Add the onions to the marinade, and steep for 20 minutes. Remove, and arrange them with the chicken slices. Pour the remaining marinade over the onion rings and the meat. Arrange the strawberries on the plate, steep for another 20 minutes, and serve.

Wine Marinade

3 tablespoons salad oil
2 tablespoons white wine vinegar
5 tablespoons white wine
1 teaspoon sharp mustard
  Salt to taste

In a large mixing bowl, combine all ingredients.

Index